Latham Smith

Ye outside fools!

Glimpses inside the London stock exchange

Latham Smith

Ye outside fools!
Glimpses inside the London stock exchange

ISBN/EAN: 9783337109974

Printed in Europe, USA, Canada, Australia, Japan

Cover: Foto ©Suzi / pixelio.de

More available books at **www.hansebooks.com**

YE OUTSIDE FOOLS!

GLIMPSES INSIDE THE

LONDON STOCK EXCHANGE.

BY

ERASMUS PINTO, Broker.

"The population of Great Britain is thirty millions, mostly fools."—THE SAGE OF CHELSEA.

"Some men has plenty money and no brains, and some has plenty brains and no money;—surely them as has plenty money and no brains was made for them as has plenty brains and no money."—SIR ROGER ORTON.

"'O, cives, cives, quærenda pecunia primum est;
Virtus post nummos.' Haec Janus summus ab imo
Perdocet, haec recinunt juvenes dictata, senesque."—HORACE.

"Nòsse haec omnia salus est adolescentulis."—TERENCE.

NEW YORK:
LOVELL, ADAM, WESSON & COMPANY.
1877.

LOVELL PRINTING AND PUBLISHING COMPANY,
PRINTERS.

LAKE CHAMPLAIN PRESS,
ROUSES POINT, N.Y.

TO THE READER.

Ye " Outside Fools," who haply cast an eye
Upon these pages, read them honestly ;
Let not the Title chafe your noble minds,
But let each learn the truth that here he finds.
All fools are equal, taken class by class,
Each " Outside Fool " may find an Inside Ass.
A murrain seize that fool who sneers at all,
As though he stood on some high pedestal.
Dig out that darling *Ego* from thy heart,
And then thou mayest act a manly part.
Let not this book one angry feeling raise ;
It means no harm—no venom it conveys.
Nay, he who writes is but as he who reads :
The pen tells truth, no better are the deeds.
Read, then, my merry blades, with rest of reins,
For an ye learn or laugh, 'tis worth my pains.

THE

AUTHOR'S DEDICATORY EPISTLE OF HIS BOOK

TO THE

MOST HONORABLE AND RESPECTABLE

CORPORATION OF JOBBERS AND BROKERS

OF THE LONDON STOCK EXCHANGE.

Dear Brothers of our "Inside House,"—I dedicate my book to you with all respect. I feel for you. John Bull is rather prone just now to listen to the demagogic howl. He has not quite recovered from that learned legal lion's roar who shook the dewdrops from his bristling mane and made respectability shrink back aghast. The nation's nerves are not so strong as they once were. Finance and luxury have worked this ill. I am afraid lest some one of the "Outside Fools" should gain the ready ear of old John Bull before he has got over the effects of his last Turkish bath, and make him treat you as you don't deserve. What means this idle talk about commissions to inquire how we work inside? And what the scurrilous abuse of crazy "Outside Fools" who've lost their money through their ignorance and greed of gain?

We jobbers, then, and brokers are much worse than lawyers, doctors, parsons, bishops, and pawn-brokers, are we? So say the "Outside Fools."

I always thought man was a gambling animal. At any rate, I have the names of every class upon my books, and holy men's the most. Aha! It's not the gambling that they hate, it is the loss. Oh, then, I see! *Hinc illae lacrymae.* Is this another species of free trade, or what is it? The parson has to learn to preach, the doctor how to purge and bleed, the lawyer how to cheat, the grocer how to get good butter out of rancid fat, and sugar out of sand, the carpenter must learn to use his tools; but any dolt may speculate, and, if he lose, abuse in coarse and vulgar terms a set of men who do at all events know what their business is, and, like the cobbler, all stick to their last.

If I well know the art of chemistry, and the virtues of the *Cocculus Indicus*, and by my knowledge undersell the brewer who puts malt and hops alone in what he sells, what then?

The man of malt and hops should surely learn the tricks of chemistry; and all you merry toss-pots should more closely study all the properties of beer.

Suppose I'm called in to a patient who is suffering from hypochondria, and find him some genteel and maybe new disease, although the man's not ill, what then?

Will the blunt Galen who with brutal clownishness says, "Take a ten mile walk, give up your beer," deserve his fee as well as I? He laughs at those by whom he lives. I sympathise with them and understand their wants. And if I gratify the wish of "Outside Fools" who think they know more businesses than one, and speculate, am I to blame?

What should be done? Why, this. If "Outside Fools" will speculate, and I feel sure they will until the crack of doom, they ought to learn the use of all our curious tools—our pocket-orders, syndicates and rigs, footballs, and puts and calls.

Well, cheer up, "Outside Fools." My brothers of the "Inside Hall" have chosen me to tell you all I know, and as I was a sinner, not a saint, you'll see the shady side of us, and ought then to be satisfied that all the rest are not so bad. I am empowered to say that all of us allow that some improvement might be made in the minor details of our beautiful system, the elaborate production of many minds through many ages. What of this?

The Church seems in a queer condition now.

But just because the Church and Stock Exchange are open to reform, are we to vilify the brokers and the parsons with low, coarse abuse? We both like dragon sovereigns, who does not? but holy thoughts prevent the parsons learning quite as much about the coins as we have learned.

Our system may be open to improvement, but I really do not see that speculators who will leave their shops to come to ours need pity when they lose. The thing's absurd. No doubt there are black sheep on 'Change, and I am going to show you two or three, but so there are in any profession, trade, or business you can name. What know you of first motives and temptations? Who made *you* the judge of men? My honorable brothers say it is now time to tell the outside world more of their ways, and then it will be seen which class is more to blame. You "Outside Fools" have got hold of the wrong end of the stick.

It is not we who do the greatest harm. It is the great financiers. I don't myself believe that there is such wide difference between the way men stand against the devil's wiles, and "Charity" allows me to think so; but if there be, these great financiers, who can resist the wonderful temptations to which

DEDICATION.

they are exposed, don't prove the Gospel truth, "How hardly shall a rich man enter heaven." It is not well that men should grow too rich by any means; but when unwieldy sums have been amassed by cleverly-planned juggles, artfully-constructed bubble-schemes, when thousands of struggling honest men, ladies with limited incomes, and countless others who don't speculate and can ill afford to lose a pound, attracted by the dangerous and seductive terms, *Investment* and *Industrial Enterprise*, are brought to beggary while these financiers batten on their earnings, something should be done to stay the ill. These loan-mongering and financing tricks have given these men a place which surely they do not deserve—a place among the merchant princes of our land, who have made fortunes fairly by developing the resources of their country, or of other lands, by discovering some novel combination of the raw material, and so finding honest paying work for thousands of their fellow-creatures. Yes, the wealth of these producers does good to others, if not to themselves, whereas financiers' money is the nation's curse, and, I believe, brings but unhappiness to them.

And what's the cure? More wide-spread knowledge of the way in which they work. But they buy all the money articles, the only source where information can be got. Until you know this fact, dear "Outside Fools," you never will be safe.

And here again, we have no right to execrate the men. The system is at fault. Suppose you had a family to keep, and knew that if you did not work your own employers' will, some hundreds would be glad to step into your shoes, pray, would you find it easy to resist?

I call, then, upon *you*, ye members of that honorable Fourth Estate, to all combine, and stamp the evil out; if ye combine, the power of capital will fail to poison and pollute those admirable streams from whence our nation draws its daily education, its financial food.

And you, ye men of wondrous wealth, spend more in slaying dragons with your means. That ostentatious charity, for which so many rich men take their value in another form, does little good to you at least.

Nay, rather follow the example of that worthy baronet, just gone to rest, whose family's proud boast should be, that with such opportunities to make he chose to spend, and died beloved by very many friends. Ye have a fearful power to wield. See that ye use it well.

And, lastly, you, ye " Outside Fools," give up your querulous complaints of brokers' want of honesty, and jobbers' tricks. Learn how the game is played, or give it up. Give up your greediness and folly, and if you must gamble, have some principle and plan. Don't try to pick the brains of other " Outside Fools " or take their tips, but learn and work like honest men. I am instructed to assure you by my brother brokers that all honorable members of the London Stock Exchange will gladly hail the day when fewer fools shall come to speculate in their insensate way.

Dear brother brokers, and you jobbers, I return you thanks for your great kindness in selecting me to speak for you. I promise you I'll do my best, nor will I let class-feelings hinder me from telling truth.

I am, dear Brothers,
Your most humble and devoted slave,
ERASMUS PINTO.

CONTENTS.

CHAPTER I.
My Birth and Origin.—"Stemmata Quid Faciunt?".... 17

CHAPTER II.
I am offered the Post of Confidential Clerk to the Firm of Seesaw and Turnabout 20

CHAPTER III.
I Pass my Examination to the satisfaction of the Firm.. 21

CHAPTER IV.
The Game of Hide and Seek between Dr. Bleedall Grabfee and Mr. Nathaniel Seesaw................ 36

CHAPTER V.
Mr. Nathaniel Seesaw's Advice to his new Confidential Clerk.. 41

CHAPTER VI.
Mr. Seesaw instructs Erasmus Pinto how to deal with Lady clients... 44

CHAPTER VII.
Mr. Nathaniel Seesaw warns Erasmus Pinto against Speculating in Unsafe Stocks...................... 48

CHAPTER VIII.
Mr. Turnabout's quaint test of a young man's fitness for the office of Confidential Clerk................... 52

CHAPTER IX.
Erasmus Pinto goes to dine with Mr. Nathaniel Seesaw. 54

CHAPTER X.
Mr. Nathaniel Seesaw's House and Position........... 67

CHAPTER XI.
Clara Seesaw... 69

CHAPTER XII.
Mr. Levi Gusher, of the " People's Bellowgraphic." 71

CHAPTER XIII.
Dinner—A Cynic's ideas of Romance, and the remarks of a learned Critic 73

CHAPTER XIV.
Omne tulit punctum qui miscuit utile dulci 77

CHAPTER XV.
Across the Walnuts and the Wine 80

CHAPTER XVI.
A Bold Stroke for a Wife 83

CHAPTER XVII.
The Honorable Walter Loftus' Tip 87

CHAPTER XVIII.
Lunch and a Doctor's Widow's Prescription 91

CHAPTER XIX.
Stephen Jobberstock's option turns up trumps, and the house is checkmated by Dizzy, Derby, and Sidonia. 96

CHAPTER XX.
Erasmus Pinto reassures the broken spirits of his Firm. 101

CHAPTER XXI.
The Telegraphic Cable of Love.—How the Cables of Love worked.—" Naturam expellas furca, tamen usque recurret" 105

CHAPTER XXII.
The Telegraphic Messages of Love 112

CHAPTER XXIII.
Clara Seesaw's Ideas on Love 114

CHAPTER XXIV.
Erasmus Pinto's Remedy for the Great Want of the Age. 118

CHAPTER XXV.
The General Matrimonial Alliance Association (Limited) 120

CONTENTS.

CHAPTER XXV. (Continued.)
An Object of Love selected by the Odic or Magnetic Current.... 128

CHAPTER XXVI.
All About a Fall, a Corinthian, and a Tea-party....... 137

CHAPTER XXVII.
All About a Cook, a Bath, and The Consequences......... 142

CHAPTER XXVIII.
A Discovery 146

CHAPTER XXIX.
Qualms of Conscience felt by the late Nathaniel Seesaw, Esq., about his business as a Broker............... 147

CHAPTER XXX.
The late Mr. Nathaniel Seesaw's Posthumous Views on the Causes of Speculation 150

CHAPTER XXXI.
On "Bearing" and "Bulling"........................ 157

CHAPTER XXXII.
A Doctor's View of the Rights of Property............. 172

CHAPTER XXXIII.
A Broker's Idea of a Gentleman and a Snob............ 179

CHAPTER XXXIV.
The History of Octavius Marmaduke Bubchook, Ex-M.P. for Rottenboro'............................ 186

CHAPTER XXXV.
Dr. Sana Mens' Views of Extraordinary Crimes 189

CHAPTER XXXVI.
Octavius Marmaduke Bubchook, Esq., becomes a Bull of Peru... 191

CHAPTER XXXVII.
O. M. Bubchook, Esq., in Account with Messrs. Seesaw and Turnabout 198

CHAPTER XXXVIII.
Octavius Marmaduke Bubchook, Esq., becomes a Bear of North British Railway Stock 200

CHAPTER XXXIX.
The History of Mr. and Mrs. Silas Snoad, and Dr. Sana Mens' Views on Teetotalers 206

CHAPTER XL.
Dr. Sana Mens on the use of the wonderful words Μηδεν Αγαν.................................... 208

CHAPTER XLI.
Dr. Sana Mens gives further valuable advice how to improve the quality of Tea and reduce the price of Meat 210

CHAPTER XLII.
How to prevent the Plague and Check the Overgrowth of Population 211

CHAPTER XLIII.
The Excellent and Mysterious Investment of Mr. Silas Snoad, and what effect the Want of a Narcotizer had upon a Cabman 213

CHAPTER XLIV.
The Discovery of Mr. Silas Snoad's Mysterious Investment 216

CHAPTER XLV.
The Wonderful Ships that were to sail across the Land on Wheels...................................... 218

CHAPTER XLVI.
The Rise in North British continues.................. 219

CHAPTER XLVII.
The Mistaken Views of Outside Speculators.—Mr. Octavius Marmaduke Bubchook closes his Bear........ 222

CHAPTER XLVIII.
The Profits and Losses of O. M. Bubchook, Esq., and how he sold his Lombard Shares.................. 225

CHAPTER XLIX.
The Moral of Mr. Bubchook's History and Death, with Mrs. Bubchook's Curious Remarks.................. 229

CHAPTER L.
Dr. Sana Mens' Remarks on Health, Happiness, and Religion 231

CHAPTER LI.
The Curious History of a Clerical Guinea Pig 234

CHAPTER LII.
Showing How to Catch an Old Man in the Matrimonial Net.. 238

CHAPTER LIII.
The Favorite form in which the Evil One tempts Holy Men to Speculate................................ 242

CHAPTER LIV.
Certain Valuable Suggestions offered by Nathaniel Seesaw, Esq., the Representative of the Brokers and Jobbers of the Stock Exchange, to the Bishops and Clergy of Great Britain............................ 245

CHAPTER LV.
The Reverend Josiah Fetchem meets with a certain deference from the Rectors and Vicars, which is a sort of paradox................................... 247

CHAPTER LVI.
How Josiah Fetchem made an Investment in the celebrated Emma Mine, with an account of Dr. Sana Mens' Views on the Goodness of Human Nature... 249

CHAPTER LVII.
A Description of Great Whopplidde-in-the-fen and of the Rector, the Rev. Jedediah Tring.................. 257

CHAPTER LVIII.
A Description of Miss Louisa Pantosniffle's Curious Dress, and of Madame Emma La Fargue, with other great Whoppliddians 259

CHAPTER LIX.

How the Great Whoppliddians determined that the Reverend Josiah Fetchem should marry one of the Ladies of their Parish, and how bets were arranged about the Event.. 263

CHAPTER LX.

A Description of Church Music at great Whopplidde-in-the-fen, the Parish Clerk, and the Rector's favorite Theological Works 266

CHAPTER LXI.

An account of the Creed held by the Rector of Great Whopplidde-in-the-fen, and his Views on the Title " Reverend "................................... 270

CHAPTER LXII.

The Reverend Josiah Fetchem arrives at the Rectory of Great Whopplidde-in-the-fen with Emma on the Brain.—The Craving for Mystery a Prime Cause of Speculation.—The Success of Quack Medicines.—The Danger of the Stock and Share List........... 271

CHAPTER LXIII.

The Man to be Distinguished from the Good he does.—Egotism a Foe to Education.—Remarks on Socrates. 276

CHAPTER LXIV.

How to Angle for an Amatory Fool, and make a Priggish Rector your Fast Friend..................... 280

CHAPTER LXV.

The Reverend Josiah Fetchem has a very Curious Dream. 281

CHAPTER LXVI.

Treating of the Three Odors peculiar to Religious Sects... 283

CHAPTER LXVII.

Treating of Habits, Secondary Automatism, and the Assertion of Philosophers that " When the Sum of the Conditions of a Case are known the result can be predicted with certainty ".................... 288

CONTENTS.

CHAPTER LXVIII.
A Philosophical Discussion between Nathaniel Seesaw, Reginald Meekin, and Dr. Sana Mens.............. 291

CHAPTER LXIX.
Containing Apologies to the Reader and a Veritable History of the Startling Effects of Congenital Automatism upon a Dogmatic Bridegroom and a Scientific Bride................................. 301

CHAPTER LXX.
Treating of the Startling and Never-before-imagined effects of unconscious Cerebration on a Clerical Guinea-Pig.................................. 309

CHAPTER LXXI
The Rev. Josiah Fetchem returns to the City and finds his Emma Shares declining.—Madame Emma La Fargue prepares for her Wedding 318

CHAPTER LXXII.
The Bride Elect meets with a Terrible Accident, and a very singular discovery is made................. 319

CHAPTER LXXIII.
Death of Madame Emma La Fargue, and decline of the Emma Mine..................................... 322

CHAPTER LXXIV.
A Broker's Classification of "Outside Fools," and a Doctor's Opinion of Josiah Fetchem's Mental State. 324

CHAPTER LXXV.
The Reverend Josiah Fetchem tries a Change of Pulpit; and meets with a most curious and distressing Accident.. 328

CHAPTER LXXVI.
Containing a Broker's Apologies to a Learned Critic.... 334

CHAPTER LXXVII.
Erasmus Pinto's Advice to Investors and Speculators .. 340

CHAPTER LXXVIII.
On the Working of Options.......................... 356

CHAPTER LXXIX.
English Railway as "Media" for Speculation and Investment.. 365

CHAPTER LXXX.
Why the Great Trunk Lines are preferable as Speculative "Media" to the Smaller Ones..................... 369

CHAPTER LXXXI.
Cautions to Intending Speculators and Investors in Railroads.. 380

CHAPTER LXXXII.
A Brief Account of a Stock that has lately been the Joy and Grief of the Speculator by Machinery and the Ruin of the Speculator without..................... 387
Outside Criticism...................................... 407

CHAPTER LXXXIII.
The Scale of Commission 427

CHAPTER LXXXIV.
Queries.. 428

YE OUTSIDE FOOLS.

CHAPTER I.

MY BIRTH AND ORIGIN.—" STEMMATA QUID FACIUNT?"

As I do not write so much for the "great unwashed," the *tunicatus popellus*, who have nothing to lose, and who therefore can whistle safely in the presence of financial robbers, as I do for those who belong to the upper ten thousand, for the well-to-do professional man, the tradesman with a thriving business, the widow, orphan, or minor, and all those who through somebody's departure from this vale of tears have become possessed of means to invest or speculate with, it seems to me quite necessary to say a few words about my origin. An old Roman said, "Virtue is the sole nobility;" but you and I, dear, well-to-do "Outside Fools," know what nonsense that old Roman talked. Birth, your reverences, has its weight in financial matters, or why does Lord Claudius Guinea Pig make such a good thing by representing the interests of shareholders in various companies about which malicious detractors would say he knew—well, about as much as the prospectus itself and the guineas he receives at board meetings. As, therefore, I have made such a good thing out of you outsiders, I tell you this, even if you have not been humbugged by a real live lord, yet you have lost your money to one descended from a king. This should surely be some consolation. We are a Clayshire family, and can trace our descent in direct line from Edward the Fourth. Cecilia, daughter of that monarch, married Viscount Wells Pinto. Mr. Thomas Pinto, a Clayshire Squire, was a lineal descendant of this Viscount Wells Pinto, and my father's mother was a great grand-daughter of the Clayshire Pinto. Now, although my father had the same thin aristocratic figure and regular features peculiar to the Pintos for generations, he was not such a fool as not to see that money is a first-rate setting to aristocracy, and consequently when he met with a wealthy stockjobber's widow, who weighed fifteen stone, if she weighed an ounce, and had fifteen thousand guineas, he forgot his splendid pedigree, and went in for her and her guineas. The marriage was a tolerably happy one, as I have often noticed is the case where the contracting parties are apparently almost totally opposite in disposition and appearance. The only issue was your humble servant Erasmus. So that, on the paternal side, at least, I escape the stigma of being "not born," as the insolent Prussian aristocrat would say of the worthy people who did not happen to belong to his class. As my mother's money had all been made on 'Change, out of the "Outside Fools," it was decided that as soon as I was old enough I should be apprenticed to Messrs. Seesaw and Turnabout, of Change Alley. I had early shown symptoms of financial acumen beyond my years, having when only ten procured a penny with a head on both sides, one of a man, the other of a woman, to toss with, and being able to beat all my schoolfellows at odd man out. At twelve years of age I understood the mysteries of the Three Card Trick as well as any professional frequenter of race-courses. At fifteen I left school and entered the office in Change Alley, as junior clerk. My duties consisted chiefly in carrying telegrams into the House, writing out contracts for clients, and running on any useful errand. But although thus engaged, I kept my eyes and ears well open and acquired more knowledge of human nature in those three years than I should have done in twenty at Messrs. Birchem and Prigge's establishment for young gentlemen. During these years of my apprenticeship I saw much that made me think the relations between broker and client both curious and instructive.

Whenever a stock intrinsically good was unduly depressed from temporary or exceptional causes, and any of our clients expressed a wish to buy, both See-saw and Turnabout would shake their heads gravely, look wise, and say, "You know we can't advise," or, "No doubt there is merit in the stock, but good people are selling, and we hear that the dividend will be disappointing," and similar phrases, that might mean anything or nothing, but which had quite enough influence to stop a client from operating in what he really knew nothing of, as is the case with nine out of ten speculators. If, however, a fair rise had taken place in the same stock, they were always willing to buy, and never said anything to dissuade their clients from acting. When a client wished to sell a bear of a rotten security, one of the partners would say, "I never knew a bear make money outside," or, "The stock ought to fall certainly, but the Baron is in, and it is of no use fighting against him." If, however, the same stock had fallen heavily, and a client thought of selling, one of them would say, "I am a wretched speculator myself, but I shouldn't wonder if you are right; the market don't look very gay just now." Any one of which remarks is sufficient to make a client act, so eagerly do they swallow anything that falls from a broker's lips. Whenever the markets went very much against those of our clients who did not attend personally, we used to send them telegrams freely without charge, while, unless express orders were given, no telegrams were sent when the markets were going decidedly in their favor. The result of this was that many chances of profit were missed, and many heavy losses were incurred by clients either buying back their bears at the highest, or selling their bulls at the lowest. I noticed also that most clients made a profit in their first account with our firm, especially if they were green hands, or had left other brokers and still retained good balances at their bankers. The inference, dear "Outside Fools," I will leave you to draw. The next chapter will contain an account of an important event in my life.

CHAPTER II.

I AM OFFERED THE POST OF CONFIDENTIAL CLERK TO THE FIRM OF SEESAW AND TURNABOUT.

ONE afternoon, after an unusually busy settling day, Mr. Seesaw called me down into his sanctum, and having carefully shut the door, he thus began:—

"Both Turnabout and myself have long seen, Pinto, that you are a youth of more than ordinary discretion and perception, and, unless we mistake your character, you look upon wealth as the great desideratum."

I bowed, for Seesaw certainly expressed my sentiments exactly. The only part of Horace that I could remember at school was this, "Get money by right means if you can, if not, by any means you can."

"As our present clerk, Jabez Suavity, has been compelled to resign through ill health at this busy season of the year, although you are young, we are ready to appoint you to the vacant berth, provided you can pass the preliminary examination to which both myself and Turnabout have always subjected our confidential clerks; and as I have no doubt that your father would not object to paying the one surety that may be paid, we would find the other at the proper time, and so you could be made a member. You may go now," said he, "and mind you are here to-morrow morning before ten o'clock, to be thoroughly catechized about the duties and difficulties of a broker."

I bowed and withdrew.

CHAPTER III.

I PASS MY EXAMINATION TO THE SATISFACTION OF THE FIRM.

THE next morning I entered the partners' sanctum precisely at a quarter to ten o'clock, and found them both there expecting me. After the usual salutations, Seesaw proceeded to put the questions to me, while Turnabout sat, pen in hand, ready to copy down my answers. Both questions and answers might be perused with advantage by a commission appointed to inquire into the duties and privileges of brokers and jobbers. I will give them in the order in which they came.

Are the interests of brokers and clients identical? Only in theory. Why so? Because, if clients generally made money the House must lose it, and consequently both brokers and jobbers would be ruined. How, then, is this prevented? By concerted action on the part of both jobbers and brokers, just as in the cattle and coal market the middlemen and dealers combine to prevent the consumer from buying directly of the producer. For instance, the broker frequently lets the jobber know what his client wants to do, and the price is regulated accordingly. Can you illustrate by example? Yes, sir, if I may quote a case from your own experience. If you know of one you may.

"Arthur Buncombe, Esq., barrister-at-law, who, although a financial fool, was far above the average in general ability, and who was certainly clever enough to often defeat the ends of justice by his florid style of rhetoric and moving appeals to the weak side of a British jury, especially in Breach of Promise Cases, that last refuge of impecunious woman with neither feelings to be injured nor modesty to be shocked, conceived the idea that Caledonian Railway Stock was going to have a great rise. Now, as you know, sir, this was a very good idea, for although Caledonians had only declared a dividend of two per cent. and stood at ninety, it was well known in the

House that the cost of working had been increased enormously at the expense of dividend, and it was suspected that this was done even more than was necessary, so that instead of having a sickly market with no strength in it, when improved prospects set in, the weak bulls might all be cleared out, and a fair proportion of bears be innocently waiting to be pickled, never dreaming of the next dividend being more than three and a half or four per cent. Now, sir, of course you and I know how groundless any such suspicions are; but I cannot help thinking that directors must be more than mortal if they do not feel a secret joy in perusing the puerile calculations of the 'Outside Fools,' based on traffic returns that are often not correct by twenty per cent., and made irrespective of the most important and fluctuating factor in the reckoning, viz., working expenses. And do you not think, sir, that it is a great temptation to a chairman, who may be a believer in the stock of his line, to make things pleasant by deferring certain bills till next half-year, and charging sundry items to capital account which should go against revenue? or, if the evil one have tempted him to sell his shareholders' property short, as the Americans say, to be most strict in keeping up the rolling stock in a wonderful state of efficiency, to reduce all outstanding accounts, and charge everything remorselessly against revenue?"

"Pinto, I think it a temptation that no mortal man ought to be subjected to; but why tantalise me? I am not a chairman, not even a director, more's the pity; but go on with your case."

"Well, sir, Arthur Buncombe, Esq., barrister-at-law and special champion of ladies in search of Breach of Promise dowry, sold all that Great Portmanteau stock which had just issued to delighted and besotted shareholders only seven millions and a half more of its ordinary rubbish at twenty-two and a half, which has been administered by some of the most eminent railway financiers in England from the first down to the present time, and not content with parting with this valuable property, the obstinate man persisted in buying Caledonians, to our great disgust and to the greater disgust of that 'Happy Family' who earned their honest living by selling Great Portmanteaus to an ungrateful public. You know, dear Mr. Seesaw, we were always bears of this valuable property, and found it so convenient to have a client of the bullish kind who could be frightened out just when we wished to close. Oh! was it not a shame? In spite of all your clever little conversational traps, this Buncombe bought ten thousand Caledonian Stock, and as we knew from Glasgow sources that the dividend was much more likely to be five or five and a half than three and a half, which calculators made it, we were afraid lest he should rob the House of fifteen hundred pounds or more. This case, sir, required real genius to manage it. Yes, sir, and, with all due deference, I feel proud to think that it was a clerk and not a principal who managed it. Poor Jabez Suavity, into whose shoes I hope to step, cut this broker's Gordian knot. One morning as he and Buncombe were going across to Capel Court from Change Alley, Suavity remarked quite in a casual way,—

" 'I have an order here to sell fifty thousand Caledonians at best. The Glasgow Syndicate are trying to depress the stock and make the bulls pay a heavy contango, or clear out, in order to buy back their stock at a lower price just after the account. I think well of Caledonians myself, but if you like to sell your ten thousand and buy back when they have dropped, I can add yours to the order and bang the market at the opening.'

"The clever Buncombe listened, was persuaded, sold his stock unto yourself, dear sir, yourself, the adroit framer of the Glasgow telegram. Alas! poor Buncombe! Caleys never dropped at all, but ere an hour was gone they rose full three per cent. The barrister lost heart, coquetted with his early love once more, and lost his all in worn-out Trunks. Jabez Suavity, who had a comic vein and funny hatchet face, told me this tale over a pipe and glass in the evening, and I laughed so much that an attack of liver was completely cured. Though Buncombe was ruined mainly by this trick, he, like thousands more, never dreamt that Suavity was not misled himself, or that the interests of broker and client were not identical."

"Suppose you were called upon to rebut the assertion that brokers do not care whether their clients make money or not, what would you say?"

"I should reply, 'The jobber lives by his turn, (and well he may, for it is two per cent. sometimes), and the broker by his commission,' and I should argue that when money is lost or won, it is only one portion of the public who lose it to, or win it of, another. This answer would satisfy all who had not learnt its fallacy by experience."

"Show the fallacy."

"A large portion of the public are producers, and in the aggregate they always possess more or less money to invest or speculate with. Periods of trade

B

depression may occur and panics interfere with the amount of this production; but still, more or less, it is always going on. Now, when the general public make heavy losses through speculation or investment, it is very seldom that another section of that public is the gainer; but it is the financial acrobat, the loan-monger, the promoter, tout, or jobber, who, knowing beforehand when the mania for a certain class of investment or speculation is sated, unloads at the highest price while the public is stuck with the stock and has to bear a heavy fall, from which too often there is no recovery. Of course there are among the public a few speculators who are possessed of ample means and large experience; but in the City the speculative roach is almost always swallowed by some baronial pike, who, having made a meal of one good shoal, waits in his lair till the next swims by. Directors, bankers, brokers, jobbers, and accountants make money, not because they are cleverer than the outsiders, but because they have better means of getting good information and use it to the fullest extent."

"But if we do not care whether our clients make money or not, and if they keep on losing continually, how is it that we still find clients to deal with us?"

"Because in this country, with its fogs and damp, people suffer so much from liver, spleen, and hypochondria, that the exciting game of speculation acts as a medicine upon the sluggish secretions. Even the immortal professor of the healing art did not find his own pills strong enough, but must needs take a Turkish bath that cost a hundred and fifty thousand pounds. Beware, ye takers of those famous pills, this loss will have to be made up out of your slow secretions! Because, again, the old simplicity of living is now obsolete, and no one tries to live on four per cent., but all co-operate, or speculate, or else invest in foreign I. O. U's., that pay them ten per cent. for a few months or years, and then pay not a cent. Then, clients leave one broker and try another, just as our clients leave us and try another; and a fresh crop of "Outside Fools" is ever springing up, who know nothing of the interesting game, but enter the arena with all the ardor of novices."

"Explain how a clever and spirited broker who would feel ashamed to live on a paltry eighth or quarter per cent. commission may increase his earnings in that way."

"He ought to make a careful selection from the jobbing saints, not sinners—they have not that decorous hypocrisy the others have—and either enter into amicable relations with them, or form a Stock Exchange Partnership. A broker of this sort should never bring out a closer than a half per cent. price in anything, should praise the stocks dealt in but little and with a two per cent. margin. It would be well for him to have a brother or at least a cousin as a jobber in the house. If also he knew two or three gentlemanly-looking old foxes who have been through the fire of experience themselves, who still have means to dress well, and can put on that jovial, frank, honest, sympathetic look that human nature loves so well, let him pay these worthies to become habitués of his office and act as decoy ducks to the speculative neophyte. They should promulgate their views to one another freely, and the broker would do well to take large dummy orders from these gentlemen, for man is not only a gambling, but an imitative animal: The speculative Verdant Green will drink in the oracular views he hears from them with eagerness, and of course they will talk against the stocks he ought to buy, and in favor of those he ought to sell; but will occasionally argue and differ from one another only to yield at last to the view required. They must be, or pretend to be, good judges of wine, cigars, horses, and women. Not many 'Outside Fools' would see that they had fallen among thieves in this amiable family party, and the broker's gains would grow apace."

"But how would you act if a client insisted upon having a close price made before he dealt?"

"I should first try to read him, as the jobbers try to read those brokers with whom they are not in collusion. Suppose I read him a buyer, I should say, 'Things look goodish;' 'they tell me rails are going better;' 'I don't know what to think of Foreign Stocks, do you?' By these little conversational experiments any broker who has the least claim to be considered a judge of human nature will be able to make out what nine out of ten of his clients want to do, and then he can bring out a quarter price, or if his man be an old hand, an eighth. Thus, suppose a client wanted to buy Westerns, and would not take a half per cent. price, I should make him $115\frac{3}{4}$–116, the real market being $115\frac{1}{2}$–$115\frac{3}{4}$, so that he would give 116; whereas if he was a seller, I should make him $115\frac{1}{4}$–$115\frac{1}{2}$, and he would only get the lower price. If I happened to read him wrong, I should make a dummy entry in my book, show it to him when I came out, and say, 'There, that's what I've done; you can have it or leave it. Just as I went in,

Dolorous George bid for or offered twenty thousand Westerns, and the market changed.'"

"Do contango and backwardation afford any scope for clever management?"

"Oh yes! they both alter so quickly and so many times a day, according to the amount of stock in the market, or according to the dealer's books, that nothing is easier to overcharge a bull and get a bear from an eighth to three sixteenths less than he ought to have."

"Give your views on limits."

"These are the most fruitful and amusing sources of gain to a broker. Every limit cleverly worked is equivalent to a put and call option, and the client, who is a mere peg on which the broker may hang his dealings round about the limit, can be shot at till the broker is tired of shooting. This can be done to the great benefit of the broker's pocket and liver, in all cases where the market does not run away from the limit, and as each broker has many clients, there will always be one or two daily targets for him to practise archery at. You see, sir, I have learnt all this from Jabez Suavity, who had only one fault, and that was, to chatter freely after a glass or two of grog."

"Yes, young man," said Seesaw, somewhat severely, "Suavity has chattered to you much more freely than I should expect you to do to any one, if you become our confidential clerk, and hope to become a member of the House. Suppose these little stories got abroad, how many 'Outside Fools' would grow alarmed, and know more than is good for us! Take the hint, Erasmus Pinto."

I bowed, and said I would.

"I think, sir," continued I, "that I could illustrate the working of limits best from another case in your own experience, which Jabez Suavity detailed to me. Have I your permission?"

"You have."

I thus began,—

"The Rev. Titus Marrywell, M.A., incumbent of St. Narrowcreed's, Brighton, finding that his wife's money, although a very nice little fortune, only brought in four per cent. per annum, being invested in a mortgage on land, took the advice of a brother parson, who also had a wife with a nice little fortune, called in the mortgage, and bought Turkish Bs. and Cs. As Sadyk Pasha was then making his tour through the countries of the Christian dogs to rehabilitate the Sultan's waning credit by the Imperial Operating Bank Scheme, these Bs. and Cs. were very lively, and rose two per cent. within a week after the parson bought. When they had relapsed a half per cent. we wired him thus, 'Bs. and Cs. have risen two. Some heavy selling now, and market weak. Reply.' The Rev. Titus did reply, 'Sell all my Bs. and Cs. at best.' We sold them to ourselves, as now the market seemed inclined to turn. Next morning, on reading the Misleading Journal, he found that Bs. and Cs. had risen four per cent., of which he had secured just one and a quarter per cent. as profit. With our contract we had enclosed a note, stating that some very good buying had unexpectedly taken place from Paris after we had sold, and that the market seemed likely to improve further. We therefore advised him to wire us first thing in the morning if he had anything to do, and to leave limits with us, so as not to miss the fluctuations that might occur. Now, as you are aware, sir, although more parsons than almost any other class were dabbling in Bs. and Cs. and other Moslem rubbish, which I should have thought a good Christian would have been afraid to touch, yet the bishops, with that masterly inaction for which they are so justly celebrated,—and although none know better than they that more truth hovers round about a sovereign than round anything else, even though Satan may be inside the coin,—never sent even one pastoral to the clergy of their diocese to warn them of the perils of fishing for sovereigns in such dirty waters, and the danger of bringing their cloth into disrepute with unconverted 'Outside Fools.' As, then, the Rev. Incumbent of St. Narrowcreed's had made a fair profit out of his first transaction with the sons of Belial, and dreamt over-night that he was a holy vessel chosen to spoil the Mahometans, he was down at the telegraph office full five minutes before it was open. In turning the corner he nearly ran into the embrace of the Rev. Lovejoy Cherubum, rector of St. Petticote's, an apostle of the Broad Church, a muscular Christian, with a portly mien, ruddy visage, and cheery voice, one who thought evil of no man, not even of the Turk. These two worthies of such opposite sects were both, oddly enough, bent upon the same errand. The gadfly of speculation had stung their reverend souls, and each blessed Mahometan extravagance and the insane policy of the British government which built up the rotten edifice of crumbling Turkish credit and gave to foolish usurers full ten and sometimes twelve per cent. for years, until they thought the game would last for ever. 'How d'ye do, Marrywell?' said he of St. Petticote's. 'I am going to wire my broker fellow to buy a couple of thousand Bs. and Cs.' 'Going to buy Turks yourself, eh?' replied he of St. Narrowcreed's, with acid look and sanctimonious whine, coining a holy falsehood on his ready tongue. 'Brother Cherubum, all Turks and godless infidels I hold in righteous abhorrence, as my creed enjoins. *You* may lend money on usurious terms to these lost heathen; but *we*, chosen vessels as we are, may not traffic thus. An aged aunt of mine, a God-fearing and holy woman, bids me attend her sick bedside. I telegraph to say I shall be there as soon as trains allow.' Thus having lied, the Rev. Titus gave his message to the clerk, and bowing stiffly to his brother parson, sneaked away. Then Cherubum called to the clerk, who came back with the other's message in his hand, and as the writing happened to be turned right way, the rector, not displeased, nor yet astonished much, read this to the sick aunt, 'If Bs. and Cs. should open good, buy five thousand at the best, first thing. If they improve two per cent., then sell. Suppose, after selling, the market relapses much, buy again at discretion, and if before the close they rise again, sell all.' 'Aha! the fox! I thought as much,' said Cherubum to himself, as he wrote out his wire, to buy Bs. and Cs. himself."

"These men, whose creed allows so very few a chance of being saved, are very often hypocrites."

"But, my dear Mr. Seesaw," said I, "do observe the blooming innocence of this Rev. 'Outside Fool.' For a commission of one pound five per thousand stock the Firm of Seesaw and Turnabout were to make for this greedy and ignorant pillar of the church two or three hundred pounds in one day, and to give him the benefit of their own discretion and experience for nothing. Will not these outside dolts ever learn that a broker only wants them for their commission, or as pegs to hang his own dealings on, and that if money could be made as easily as they mostly think, the broker would make it for himself without the trouble of being pestered with prigs and idiots, who think they know what he has failed to learn thoroughly all his life? But how did you work? This is how. There are dealings at half-past ten in the Foreign Market very often; and this debatable half-hour from half-past ten until eleven can be made a sort of put and call option by a clever broker, because, if he has orders to buy, he can execute them then, put them down to himself if the market goes right way, or put them down to his client, if it goes wrong. At half-past ten Bs. and Cs. opened at $81\frac{1}{2}$, the price at which they closed the night before. As you had an order to buy five thousand, first thing—which 'first thing,' means as soon as there is dealing in the market, or at the official opening, when the rattle goes, as the result may require—you bought five thousand at $81\frac{1}{2}$. Before eleven o'clock, which may also be called 'first thing,' your purchase showed a profit of one per cent., *i.e.*, fifty pounds on the five thousand. You then sold the five thousand to the Rev. Titus at, not eighty-two and a half, which was the exact market price—for in these Bs. and Cs. there is a one per cent. price always sent out, and sometimes two, a splendid trap for 'Outside Fools,' although it is quite possible to deal closer, if the broker wants—but you sold to him at eighty-three, so that in addition to the fifty pounds profit and your commission, which was six pounds five, you had sold at a half per cent. above the market price, which margin of a half per cent. you of course shared with the jobber, who was a partner and a friend. Yes, sir, this half-hour, as you well know, is a mine of wealth to a broker who has plenty of morning orders and a conscience possessing that true aristocratic pliability unattainable by the herd. Of course you wired the parson the moment the market looked like going flat, telling him that, having an order to sell from a client, you had given him the turn and bought the five thousand cheap. Of course, too, when the usual rumour dodge was started, and the 'Outside Fools' who haunt the Telegraphic Exchanges and Speculating Club Rooms, for the purpose of swallowing, as something true and sent express for them alone, the downright lies or garbled facts that the financial pike gets posted up to catch his daily meal of roach with, you wired thus, 'The market is very flat, and it is said that Sadyk Pasha's mission has failed.' And of course the Rev. Titus wired back to sell at best and buy back on a drop. Of course the rumors were false, and instead of a drop there was a rally. You of course wired the news. Titus, being a novice, thought the market must go better, and wired back to buy at best, which you did again a half above the market price. But I need not say more about this speculating pillar of the church. He went on with his limits and you with your working of them until you and the Bs. and Cs. had cleared him out."

"Very good," said Mr. Seesaw; "but some clients insist upon having a limit left in the House. How would you act with them?"

"I should say, first, that I never left a limit in the House, because my client would, of course, never get any better price than the limit, whereas, if he left it with me, he might do so. Of course, sir, you know that our clients, somehow or other, never are lucky enough to get a better price than the limit left; but still, in theory, this would be a fair objection to make against leaving limits with the jobber. Suppose a limit were left in the House to buy Brighton A. at 110, and a bad accident were reported suddenly, the jobber would of course sell directly at 110 although, almost at the moment he sold the stock might be quoted 108, or even lower. Now, in theory, the broker would protect his client and buy at a lower price; but in practice the client would never, or next to never, get any such protection. If, however, a client should still insist on having the limit left in the House, nothing would be easier than to leave it with a jobber with whom you had established 'Amicable relations,' and he would share with you the further margin of profit, when there was any, and would, in all cases where the limit was only just reached, act for himself as against a put or call protection, and you would together share the profit, and report to your client that another quarter, eighth, or sixteenth, as the case might be, was needed to get the business done. Thus, suppose a limit be left in the House with a friendly jobber to sell 10,000 Great Easterns at 51, the moment they touch 51 the 10,000 would be sold. But if the market should afterwards relapse, as in many cases it would, you and the friendly jobber would buy back the 10,000 at whatever profit you could get, and report that the price was never quite 51 buyers. Of course, an experienced client might insist upon having it put down at 51, if the official quotations marked a half per cent. above that price; but you know, sir, that a client has little chance against the committee, and the jobber would of course declare that he did not know they were buyers, and, moreover, if one or two did complain, how many more would not?"

"Very true, Mr. Pinto," said Seesaw, peering curiously at me from under his shaggy eyebrows; "but how would you play the game of Hide and Seek with a client, when, as the Americans say, a soda water rise* was taking place in his stock, or when there was a panic fall, and he wanted to cut his loss quickly?"

Here Turnabout said to Seesaw,—

"Give the boy a glass of old brown sherry, and take one yourself," and this made a break in my examination. I will commence a new chapter with my answer, which I was enabled to make from another anecdote told me by Jabez Suavity.

CHAPTER IV.

THE GAME OF HIDE AND SEEK BETWEEN DR. BLEED-ALL GRABFEE AND MR. NATHANIEL SEESAW.

"WITH your permission, sir," resumed I, "I will illustrate again by a case from your own experience, which Suavity told me, and I will relate it in his words as nearly as I can. He had dined with the doctor and knew his history. Septimus Bleedall Grabfee, M.D., lived in a comfortable house at Kensington. He had married a wife in India who had seven thousand pounds, besides personal attractions. Being

---

* A *soda water rise* means one that is very soon lost; a more sustained rise our Transatlantic cousins term a *whisky rise*.

without encumbrance, as the married servants' advertisements with unconscious satire aptly put it, and being blessed or cursed with a clever, restless brain, he conceived the idea, in which he was encouraged by his wife, of making a large fortune on 'Change. 'One would have thought,' said Jabez Suavity, ' that a man who possessed a wife whose personal attractions were set off by seven thousand pounds' worth of the root of all evil, and a decent practice, might have been content to live on his income and her property. But no, for dear is 'Change unto a busy brain; and so he joined the swelling ranks of "Outside Fools." And fortunate for us it was that he was hit so hard at first, for he would otherwise have beaten us at our own game. He was so well up in the merits of the various stocks, had such excellent perception, could diagnose a market so cleverly, that I do believe we should have failed to clean him out, had he not believed us honest and read newspapers too much. That jolly, young old, rollicking buffer, Reginald Meekin, whom he happened to meet at the "Grand" at Brighton, introduced him first to us.' One morning he came up to town post-haste, having heard from a trustworthy source in America that the Leery Directors were going to be turned out, and more money extracted from the Britisher—ostensibly for steel rails—really, for a fresh lining to the pockets of the Leery Ring. Now this information was good, but the doctor had delayed operation until several besides those behind the scenes had learnt the move. However, on this morning the doctor gave Mr. Turnabout an order to buy five thousand Leeries at the best, as soon as he could get them, and instructed him, in case he could not go down to the House at the opening, to send the order to you, sir, by Suavity, as you had already gone to watch the opening of the Foreign Market. 'Now, youngster,' said Suavity to me, 'keep your eyes skinned and your ears open, for what I am going to say is worth money. Whenever a client gives an order, look out for an alternative in it, for a single "if" in clever hands, can be made a put or call option. The doctor, you will remember, gave the order to Turnabout, and instead of holding his tongue, he must say, "If you cannot go down to the House, send the order to Mr. Seesaw." This alternative, and the fact that Leeries are dealt in before eleven, gave us a very handsome sum. Turnabout went down to the House, unknown to Grabfee, who had gone to the bank to cash a cheque, found Patsy Nickel bidding away for Leeries, which opened a dollar better, with a very strong market. He, of course, seeing the market good, bought five thousand at once, and told Mr. Seesaw that he was not to come out when called, but stand in the Leery market and sell the shares, unless they dropped, when he was to come at once to the office and report the purchase for Grabfee. After this comfortable arrangement, and having, further, left a copy of the order to buy with the Cerberus in Capel Court, to be delivered as soon as Mr. Seesaw came out, Turnabout went placidly to the nearest wine cabin and indulged in sundry glasses of his favorite old brown sherry. Having returned from the bank to the office, and waited for a quarter of an hour, the doctor got uneasy and went down to Capel Court, where he heard that Leeries were rising a dollar every five minutes. This made him wild, and so he set the Cerberus, who keeps the gates of Tartarus, a-bawling, " Seesaw ! Turnabout ! " till he was hoarse, —but half-a-crown soon cured his sore throat.' As long as the Leery market kept on the rise, you played at Hide and Seek amid the excited dealing throng, and listened not to Cerberus. Grabfee got wild, and sent off Suavity, who just came down the court to look for Turnabout. 'Meantime the Leery market paused, looked " toppy," as the saying is, and Hide and Seek no longer paid, so out came Seesaw, saw the doctor with well-feigned surprise, received the slip from Cerberus, and said, " The shares have risen doctor, just four dollars and a half, and still look very good ; but what a pity I did not get this before." "Go in and buy at best ! " said Grabfee, nearly blind with rage. He went and sold the shares that Turnabout had bought first thing to the doctor, at a profit of four dollars a share, thereby making a profit of nearly four thousand pounds which Grabfee should have had. The shares of course would have been sold to him before, if they had dropped instead of rising, as they did. An hour afterwards Leeries dropped a dollar and a half, which movement you promptly reported to the unhappy disciple of Galen, who, disgusted at having lost a chance of making four thousand pounds, and seeing already a difference against him of fifteen hundred pounds, sold all his shares and went off in a huff. Now Pinto,' said Suavity, 'you see how useful Hide and Seek is to a broker, and you ought to see how beautiful a thing is partnership; for each partner can blame the other, as is often the case with man and wife ; but the client can blame neither without the other coming to the rescue.' "

As it was now close upon eleven o'clock, Seesaw said to Turnabout,—

"Pinto has answered our questions with sufficient ability to warrant our appointing him to the vacant office of confidential clerk, so if you will go down to the House and execute the morning orders, I will have a little further conversation with him, and learn how he became so well posted in our private affairs, and I will give him some good general advice."

"I know sir," said I, "that you would be surprised at my being able to relate these anecdotes; but as there now is no chance of Jabez Suavity's resuming office, it can do him no harm, and may do me good. He was a model of reticence, except when he had taken a glass too much, which on occasion he would do; and then he was one of the most amusing and talkative fellows out. He told us these little stories one evening, when Sam Chenery, Harry Lee, and I, were at his rooms in the Queen's Road, Haggerston, having a game of whist; and so graphically did he describe, or rather act, your calm surprise when you first saw the doctor, the innocent look with which you took the order from Cerberus, and the excitement and fury of Grabfee, that we were all convulsed with laughter, and poor Sam Chenery broke a bloodvessel and lost his chance of winning the One Mile Handicap at Lily Bridge, for which he was first favorite.

CHAPTER V.

MR. NATHANIEL SEESAW'S ADVICE TO HIS NEW CONFIDENTIAL CLERK.

" WELL, Mr. Pinto," said Seesaw, "you have certainly given very creditable answers to my questions; but this is partly owing, I perceive, to the instruction you have received from Suavity, who I never should have thought to be so indiscreet. You must clearly understand, young man, that if we appoint you, and you wish to advance your interest, you must consider, as Talleyrand used to do, that words are given to a clever man not to express, but to conceal his thoughts, and that any chattering in your cups would surely ruin you with us. The mainstay of our system is secrecy, and a few little anecdotes, such as you have recounted, would teach an 'Outside Fool' in five minutes more than he has any business to learn in five years. I have taken a fancy to you, and if you play your cards well, you may soon be a member of the Stock Exchange, if not a member of our firm."

I bowed, and assured the worthy man that I never drank anything but claret and an occasional glass of light sherry, and was blessed by nature with a most secretive disposition.

" Well, then, I will now give you a few useful hints about the way of dealing with clients, and tell you what views I hold about the stocks which one would only like a client to deal in. With regard to manner, it is difficult to lay down any rule, for you will have 'Outside Fools' to deal with of all dispositions and classes, from the baronet or now and then an impecunious peer, who sits, as Guinea Pig, upon some company's board, down to the coachman or the lady's maid, who see their Eldorado in some worthless foreign mine. The ideal broker instinctively sees all his clients' characters and weaknesses, and with a graceful versatility can be, or grave, or gay, to suit the man he operates upon. But this is genius, and without flattering myself, Pinto, I think I must possess a portion of this genius, for I was offered three hundred a year by a successful novelist if I would let him come into my office and take a few daily notes while I was operating with my artistic skill on various 'Outside Fools.' Of course I laughed it off: three hundred pounds a year, forsooth! it would be worth a thousand, if not more. However, it is not every man who is able to be a Seesaw, and you must try to imitate me as much as you can. In a general way, it is good to be genial, rather jocular, but never coarse, as too many of our common brokers are—to wear an air of candor and of courtesy, and most to novices. When asked to give a definite opinion about a stock, if possible I put the question off, or answer thus, ' My dear sir, I hear so many opinions, and am so busy, that I have not time to sift them. Your own judgment will often prove better than mine. If you will believe me, we know no more inside than you do outside.' This flatters ' Outside Fools.' Suppose a client gives a view about a stock in your office, profess to be struck with its originality; act the rôle of learner rather than instructor, and if one of your paid habitués can lecture well, encourage him to talk. As some shrewd ancient poet somewhere says, ' More fish will swim into the ponds, and they will be well stocked ere long.' Nothing is more fatal to success than a cold cynical demeanor, or a clownish bluntness that calls a spade a spade. It is wise to have a fund of West End anecdotes, to know the latest scandal in high life, to keep a box of really good cigars, for shillings spent in this way oft bring pounds. Take each client aside, and whisper confidentially, while others are looking on, for most like this, it makes them seem important; and do not make the grave mistake of neglecting smaller clients entirely for ones who deal in fifty thousand at a time. Many brokers spoil a business by this fault. It is not a bad thing to have a fashionable tailor come round to your office,—to have samples of wine about, and to ask your client's opinion about them. When you have brought out the morning prices, your remarks must be discreet and to the point. If orders are slowly given, you might observe, if the office be clear of investing fogies, 'There really is not much doing, but the tone is good. I bought a couple of thousand Egypts for Turnabout, who seems to believe in the stock; but don't you follow him. We are both nearly always wrong.' The fish will rise to this bait, disregard the caution, give you one or more orders to buy Egypts, when of course you will sell to them yourself on a weak market. If you have sufficient 'Amicable relations' established, put a jobber's name upon your contract; the novice has never heard of Stock Exchange Partnerships, and will think collusion is impossible. It is wise to grow a heavy moustache. The mouth is such an awkwardly expressive feature. I have known a beautifully childlike expression of honesty and benevolence on a really clever broker's face quite marred by one small sinister curve hovering about the mouth. Oh, yes! grow a moustache: Hair was given to conceal, not to express."

CHAPTER VI.

MR. SEESAW INSTRUCTS ERASMUS PINTO HOW TO DEAL WITH LADY-CLIENTS.

AFTER a brief pause, Seesaw thus began again,—
"Suppose you are consulted by any widows, orphans, or single ladies, with money to invest, don't put them into Consols, Colonial Government Securities, or Indian Railways, unless compelled; but choose them a good lively stock that pays from seven to ten per cent., such as Turkish, or Egyptian, or Imperial Ottoman Bank. Peruvian, also, is an excellent bait. Many 'Outside Fools' have had slight misgivings about Turkish Stocks, have not been quite sure of Egyptians, but I have scarcely met with one who could see through the guano swindle, who was not dazzled by the much-vaunted value of that country's curious asset, ever increasing while we sleep, a sublime gift of nature which, as yet, has made the lucky half-breeds who possess it independent both of industry and honesty. Even our naval commanders seem to see through spectacles here. Yes, you will do well to put any of your fair clients into such sound securities as these. No fear of their fathers, brothers, or guardians coming down upon you, for they are all engaged themselves in the same interesting but not exactly safe game of usury. Those who have had their dividends for some years,

and who know a friend who has heard of some other friend having had a Bond drawn off at par encourage the new speculators to hope for similar success. Of the three I should choose Egypts as the soundest—indeed, so sound are they, that the Khedive cannot keep himself from buying up large quantities of his own stock and paying for it with money borrowed at a higher rate of interest than the Bonds themselves pay. Well, we will suppose that the tip has gone round to the brokers that a rig is coming on in Egypt seventy-threes, and that investors are much needed to assist the rigging syndicate. Put all the ladies in you can, and having selected Egypts, warn them against Turks and Perus, for when the crash does come, they will remember what you said, and trust you more. Lady-clients give much more trouble, require more consultation, and never seem to think you have any other fish to fry. You may recoup yourself for such a loss of time in sundry ways. When your fair one has taken up her stock, say in a casual way, 'Of course you will take a profit, and buy again if the stock falls. Keep your Bonds in an iron safe, for if they be lost, or burnt, the governments are much too pleased to give fresh Bonds;—when dividend time comes round, they must be left three days for examination.' Your fair clients will be alarmed at these dangers, and will say, 'I have no iron safe, and should not know how to manage.' Offer at once to keep them, collect the dividends, and advise about selling and buying back. This will pay you well. As the Bonds are to bearer, you can borrow money on them as you please; if your client's Bonds be drawn you can substitute undrawn Bonds with ease, and pocket the bonus, for it is ten to one they never took the number down; and last, though not least, you can, having discretionary limits, buy and sell them over and over again and pocket nearly all the gains, while, if you should be so awkward as to act at the wrong time, all you have to do is to write a diplomatic note and say, 'Certain rumors were afloat, and thinking that ladies ought to run no risks, I sold. The rumors have fortunately been proved false, and the stock has risen again. Shall I buy back again?' In case they should refuse to do this, send them the quotation of some other lively stock that you can recommend, and say that, as the market went the wrong way, you will charge them no commission. Women like to be written to; don't grudge your time. The poor souls will repay you at least fifty per cent. Let your motto be, 'I throw a sprat to catch a herring with.' Country clients are preferable to those who attend personally. It is true they deal more seldom, but you can charge them at least twice as much commission, influence them much more by your correspondence, and escape the worry of those numberless inquiries which so often result in no business, and from that annoying buzzing about a man to which the clients who attend daily are addicted.

" When any of your clients become defaulters, treat them leniently, and waste no time in law, for of course some of them must in time fail, whether honest or dishonest, contending vainly as they do against a beautiful and elaborate system about which they know next to nothing, and where the odds are so much against them, without reckoning that indirect personal influence a clever broker brings to bear, which often is the greatest odd of all. You must have noticed yourself, Pinto, how much and frequently such words as these have told on our clients' dealings, 'What a swindle that Brighton A market is! I should not wonder if the dealers did not refuse to carry over next time. If I were a speculator, and did not mind paying a little out, I should make a fortune here. I think British will soon be quite unsaleable.' But these remarks must not be made, so to speak, *at* your client, they must appear spontaneous and as if made by one who could not bear to see a swindle going on successfully. Of course the result would be that your clients would become bears of two rising and improving stocks, against which all that any one could justly say would be that they had improved much and risen much to correspond with the improvement. Never go to law. You may depend upon it that an 'Outside Fool' will speculate until he has lost all. Besides, it would do your connection harm, and in this world of many ups and downs, the lame duck* may get cured of its lameness and come back to dabble in the dirt again. My plan is always this. I say,—

" 'Pay me what you can, dear sir. I would write off the debt were I a richer man; but I have a family and cannot afford the luxury. And pay me when you can. I know you are a man of honor.'

"You would be surprised how my defaulting clients have worked to pay me what they owed."

---

* A lame duck is one who cannot pay his differences.

CHAPTER VII.

MR. NATHANIEL SEESAW WARNS ERASMUS PINTO AGAINST SPECULATING IN UNSAFE STOCKS.

" OF course you will occasionally speculate yourself. To do this safely you must follow principles, not ideas, or even with your superior knowledge of the business and better information, you will be ruined. If you take my advice you will never buy a share in a mine, English or Foreign. The really good English mines scarcely ever come upon the market, and good foreign mines more seldom still. Even if a really good mine is worked by a public company, just as a good racehorse is sometimes not allowed to win, so it is not allowed to turn out well. Such prizes as Cape Copper, Devon Consols, Van, and St. John Del Roy are the baits which catch the ' Outside Fools,' who forget that among the thousands of utter failures these are the only prizes. Take no shares in industrial companies, unless fully acquainted with the concern. Success here depends upon the management, often upon a single manager's honesty, business capacity, or sobriety. Cable shares are as yet in their infancy, and should only be touched by rich men who can afford and ought to pay for the experiments of science. Any day a new cable may be invented that may do its work much better and cost half the money. Still they are dangerous to bear, for the reason that the persons who now hold most of them are powerful and rich. Foreign governments, with the exception of France, Russia, the United States, Portugal, and one or two others, only pay their interest by fresh borrowing; and as the above-mentioned countries' Bonds only pay an average of five per cent. on the price, with some not inconsiderable chance of a depreciation, I cannot see the use of buying them. A great deal of fuss was made about the honorable way in which Russia paid the interest on her bonds during the Crimean War; but surely a country backed up by the greatest capitalist would not kill the goose that laid the golden eggs. The truth is, foreign loans are very much like mines, and their credit depends quite as much upon the name of of the financier who endorses their bills as upon the resources of the country.

Why, when the young Alfonso ascended the throne of bankrupt Spain, and a very large fish had bought the Bonds, we read such articles on Spanish stocks that, had we not well known that all those columns were a mere financier's puff, we must have bought. No abuse just now seems bad enough for brokers and jobbers; but surely the magnates of finance, who bleed England by the power of their names of such huge sums for countries to develop all their railway system for strategic purposes, or for empires, almost unknown to the lenders, to spend the money as they please, do far more harm than we. *We* only execute fools' orders, and are looked upon as almost thieves. *They*, by the credit of their names, induce some millions to put money into these foreign I O U's who do not speculate. We help the speculator to lose his money with us which he would surely lose with some one else. We are execrated; they are lauded to the skies. And why? Because none dare tell truth where all this root of evil is. Russians would be a first rate bear, but you cannot carry over; the stock

C

is always scarce. Some day a fall of twenty per cent. will come, the great man will have sold his first, and then you will be able to carry over as a bear with ease.

No, Pinto, don't touch foreign loans yourself, but let your clients try their best against the wire-pulling usurers who rule the roast. Would you deal for yourself in the stocks of so-called governments, that first sell enormous bears of their own rubbish, then spread rumors of repudiation, then buy back their bears, deny the rumors, then sell bears again upon the rally, then repudiate? or pay half the dividend due to their creditors, and claim the whole upon the stock they hold themselves? Oh! come, ye 'Outside Fools,' these are the stocks for *you*. Call us hard names, but catch *us* in these traps you never will again. Oh! if you but knew the size of the commissions large financial houses get for selling their good names and catching those silliest of all, investing fools, you would not think our charges much! I speak with feeling on this topic, Pinto, and I'll tell you why. Perus and Turks have never caught me yet, but set a thief to catch a thief, they say. With shame I own it, I, Nathaniel Seesaw, backed up by a system of elaborate chicanery, no fool to wit, was beaten by the wily African and his financing touts and juggling band. Seeing that sleepy old gentleman John Bull let foreign countries on the verge of bankruptcy dip their hands so freely into his pockets, I was caught by the idea of the Mahometan buying up his own stock with the bondholders' money and then issuing a fresh loan at the higher price. It really was a grand idea. Some clever rogues were caught in that Egyptian trap of 1873. I was not the only one; there is some solace there. Knowing that the syndicate was powerful and rich, which was to float the loan of 1873, I bought a large stake in the loan of 1868 at 91 in 1872. It had been nearly 96. No doubt I was an awful ass, but I was unlucky enough to know one of the syndicate, and that is how it was. The loan came out for £32,000,000, in 1873. I never had a chance to sell. The public did not take the bait; the syndicate were sold instead of selling "Outside Fools." My 68 loan was at 75. Yes, Pinto, and I've got it now. Why did not my friends shave my head, and keep me in close confinement till that Egyptian bubble burst? Ah! why indeed! I fear I shall never recoup myself for that mad act. So learn from my experience, and never buy a foreign Bond, for when a heavy drop occurs, you don't know where it will end, the intrinsic merit is so small.

If you speculate, buy English Rails. This is a property, it is indestructible, and in time is sure to recover, unless the country should go to the dogs. The price Rails have been once they always reach again. Of course directors may be found who play their game to suit themselves, defer some bills to next half-year to swell the dividend, or drag some in to keep it down, charge sometimes more and sometimes less to capital account, create fresh capital too much, and dip their own hands in the till; but the day is fast approaching when directors and their speculative friends, with the aid of noodles' proxies, will no longer be able to hoodwink or gag a meeting, but will be required to give a good account of their stewardship, to foster no underhand competitive schemes, brought forward only to depress the stock, and then be suddenly withdrawn, to really fuse, or not pretend to fuse, and aim at closing capital accounts.

All this is coming, but it must have time. The only danger is that, when there is no foreign rubbish left, the great men of finance should buy these Rails enormously, buy articles to crack them up too much, and then produce a panic by their sales. This, too, is on the cards. At present the *Misleading Journal* tries to prove all Rails too high, and that a panic is to come. You see the big ones like to buy their good things cheap. Yes, Pinto, if you speculate, buy English Rails, and when you read a savage article against these English Rails, buy twice as much as if no article appeared. You'll make a trifle so. In conclusion, remember this. To speculate successfully there are three requisites—judgment, nerve, and money. Judgment is to some extent a natural gift; nerve may be increased, if not acquired wholly, by sobriety and persevering energy; some little money must be had to start with, unless you run an unfair risk and make a fluke. I must now see to business. You will do for us I think."

CHAPTER VIII.

MR. TURNABOUT'S QUAINT TEST OF A YOUNG MAN'S FITNESS FOR THE OFFICE OF CONFIDENTIAL CLERK.

At this moment John Turnabout entered the office, his great red face glowing with excitement, or—the favorite old brown sherry. The playful wags inside the House called him "Butcher Turnabout." In some respects he was a worthy soul; but nothing could convince him that the nation was not made for the Stock Exchange, instead of the Stock Exchange for the nation.

"Well," cried he, " to be, or not to be?"

"Oh!" replied Seesaw, "Pinto will do for us; he has answered all my questions more than well, and listened to my homily on stocks with most attentive ears."

" I should like to put one to him myself," rejoined John 'Butcher' Turnabout. "It is an odd one, but the man who answers it as I think that he ought may be trusted anywhere with anything. I never yet found one of Pinto's age who could so answer it. Suppose, young man," said this funny old broker to me, "you were travelling alone in a first-class carriage on one of the metropolitan railways, and a young lady with pretty trusting face and winsome ways, and figure freely shown by the new-fangled style of dress, which an old man like me would think suggestive, if not immodest, were to step into the same carriage, and seating herself opposite to you, say, 'Pray, am I right for St. John's Wood?' what would you do?"

For a few moments I was fairly staggered by this novel question; but soon recovering, I thus replied,—

"I should answer my fair questioner with the suggestive dress in these few words, 'I really am not sure, but I'll get out and ask a porter.' Suiting the action to the word, I should have the rudeness to forget that I had seen the lady, should spring into the nearest carriage in which the other sex was not, and ride in safety to my journey's end. 'You see, sir,' as an intelligent, though ungrammatical porter once remarked to me—' you see, sir, they 'as quite a weakness for perfessional men a-travelling alone in a first-class carriage.'"

"Bravo, Pinto," said the funny butcher; "a man of your age, who is proof against the seductive wiles of such a dangerous man-trap, is safe enough for me; you now are one of us. Off to your desk and wire the country clients well to make up for lost time."

I bowed, and wired, well pleased that I was safely through this odd ordeal, and wondering much at the butcher broker's grotesque test of my trustworthiness.

CHAPTER IX.

ERASMUS PINTO GOES TO DINE WITH MR. NATHANIEL SEESAW.

NEXT day, when business was nearly over, and when I had wired at least half a dozen country clients out of good stocks on a rising market, and into South American rubbish on a falling one, Mr. Seesaw said to me,—

"Come and take your dinner with me this evening, Pinto, and we can have a quiet chat. There will be no one else but my daughter and Mr. Levi Gusher, of the *People's Bellowgraphic*, and he has an engagement soon after dinner."

We left the office just in time to catch the five o'clock express to Chalk Farm. Seesaw lived in the Adelaide Road, some distance from the station.

"I did live at Brighton," said he, after we were safely ensconced in an empty carriage and had lit two of his particular Partagas; "but I could not stand the wear and tear of travelling up and down every day. What a place that Brighton is! It will soon be nothing but one vast suburb of London; all the world seems to go to Brighton now, and a good part of it to live there. I hear the Beckenham scheme is to be on again. Metropolitan promoters, I imagine. What nice little profits the Baron and Sammyvell ought to have made out of their Brighton bulls. There is a pot of money, Pinto, to be made out of that threat of competition, hackneyed trick as it is. Even the great wire-pullers on the bull side like it, because they can clear out all the weak and timid holders so, and get a firm basis for a further upward move. Of course the bill will be withdrawn, as it was a few years ago, and about the same day. Now, Pinto, if you and I had made such a haul out of the stock as I dare say those two and their party have, we should go to the promoters of the rival scheme and say,—

"'Come, now, gentlemen, what do you expect to get? You know as well as we do that if you do deposit the money you will never get the bill passed, and however much the public may like the idea of cheaper fares, through competition, they will never take shares in the new company. Of course, as large quantities of Brighton stock are still in certain persons' hands, waiting to be absorbed by the public at the proper time, you have a strong position, for the pot might boil over, if it went on far enough. But you would only gain a little by selling the stock, which would not drop much till the bill had really passed, and pass it never will. Suppose we say five thousand each for A, B, C, and two for all the rest, you then might buy the stock before the scheme is publicly withdrawn and make a certain profit in addition to the *douceur* we propose to give. Of course you are strong enough to get the shares quoted at a fictitious premium, even now-a-days; but really there's no chance.'

"Yes, Pinto, that's what we should do. Is it not a pity that the Brighton Directors are so entirely devoted to their shareholders' interest and the promoters of the rival scheme so anxious for a problematic public good as not to see their own? Oh! it is a pity! Why, if they took the money, both might agree to pay a worse dividend this half, pay bills that need not be thought of till next half year, spend more on rolling stock, and get the A's down ten per cent., then next half year, when all the calculating idiots would go for two per cent., come out with three and a half or four. Oh! Pinto, if we had the chance of such a pretty little game, we soon should have swell mansions at the West End then, yes, and at Brighton too.

"Then there's that Chatham Fusion Scheme. I grieve to see two champions so careful of their reputation for acumen so determined to exact the uttermost farthing from each other's shareholders that one hundred thousand pounds a year that might be saved is lost to both. The shareholders will try to make them fuse at this next meeting, I should think. And, Pinto, if they fuse don't put your money in the stocks, except for a soda-water rise, for Parliament will never pass the fusion scheme unless they promise to reduce the fares, which, to my mind, are quite absurdly high. No, Pinto, choose the great trunk lines, not these close boroughs, where so much is dark, so many schemes afloat. But just suppose that you and I were the two Kings of Brentford, Pinto, what a pretty little swindle we should start. In the first place, we should permit, not instruct, mind, some well-dressed gentleman with a good store of native impudence to circularise the public with the details of the scheme. We should let most of the very rich shareholders into our plot and none of the poorer ones. Then we should, of course, having bought large quantities of stock before the public mention of the scheme, sell gradually all that the market would absorb. There then would be a hitch, or first a rumor only of a hitch; we should buy back again, and take quick profits, after other rumors had replaced the former ones. Thus to and fro with loaded dice would Messrs. Seesaw and Pinto play until their pockets were quite full. When pressure from without became too strong, we then should fuse, and sell huge bears at quite the top, then have a virtuous fit, reduce the fares to please the public and the government, and close our bears at the right time. Aha! ye shareholders of those southern lines, ye may bless your stars that ye have such men as ye have to look so closely after your real interests, for we should soon have shown you what besotted fools we thought you were."

I pressed old Seesaw's hand in silence; he was really eloquent.

"Yes, Pinto," said the worthy man, "I should have got back all my Egypt loss, for with such profits I could well have afforded to sell even at the present price. But let us cut the shop; it makes me ill to think what fools directors are to miss such splendid chances so. What do you think of matrimony, Pinto—eh?"

"My dear Mr. Seesaw," said I, " it is a subject that I hardly dare to think upon. If I lived in one of the colonies, where a sheep could be bought for half-a-crown and a bullock for half a guinea, and where surplus corn is used to light the ovens with, I should not only think of matrimony, but speedily take unto myself a wife and set about increasing the population. In a new country, population is surely the one great requisite. But in one like this, where your butcher will scarcely let you have a pound of good meat for a shilling, and where your baker sells you a sickly compound of inferior wheat adroitly blended with the Rock Potato, or other worse adulterating agents, where house-rent, food, and taxes are ever growing more expensive day by day, while earnings keep the same or else grow less—except for colliers, who work three days in the week and drink champagne the other four, and for the communistic artisan, whom agitators for their selfish purposes seem bent on keeping ignorant, by raising the education cry in their own vicious way—where servants now are the real mistresses, where the million or more surplus ladies, as a certain person lately somewhat insolently termed them, are seriously discussing the question, whether it would not be better to go out to service and be well fed, with plenty of pocket-money, besides being able to badger the snobs upstairs, a privilege which, I can assure you, is not to be despised.

"As for 'Lady Helps,' whatever that very silly term may mean, I suppose they would establish 'amicable relations,' as we say on 'Change, with the unmarried males they might come in contact with, and although the mistress of the house would probably be furious, I daresay it might be good for the nation at large.

But this question is too deep for me, I leave it to the female Solomon who keeps writing to the papers on these interesting topics. I would rather be a servant in a luxurious family belonging to the upper ten than a governess; for my lady does not get five shillings bonus when she pays a bill of two pound nine, whereas, unless I were a downright fool, I should get this in Regent Street at least. Hence spring co-operative stores. But I am getting away from the subject. How dare the thousands of men who have inelastic incomes of from two to three hundred a year think of marrying a wife who must be elaborately tied above and below so that sitting down would be impossible, while to save her life from a mad bull she could not spring aside without the danger of most disastrous and splitting results? How dare they face the hungry if not healthy baby almost sure to turn up rather more than once a year? How dare they face the chance of twins and still more wondrous and alarming natural or unnatural feats? How dare they face the awful doctor's bills, the scarcely ever absent nurse? Ah! how indeed?

"It appears to me, sir, that whatever cant may say in such a country as this over-populated, under-educated, and luxurious Island is, it is almost as much an intelligent man's duty to abstain from committing matrimony until he can afford it as it is to abstain from drink, or any other vicious habit. Suppose, you say, 'There is emigration.' True, there is; but emigration takes from us the vigorous and strong, and leaves us but the weak, the *bouches inutiles*, and an ever swelling class with brains and education too, well fitted for professions, but not able to find one that pays and is not over-stocked. In truth, dear sir, I feel that the greatest benefit that I could bestow on my own class would be, instead of marrying on nothing and depriving some one else of his fair share of food and love, to slink away unnoticed from this vale of tears and make room for some poor devil who, most likely through no want of his, is nearly starving through the want of remunerative employment. Yes, sir, food and love, I take it, are the two real requisites for happiness in life, to which in cold countries a trifle of clothing may be judiciously added; but surely there is no need for such grotesque and elaborate architecture in modern dress, with all that quaint cockscomb behind. If single ladies knew how these astonishing devices terrify the marrying man with a small income, surely they would in charity defy the milliners, and once more let the lady strike the eye more than the lady's dress.

"Now, dear Mr. Seesaw, money, which in the city certainly seems the root of evil, can purchase food, the first great requisite for happiness, and even if it will not buy the love, it goes a long way to make it comfortable. It can surround the love with awful trains, suggestive and statuesque dresses, bijouterie, and all the nick-nacks which your lady, who would move in good 'society,' that many-headed hydra, requires. If anything stirs my bile more than another it is the reckless way in which poor curates with one hundred pounds a year, or little more, rush into matrimonial bliss, and saying, 'The Lord will provide,' straightway beget a baker's dozen of children, and then call upon the parish to help to pay the butcher's and baker's bill, and to put Tom, Dick, and Harry, and any of their brothers and sisters who may be ready, to school. Of course I do not allude to that intelligent and ever-growing class of parsons who, however much they preach against the vanity and danger of the riches of this world, with calm philosophy select some fair one from their virgin flock—a flock that is, if anything, more full of faith in their dear pastor's self than in the truths he tells—and look more to the fair one's fortune than her charms.

"Oh no, these clever parsons do not rob their fellow-creatures of their share of food or love. 'Tis right enough, for hardly shall the rich enter into the kingdom of heaven, we are told. Then what a triumph for a holy man to lead the wealthy Edith there, to spend her money, some on charity, some on himself. Whatever cynics say, it must be right. The parents, too, are right to give her to the holy man, for though he may be only as a layman is, his cloth ensures respectability. Oh yes, the parents are quite right. But the other parsons, who do not wear these prudent spectacles, although perchance more honest men and true themselves, are surely very wrong in marrying before their time, and wedding wives before they have a prospect of securing that other requisite of happiness. The value of the food supply is raised by this thoughtless matrimony and begetting of children, which the parents really cannot keep themselves. Why, sir, a fourth of all our taxes might be paid by fining heavily the rich unmarried bachelors and spinsters, and by imprisoning without a fine all those who married thus imprudently. Now I dare say, Mr. Seesaw, you think I talk thus because I have no wish to get married myself. There's nothing I should like so much; but I don't see my way at all.

"Young man," replied he, "your views are somewhat strange, but not far from the truth; yet still I can't help looking on man's selfishness in this respect with lenient eye. 'Tis true I, like the clever parson, married Mrs. Seesaw more as a financial helpmate than because I was much in love, and I was lucky, for never, I think, were more good qualities enclosed in narrow space. Thin as a lath, weak as a cat, with lack-lustre and sorrowful eyes, poor Jane Sipthorpe Sadd lived just three years after we were wed, then quietly retired to a better world and left me one daughter, to whom I will introduce you when we get home. But though there was scarcely enough material in my poor Jane to kindle so gross a flame as ordinary love, besides all her good qualities, she had just thirteen thousand pounds, which if it did not make me love, made me respect her very much. This money, Pinto, was not invested in rotten foreign Bonds, that pay you anything per cent. as long as they can keep on borrowing, not in flourishing industrial companies, where ten or twelve per cent. is paid for two or three years, and then the manager levants with all the funds, or takes to drink, not in bank shares, that favorite investment of ladies with limited incomes, clergymen, and orphans, who never think of calls, but live on all their dividends, and do not set aside a single cent. for rainy days. I wonder what the issue would have been if the directors of one of our greatest banks that lost nine hundred thousand pounds by lending money upon worthless bits of paper, instead of sound securities like English Rails, had come before their ignorant and greedy shareholders, who never thought of calls and unlimited liability, and said, 'Ladies and gentlemen, we have lent your money to men of straw, and lost it; indeed, we have lost so much, that we cannot pay you any dividend at all, and our reserve is gone.' Why, if the directors had told the naked truth, there would have been a run upon the bank, the greedy fools who held the shares would all have sold, and the credit of the bank quite ruined for a time. A man or woman who holds bank shares has no right to live on all the dividends, for all·banks must in a certain number of years be liable to break—even the Bank of England would have broken more than once, but for the aid of government—but should set aside from seven to ten, and form a sinking fund to recoup him in event of failure. No, Pinto; Mrs. Seesaw's money was not invested in these dangerous securities, but in a first-class mortgage on another person's land, with ample margin. I used to consider myself a bear of land without having any difference to pay, and I used to wish a time would come when I could foreclose and take in my bear at a low price. I should not care to be a bull of land just now. Some years of great prosperity have raised the price enormously, and made us think that land will never go back again. This is not true. There is, no doubt, an improving undertone in land; but after a period of inflated prosperity, it is dangerous to buy even solid stuff like land, unless you pay for it entirely. Suppose land has risen twenty-five per cent. in value through a series of peaceful prosperous years. A man buys forty thousand pounds' worth. and borrows thirty thousand on it. When bad times come round, his mortgage is called in, his bankers desert him just when he wants their aid, and, if he tries to sell, there's not a buyer in the field, except at such a price that wipes off his ten thousand pounds. Some day, ere very long, these borrowers on land will find out their mistake. The fact is, nothing short of the actual value of any security, however sound, is absolutely safe. But if the owner of ten thousand pounds had bought ten thousand pounds' worth of land, and paid for it whatever happened, he would be as safe as it is possible to be. In case of war, he might not be able to sell, but he would get a tenant easily; for surplus-population makes more tenants but not more land, and corn is dearer in a war; and so would land be, if all owners paid entirely for their land. Unless luxury has brought our nation to the very verge of decadence, as it did the countries of old times, land is the finest investment to be found; but one who buys when land is dear, should pay for what he buys.

"Well, Pinto, soon after the death of my poor Jane, the panic of 1866 broke out, Upperends burst up, banks came down with a crash, and among the thousands rendered penniless, the gentleman upon whose lands I held a first-class mortgage tried to raise a second mortgage to pay his calls in vain, and failed. Yes, Upperends, whom all the world had trusted so. And since their time how many more great names have proved but dross; and so it will be to the end of time. Upperends have failed, Sidonia reigns, and if the 'Outside Fools' don't learn much more quickly than they have of late, he will reign long enough to be beyond the reach of even the slightest check. He must feel very sad, this wonderful Sidonia. What supreme contempt he must feel for all the miserable fools who fall a prey to his well organised machinery. I wonder, Pinto, whether he believes in other worlds, or thinks this life the sum of happiness? Do you know, Pinto, I admire that man intensely, though I wonder how he can resist the fearful temptations his enormous wealth renders him liable to. I daresay he is anything but happy, if you knew the truth. You see, if one gets to the very top of anything, it is a dismal prospect to look down; the competition upwards is the healthy thing. Poor Sidonia! wealthy as he is, I do believe he is more lonely than such pettifoggers as Nathaniel Seesaw and Erasmus Pinto. He must know that men came to see him for his wealth, and not for himself. I should vastly like, Pinto, just to dine with him once, to see the great leviathan and find out whether the root of evil has left still some traces of humanity. Well, as I told you, my mortgagor, unable to raise a second mortgage on his land, was forced to sell. The estate, which was worth much more than it fetched, was put up for sale. As I stood in the best position, and few had money to invest, I bought it for just one thousand pounds more than it was mortgaged for, and three years afterwards I sold it at a profit of eleven thousand pounds. My losses in Egyptian stocks have absorbed most of what I had except ten thousand pounds, which is settled on my daughter Clara, and will remain so whether she marries or not. I thought before the Foreign Loans Committee gave the *coup de grâce* to all these Bonds I might get out without a loss; but now I am afraid, and know not what to do. This Egypt nut is very hard to crack. One thing is very clear, the stock can't stay where it is now. A rise or fall of twenty per cent. must be on the cards, and I must wait and grill. But I forgot; we shall meet Mr. Levi Gusher, of the *People's Bellowgraphic*, at dinner, and as he is, among other things, the Egyptian special, and keeps a 'sub' there while he is at home, he will perhaps enlighten us.

" Now, Pinto, if ever you should feel as if you could not do without the love as well as the food we talked about just now, take my advice, and go straight to the father of some nice girl who has both requisites, and say, ' I love your daughter, sir; but she has money, and as yet I've next to none. But though I have but little money, I know what its value is, and how to keep it safe. Let me try to win your daughter, and if I succeed, tie all her money fast to her so that I cannot touch a cent.' Were I the father of that girl, I should reply, 'Young man, I value money quite as much as most men do; but when I call to mind how many of my friends, respectable and energetic men, have been reduced from affluence to beggary through ignorance of what is safe and what is not, I feel that I would rather trust my daughter to a man who knows what safe investment means than to a rich man who might lose his all in some unsound security.' By-the-by, how is your father, Pinto? I heard the other day that he had sold the estate in Clayshire. Lucky hit that purchase was, so Tape and String of Lincoln's Inn told me. He would have missed that chance but for the unexpired lease, and the testator's family, who, anxious only to divide and get clear of each other, instead of keeping the estate and living on the rent, were eager to sell, and as your father's lease was not run out, they offered it to him. I never saw a man who better deserved his good fortune than your father does. He is a fine old gentleman. His only fault seems that he is so easily persuaded by other people, which often makes him suffer secretly for want of firmness to refuse. His judgment is good, but he mistrusts it and himself through poorness of blood. If I were called in as a doctor to prescribe, I should exhibit Clarke's blood mixture and port wine, to raise the good man's estimate of self, and stop his overrating other people so. Excuse my speaking plainly, but I really see nothing else that can prevent Pinto senior from keeping the money brought him by the sale of this estate. I suppose his wife's money is tied to her, is it not?"

I laughed at Seesaw's quaint remarks and remedies, and said I thought it was; and wondered to myself why he asked such a question, and talked about my worthy father so. Just then our train stopped in the station at Chalk farm. After a walk of three or four minutes we arrived at Mr. Seesaw's house, which I will describe to you in another chapter.

CHAPTER X.

MR. NATHANIEL SEESAW'S HOUSE AND POSITION.

EVERY one knows the Adelaide Road, running from the Adelaide Tavern, in the Hampstead Road, along the North Side of Primrose Hill, and intersecting the Avenue and Finchley Roads. It is a good cheerful road, with houses of a comfortable unpretentious style, not built for "Stucco Swells," but for families who know little and care less for the hollow, feverish Belgravian life, for families whose aim is to eat, drink, sleep, and go to church in a regular respectable kind of way, to whom Mrs. Grundy is an amusement rather than a terror. Mr. Seesaw's house was called "Boyfield House," after a relation of his brother, who had made a fortune in Wheal Mary Anne Shares, and being childless, was expected to leave Clara Seesaw some more of the root of evil. The house itself was replete with cheerful, well-furnished rooms, and in other respects was like many in the same road. There was no straining after effect, no tinsel, no flashy furniture such as the vulgar plutocrat affects. Nathaniel Seesaw, though a City Broker, was a man of taste and much respected in the neighborhood. He had been the vicar's churchwarden for some years, and had been retained in that office, it was currently reported, because of the very superior way in which he held the plate on Sundays, especially to all who flocked in the church without having sittings of their own. Few could resist the powerful appeal, not of their own consciences, not of the Rev. Silvertongue Richwife's eloquent discourse, but of Nathaniel Seesaw's full basilisk gaze, so cold and clear, so utterly devoid of any sympathy with the impecunious devout—a gaze that seemed to read each parsimonious thought as soon as it was formed —a gaze that often changed, as if by sleight of hand, a silver threepenny into a shilling, and not seldom half-a-crown, according to the moral strength or weakness of the victims that he gazed upon. Oh! with what sovereign contempt he looked upon the paltry giver of a threepenny, that miserable silver piece, coined surely by the Evil One to be a thorn in the side of holy men, by which so many niggard, lukewarm souls seek to evade their religious obligations. I say *evade*, for never can *discharge* be gained at such

cheap rate. With what bland smile Nathaniel Seesaw beamed on givers of gold pieces, whose disordered
livers, or the purse-proud wish to seem more charitable than others are, too often made them give the
gold. The widow's threepenny is more than your
gold pieces, ye would-be religious fools. I myself
heard the Rev. Hawhaw Chasuble incautiously avow
at Miss Ancient's muffinstruggle, that his vicar—that
is, he meant to say, the parish poor—would lose three
hundred pounds a year if Mr. Seesaw were to give
his office up.

We were now assembled in the drawing-room, and
I was introduced to Clara Seesaw and Mr. Levi
Gusher, the Egyptian special. As the lady exercised
an important influence on my career, I will describe
her first.

CHAPTER XI.

CLARA SEESAW.

> We met: what need of speech,
> To tell the heart that each
> Was dear?—a word, a look,
> And from an open book
> Of thought, we read our love.
>
> *A Fragment from the Poems of Salome Pinto.*

IMAGINE my dear "Outside Fools," a woman about
twenty-five years of age, with a very pale but not
unhealthy complexion, perfectly oval face, wavy
chestnut hair, and very large full brown eyes, that
looked at you with an honest openness, and, at the
same time, an unconscious dreaminess that made

you interested in, and at home with, their owner at once. In figure rather tall and slight, she moved with an alluring languid grace, a sort of serpentine litheness that was enchanting. There were curves and undulations about the figure of Clara Seesaw that are not possessed by ordinary women. To be in her presence soothed and delighted the senses much in the same way as it does to listen to a beautiful piece of quiet music. There was no conventional *pose*, no studied manner; she was perfectly natural, and yet completely lady like. Her dress became her, but added nothing to her beauty, which would have been infinitely more beautiful and graceful to the artist's eye in a Garden of Eden, clad only in the simple costume of our first parents. After meeting with the girls one does meet with in London society — girls fearfully and wonderfully dressed, in manner half-flirt, half-actress, or, if nature be not wholly suppressed by art, simpering and silly, bent alone on securing some well-to-do mediocrity as a partner for life—it was indeed a rare treat to see this woman, fascinating, yet quite unconscious of her power to fascinate; unsophisticated, yet well informed; charmingly naïve, and free from prudishness, yet far more modest than the conscious misses who are so afraid of seeming natural, on whose cheeks a blush is so ready to rise that men who did not know this style of girl would think she must be blushing at her thoughts. As you are now probably tired of my description of Clara Seesaw, let us turn to Mr. Levi Gusher, the City Editor, and Special Correspondent on Egyptian affairs.

CHAPTER XII.

MR. LEVI GUSHER, OF THE "PEOPLE'S BELLOW-GRAPHIC.

A VERY feminine-looking man was Levi Gusher, with a blonde complexion like a girl's, a face perfectly innocent of whiskers or moustaches, and features small and delicately chiselled. In height he was quite five feet three, if not half an inch more. And yet, though small in size, this little man had a most magnificent air, and when not in foreign parts, his dress was the envy of all City editors, to all of whom he was about as superior in neatness of person, quality and style of boots and gloves as he was inferior in power of brain. With his small well-turned head raised high enough to be quite uncomfortable to the back of his neck, this little fellow would gaze abstractedly into space like one whose brain is laboring to solve some difficult financial problem. He wore this philosophic air for fear he should be confounded with the common herd of speculators whom he passed on his way from his office to his broker's, and from his broker's back again. This dainty person was, so said report, a favorite with women, who like either strong, passionate, manly sort of men, to whom they can look for protection, and of whom they are rather afraid, or else the man-milliner style, like Gusher, who can admire and appreciate all their little arts and mysterious finesses, who can make love to them in a pretty harmless sort of way, and who is too well-trained to show the slightest natural impulse or feeling. I confess that I felt a pang of jealousy as I saw this gifted being complacently ogle Clara Seesaw through his eyeglass, with an air that aped that of a Sultan who throws a handkerchief to some favored odalisque; but there was no cause for alarm; she evidently regarded this paragon of City editors as an amusing curiosity, and would no more have dreamt of loving such a mannikin than he of loving anything more than himself. Yet Gusher was good company, had a store of small talk and city scandal always ready, knew what Delancey, of the *Misleading Age*, and Deremuth, of the *Flesh and Devil*, were about, was posted up in all the riggers' and the wreckers' moves. 'Tis said another change in City editors is imminent. Just listen to an ex-Director's views of what a City editor should do.

"My dear sir," said he to a friend who was indignant at the way in which the pen was used to suit employers' speculative books, "you talk absurdly. It is quite a mercantile affair. I was a Director once myself, and I confess that I always used the information my position gave, nor did I think it wrong, because I know all do the same."

"But does the nation know that their Directors hold these views?" said the friend.

"Of course it does," replied the other, "and it does the same itself in trade. Each class may grumble at the way the other classes cheat, but still at heart this nation of shopkeepers likes to cheat, if it be done but legally. It's no use changing City editors; they are the puppets of the men who own the papers for which they write. One writes things up, sells on the rise, and buys back on the fall. He is kicked out. The next writes down the bad and good alike, buys when the good are down and sells when the rebound has come. Is there a pin to choose?"

The man who said these words was liked by all, and was a gentleman. Think over it, ye "Outside Fools."

CHAPTER XIII.

DINNER—A CYNIC'S IDEAS OF ROMANCE, AND THE REMARKS OF A LEARNED CRITIC.

"DINNER is served," was the welcome sound that now called us from the drawing-room. Although Gusher was so much in love with himself, and I already half in love with Clara, in spite of my previously-expressed views on marriage and population, yet both of us were not sorry to hear those comfortable words, "Dinner is served." Never mind what we had to eat and drink. There was no pretentious display no false glitter; everything was well-cooked and quite as well served, and, more than that, the wine was real juice of the grape. Our host was at one end, his daughter at the other; I and Gusher sat on either side, and a very cosy little *partie carrée* we made. I enjoyed myself very much; but I tell you honestly that one or two bright glances from Clara Seesaw's soft brown eyes could have transmuted Spanish mutton into the best southdown, Cape Sherry or Mountain Port into Madeira and veritable '47.

I had felt jaded and worn before I left the office, and experienced that wooden feeling about the forehead that springs from overwork, for it was carrying-over day, or, as Jabez Suavity would call it, "First Thieves' Day." There is worry enough on that day without the pestering inquiries of the "Outside Fools" who bother one to death to learn the making up price of this or that stock, the contango or backwardation on some other, all day long. Besides, they often want to deal before the jobbers have arranged their books and scarcely yet know how to start the game for next account. However, we protect them well by bringing wider prices out for all who try to deal. · As I felt rather done up, after lunch I ran round to a doctor's place in Finsbury Square, and paid a fee for his advice. " Rest and a tonic," said the sage. As rest was quite out of the question, and a tonic alone was of no use, I might have saved my fee. Of one thing I am sure, no Galen's mixture could have done me half the good which that delightful tonic did that began to work almost from the first moment that I saw the lovely Clara. I wonder doctors don't prescribe, " Rest and a lively girl's society;" for many melancholy patients would soon be well with such a commonsense prescription's aid. A young friend of mine, who is "born," and consequently moves in good society, and who has fallen madly in love with a pretty little hundredweight of blonde humanity, styled " Baby Clarke," the pride and ornament of Mayfair Skating Rink, thus said to me,—

" Pinto, old man, if you are low and out of sorts, try falling in love; it is the best pick-me-up that ever was invented. Ever since I have been spoony on Baby Clarke I've felt so light and airy-like, I seem to tread on air, and to have drunk some curious elixir that makes everything unnaturally fair. It's very funny, but it's very nice. Yes, Pinto, fall in love, you'll never have the blues till after marriage then."

"Pish and pshaw," says some testy old cynic of mature age, "the boy is in love, and why on earth can't he say so in as many words, and have done with it! No doubt, my good sir, you are right; but I have not yet toppled over the matrimonial precipice as you have and been much bruised with the fall. I am not yet awakened from that dream which we all have a right to dream at least once in our lives, as a foretaste of heaven. "Young man," I think I hear the old cynic rejoin, "there is more romance in a prime saddle of mutton, a ripe Stilton cheese, a bottle of '63 port, and a box of A 1 Partagas than there is in all the smiles, ay, and the caresses of a Venus. 'A chilly thing is love, without good-store of corn and wine,' the Roman poet says." Quite true, old man, but the corn and wine are more romantic with the Venus than without.

All human beings in this vale of tears require to be narcotised at times, and in a slight degree, and this is right, for else their sorrows would oft turn their hard-worked brains. Only let their motto be, "Nought in excess," those golden words of old Greek sages, the only safe "proverbial philosophy" which one might teach a child, and fear no ill result, such as the priggish and one-sided wisdom of the copy-slips will oft produce.

Well, cynical old man, your narcotic is perhaps a pint of generous '63, mine is the anodyne of woman's smiles. Some find it in intoxication of the mind, in travel, books, or some engrossing business, in which the thought of self is lost; some find it in the chasuble, the music, and the church with dim religious light; the maiden finds it often in the parson, decked out for his theatre; this narcotism in its highest and most happy form is Faith, and in its lowest and its worst it is bad beer, a dose of opium, chloral, gin, or grocer's wine. Who could have thought, old man, to look at you, with that daily expanding waist, that you, too, once had your dream? Yet so it was; the short-necked, short-breathed fair one, sixty years of age, who lies so often snoring by your side, was once a slender, graceful girl, one glance from whose bright eyes was quite enough to make you both the happiest and silliest of men.

Yes, you've had your dream, don't sneer at mine, and think your '63 the only sensible narcotic left. No sooner, however, have I answered the old gentleman's cynical remarks on love than I am assailed by one Grammaticus, a critic on the *Fangless Viper's* staff, a weekly paper which was read extensively before the *Flesh and Devil* burst on an astonished world. Grammaticus, to whom this book was shown in manuscript, on which he scribbled here and there his caustic notes, has, at all times, a liver in fine order for criticism; but all through the November fogs and dark December days 'tis charged with pus and venom worthy of Rupilius Rex. Here are his notes,—

"I cannot conceive how a low broker's clerk, in other words, a vulgar moneygrub's understrapper, dare to publish anything at all, and having dared, to trifle with his readers, if there be a single fool to read such trash, by telling them the feelings of a broker's clerk forsooth, while in the presence of his lady-love. He says he writes a book to show how "Outside Fools" are duped, to prove that members of the Stock

Exchange are not so bad as they are thought to be, and yet I, Grammaticus, find this conceited broker's clerk, instead of writing contracts at his desk, talking twaddle about himself and his feelings in the thirteenth chapter of his so-called work. Does this fool, Erasmus Pinto, think that characters like Nathaniel Seesaw, Jabez Suavity, or that dummy Turnabout, show up the men on 'Change in better light? Good lack! I have cut up some tons of trash in my time, but glad I am that this is yet in manuscript, for I should scarce find proper words to damn the thing in print."

To this elegant invective, in spite of which the manuscript will go press, I will reply in the next chapter.

CHAPTER XIV.

OMNE TULIT PUNCTUM QUI MISCUIT UTILE DULCI.

Most sapient Grammaticus, by whom even to be censured is an honor, and to be praised must be perfect bliss, whose remarks, so full of critical refinement and elegance of diction, I have copied down with care, as models for the benefit of Pintos yet unborn, accept my warmest thanks for your benevolent suggestions, and also my regret at not being able to avail myself of them. As those who could write on this subject are prevented by the root of evil, and as those who would write on it have not the experience, I, having the experience, feel bound to tell the public what I know because they ought to know it, and there's no one who will tell. I am no author attitudinising and grimacing before a sated public and a captious band of learned critics, but I am simply carrying out the latest wish of my dead father-in-law, whose posthumous notes will form portion of this narrative, and who, having cheated many in his time, desired to show intending speculators how he did this evil thing. There is something to be said, I try to say it, and what matters if it be not said according to strict rules of art? You say, my dear Grammaticus, "that I *am* a low broker's clerk," and you append a caustic explanation of the term. I *was*, not *am*, a broker's clerk, for ever since my Clara's father's death I have been a broker myself, with two low broker's clerks to work my wicked will. But it would be trenching on your province, most accurate of critics, to quibble about words. How can I be a vulgar moneygrub sprung from a British king? What though the Pintos have condescended to allow a scion of their house to enter the service of the plebeian Seesaw? has not the son of a duke, with an equally noble disregard of pedigree, deigned to enter Ethelbert and Wagtail's office? It is true they are very different men from Nathaniel Seesaw and John Turnabout; but still the stigma is the same, if there be any, which I fail to see. You are behind the times, my good Grammaticus. Plutocracy is now the real aristocracy, and will continue to be so in this country as long as butcher's meat keeps at its present price. You should see some of the names the vulgar moneygrub has written on his contracts. Any way, the broker fellow is on speaking terms with real live lords, marquises, and members of parliament. Why, I have at this moment a tiptop lady, who is a bear of seven thousand Anglos; and no fool, too, if she does not close on a slight rise, which my native gallantry will never let her do. Then, really, my dear Grammaticus, learned man as you are, I think many of the "Outside Fools," for whom these pages are expressly written, are better and more useful men than you or I. I am an optimist, and think that ignorance is vice, and hope that when the "Outside Fools" know how the trick is done, there will be fewer fools to fall a prey to knaves like me, or their own greediness. As for these little conversations about myself, Clara Seesaw, Levi Gusher, and others, they may not have much to do with the subject, but they help the reader to get over the dull passages without yawning. You spitefully insinuate that characters like myself, Seesaw, and Turnabout are no ornament to their class, and that this is not the way to clear the character of the members of the Stock Exchange. Can I point out the abuses and defects of the system by describing and panegyrising the numerous honorable members who belong to that system? Of course I cannot. Whereas by describing the black sheep like myself, and gibbetting their malpractices, I relieve my conscience and that of my lamented father-in-law, do a public good, if in an awkward way, and give more lustre to the virtues of the general body of brokers and jobbers by showing up the few dishonest men. I can assure you, for I hear it every day, that the honorable members of the Stock Exchange are earnestly discussing the best means to alter many of their rules, and stop the worst and most insidious methods of chicanery. As for my style, my good Grammaticus, puzzle not your learned brains about it, for we neither of us shall profit if you do. I should not wonder, if the "Outside Fools" live long enough, that they will weigh your merits much more justly than they used to do.

CHAPTER XV.

ACROSS THE WALNUTS AND THE WINE.

DINNER was over, dessert was on the table, the glasses were filled : Seesaw's and mine with the port of '63, destined to eclipse all other ports in body and bouquet combined, Miss Clara's and the dainty Gusher's with a still Moselle of rare and curious brand. Our host's benevolent face beamed with increased benevolence, as a good man's should when he has had a good dinner, I was serenely happy, Clara looked amused at Gusher's languid air of calm indifference, which now and then was varied by a condescending smile at her, when Seesaw broke the silence thus :—

"Come, Gusher, let us have your latest news. What are the great ones after now ? What news from Egypt ? I hear your 'sub' is there, though you are home again. You know how deeply I am interested in the Khedive's welfare, and how thankful I am for the smallest crumbs that fall from the editorial table."

The piece of flattery struck home, and this illustrious member of the Fourth Estate replied,—

" There's very little news, and not a telegram worth mentioning from Egypt yet, though I expect one every day. The only new thing I have heard is this. The Honorable Flora Rattledrum, whom doubtless you know well by sight, has lost ten thousand pounds in Turkish Seventy-Threes, and is in a furious rage with old Stephen Jobberstock, of Warnford Court, who put her into the stock. She vows that if he does not find her something good to make up for the loss she will expose him to the world in general and to her own set in particular. Now Jobberstock is in a pretty quandary, for this determined lady of title comes to his office twice a day, bullies him aloud before his clients, and often sits in the office for an hour at a time, expecting some impossible movement in Turks to bring her money back to her. Stephen does not care twopence about the world in general, but he does care much about the Lady Flora's set in particular, for the commissions he gets from her and her friends' clandestine speculations come to nearly two thousand a year, besides some further pickings from limits and contangoes. Another of Jobberstock's clients is Lady Di Hupperten, whose husband is very rich, but, as the lady herself says, so mean that she is forced to speculate to dress herself. She was a persistent bear of Anglos, and made nearly three thousand pounds out of the transaction; but she turned a bull of Egyptian just before the Turkish repudiation, and as a powerful clique were forcing Egyptian Stocks down every day, old. Stephen grew alarmed, and made her close at 66. The price did decline further just after this, but she would buy again, and instead of rising, the stock fell to 52 and a half. While it was still at 54 the lady herself got in a funk and sold, intending to buy back at a still lower price, but no chance offered, as it gradually rose to over 60.

" The worthy Stephen, finding that his connection with the wealthy lady speculators at the West End was in serious peril, and, like other brokers, being well aware that the stock would never stand at the price it was then for long, but must have a heavy fluctuation upwards, or downwards, determined to make a last vigorous effort to retrieve his fair clients' losses and his own reputation. With the aid of an

D*

Israelitish friend, without whom no speculative broker's office is complete, he procured a substantial advance on the Honorable Flora's diamonds, and also a clever imitation in paste to lull marital suspicion, and having himself lent a thousand pounds on two houses belonging to Lady Di, at Kensington, he strongly advised his clients to give a certain sum for the call of thirty thousand Egyptian 1873, if he could get the business done. It is not an easy thing to find a jobber to deal in puts and calls with outsiders when a stock is unsettled, but with patience and attention it is possible to get a few thousands done sometimes. They both agreed, although they knew no more what put and call meant than a lover does how much of his lady love is real, and how much false.

"After a great deal of trouble the business was arranged at an average price of three per cent. for the account, *i e.*, they stood to lose three pounds per hundred on thirty thousand, and to gain whatever an upward fluctuation might give them, if they sold at the right time. 'There now,' said Jobberstock to himself, 'the fools can only lose nine hundred pounds a-piece, and I have good security for that, while if an upward move should come, which is just on the cards, it will be more than three times three per cent., or I'm an ass.' This option was arranged this afternoon, and I shall watch the issue with some interest. One thing I know: it can't be many days before we get important news, and I shall have it first, or quite as soon as the leviathan, and he won't put the price up all at once, you may be sure, though rumors of all sorts may put it down. If so, don't sell."

Thus having said, the City editor rose from the table, bade us all good-night, and left. I, with reluctance, followed him—dreamt all night of Clara Seesaw as Cleopatra and Egyptian stocks at 75. As the next day had an important influence on my fortunes, I will begin a fresh chapter with what then took place.

CHAPTER XVI.

A BOLD STROKE FOR A WIFE.

THE next morning I awoke with a sense of grave responsibility, why, I could not exactly define. I felt as though a crisis in my fortunes was approaching. I had thought deeply over Gusher's anecdote and parting hint, and I secretly favored Jobberstock's view that a rise was not unlikely, even if it proved a soda water, not a whisky rise; and all the way to the city I argued the pros and cons. Except for those select few political wire-pullers and financial magnates who were in the secret, this Egyptian nut was the hardest to crack of any that had for years been offered to the teeth of speculators, and, what is more, "Insiders" were as much at sea as "Outside Fools."

I will just give the views held by the general body of brokers and jobbers, which were of course held more or less by the outsiders, for their views come mostly from other brains and not their own, and chiefly from the money articles. It will be seen at a glance that the bears ought to have been victorious according to the usual rule of probabilities.

Against the Stock.

1. The general distrust engendered by the revelations of the Foreign Loans Committee.

2. The aggravation of this distrust by the recent Turkish repudiation.

3. The certainty that the general public would refuse subscriptions to the further loans of any but the very soundest governments.

4. The slenderness of the chance that the Khedive would have the moral courage or power to break with the financial touts, and usurers, and banks that were sucking his blood, ruining his credit, and preventing him from publishing a true statement of his position.

5. The uneasy feeling produced by the explosion of sundry small parcels of political gunpowder on the continent.

For the Stock.

1. The richness of the country and the value of its exports.

2. The investiture of Prince Tewfik by the Prince of Wales with the star of India, not regarded as an empty compliment to a Foreign Prince through whose dominions it was necessary to pass, but as a definite expression of England's wish to make an ally of Egypt, to render her moral and material aid, to make the succession sure and the change consequent on the death of an enterprising and enlightened ruler less prejudicial to the country.

3. The necessity of England's doing something to show that the "peace at any price" party have not completely stultified her energies, but that she has her eyes open to Muscovite encroachment, and a feeling that Egypt, being the highway to India, and free from the perplexities of the "Eastern Question," would prove a more paying *protégée* than the ever-ailing Turk, by whom, through our own government's mistakes and large financial houses lending their

names to float the loan, so many "Outside Fools" have come to beggary.

After a careful summing up, I decided in my own mind that the stock ought to be certainly bought. But this was all very well, and the views I held might be true, but how was I to get Seesaw and Turnabout to act, unless I could give them some definite information, which I did not possess, and saw no hope of possessing?

I have already mentioned in an earlier chapter that the firm were large holders of Egyptian Stocks, bought at a much higher price, and that, if the price fell much more, it would be a very serious matter. Immediately after the Turkish repudiation became known, they had sold bears of the same amount of the stock as they held, but being so completely in the dark as to the extent of any further fall, they dare not close their bears, although the stock had dropped so much—in fact, about thirteen per cent. Now if I could induce them to close, they might net the difference, and sell again on the rally, and unless there was again a fall and they thought it wise to close, they could deliver the stock they had held so long and be clear of any further loss. I thought I saw a splendid chance of saving the father and winning the daughter. But where to get information from a source that warranted action? Where indeed? In rather a desponding mood I walked down Capel Court with some telegrams, when I spied Gusher, with his head in air as usual talking to Reginald Meekin in quite a patronising way. Now Meekin is a fine man, about a foot taller than Gusher, and dull as I felt, I could not repress a smile. The City editor did just nod to me, but with a look so frigid and so lofty that I saw nothing was to be got in that quarter, so delivering my telegrams to the Cerberus at the door, and inwardly cursing all City editors, I turned back to the office in no enviable mood. I saw, in my mind's eye, my employers ruined, the fair Clara in tears and lost to me for ever. No sooner had I entered the office than Turnabout handed me a sealed packet and said,—

"I want you, Pinto, to take this at once to Messrs. Ethelbert and Wagtail's and place it yourself in the hands of the Honorable Walter Loftus, the junior member of their firm."

Now, observe how oddly things come about, and how much stranger truth is than fiction. The Honorable Walter was under an obligation to me. I had dragged him out of a hole in the ice at the risk of my life, while skating at the Welsh Harp the year before. That service, coupled, no doubt, with the fact that my genealogy was unimpeachable, made him acknowledge me, whenever we met, and say that he hoped some day to be in a position to repay me. Of course, dear "Outside Fools," you all know the Honorable Walter Loftus. His presence is commanding, head massive and well set, forehead broad and intellectual, the eyes full of fire, and the mouth and chin expressive of great determination. He has an easy flow of conversation, and a genial animated manner. I am sure you must know him well.

CHAPTER XVII.

THE HONORABLE WALTER LOFTUS' TIP.

I LUCKILY found the Honorable Walter in the office, and delivered the packet safely into his hands, and was just turning to go, when he said,—

"Glad to see you, Mr. Pinto; will you step into my private room for a few minutes, I should like to have a little conversation with you." When the door was shut he continued, "I believe I can now repay the obligation I am under to you; but you must promise on your honor that you will not divulge to anyone else what I am going to tell you. It was understood when I joined the firm of Ethelbert and Wagtail that I was to communicate to the senior partners any early information from persons in high places, with whom, as you are aware, I am intimate. Now I am at this moment in possession of a very valuable piece of information, which I daresay the firm would not like my mentioning to anyone at all, but I owe my life to you. This news will be known to several about three o'clock this afternoon. At present not even Delancey, Deremuth, or the Baron know anything about it; indeed, I know from a trustworthy source that, having closed their bears about from 53 to 57, they have put them out again, expecting a heavy fall. Gusher, of the *Bellowgraphic*, may have a wire from his sub-editor, who is now in Egypt, but scarcely before two o'clock, and you may be sure Gusher will tell no one. With Deremuth he is intensely nettled, owing to some sharp criticisms on his money articles, and he would be delighted, as indeed would several inside the House, to see so fine a bear well pickled and strung up. I hear that many of the jobbers have agreed to close their bears together, force Egyptians up, and so make Deremuth close. Now listen well to what I am going to say, for it is no common occurrence, but one which, if I mistake not, the members of the Stock Exchange will have cause to remember for many a long day with a shudder, when they think how nearly were the snarers snared themselves,—an occurrence, I say, which will set all Europe thinking. I need not tell you how much the Khedive has been pressed for money lately, and you may be sure his so-called bankers won't relieve the pressure without plunging him still deeper in the mire of bad finance. Well, a few months ago, not liking the proposed terms for the renewal of the Treasury bills, he opened negotiations with some French bankers and the Société Generale for an advance on his Suez Canal shares. Now, as is too often the way with bankers, when one really wants their help, these worthies were very difficult to please, and thinking that their mouse was safe, they played with it, intending to devour it at their leisure. So they higgled and haggled till Ismail's royal bile was stirred, and in a huff this sharp Mahometan turned to a leading English banking house for aid.

"Meantime an agent, so the story goes, of the Emperor of all the Russias suddenly appeared in Egypt, and bid the Khedive two million eight hundred thousand pounds for his Suez Canal shares, and that, too, with many coupons cut off from the shares. What could this agent want them for? What was his autocratic master's game? But that is not our business now. Oddly enough, this Russian agent's bid was just four hundred thousand pounds more than the French syndicate had been even asked to give. This bid woke up the Paris usurers, who saw now that the royal mouse seemed likely to escape the cat this time. And then began a little auction thus,—

"'Two million eight hundred thousand pounds, I can bid for the shares,' the Russian agent cries. 'Three million,' promptly bid the syndicate of France. 'Two hundred thousand more,' the Muscovite replies. Three million four hundred thousand pounds is bid for France. But lo! upon the scene appears a bidder from that slow dull land, which ever since the Free Trade mania seized upon our minds, and so-called Liberals ruled, so many foreign countries, solvent or insolvent, have snubbed, sneered at, or plundered of her gold. He bids but once, 'Four million pounds' and down the hammer comes.

"Whatever faults the present government may have, though Slave Trade Circulars be framed by under-strappers' hands, though round men be too often put into square holes, as wittily was said not long ago, though ironclads be sunk, and none but subalterns to blame, this one act, to my mind, so sensible, far-sighted, and courageous, might condone all else.

"Why, sir," and here the Honorable Walter grew quite great in his excitement, "it means that once again old England is awake! The British Lion shakes himself free from that miserable sophistry which fain would have us think our mission is to spread free trade o'er all the world, save negro brothers' souls against their will, laugh down the volunteers, and talk and act as though wars all were ended now, as though a single haughty bully's spleen were not enough to set all Europe in a blaze, as though the Tinkering Triumvirate sought nothing but the spread of Christian grace. Oh, well it is that England wakes in time! 'Tis true, we are a race of shopkeepers, but not so lost in the pursuit of trade as to forget our shops must be themselves kept safe. More taxes, if spent as they should be spent, to make the common soldier's lot a better one, to fit our fleets of active gunboats for the coast defence, will bring no discontent. But stay, in my excitement, I forget myself. 'Tis not the time for such remarks. Of course I need not tell you, Mr. Pinto," continued he, in calmer tones, "what effect the news will have upon Egyptian Stocks, already largely over-sold, when it becomes known, which it certainly will, during the afternoon. Take my advice and act in time, but don't forget your promise not to mention this. There is no more to say. Have I repaid you now?"

With deep emotion I grasped the young noble's hand, and cried,—

"You have, indeed, a hundred-fold."

I left the office of Messrs. Ethelbert and Wagtail with far different feelings, and at once made up my mind that, as I was bound in honor not to tell my firm the news, I would act for them as they would act, supposing that they knew. By doing so I should make Turnabout and Seesaw both warm friends, advance my interests, and might win Clara as a wife. Turnabout was luckily away for the day, and Seesaw was going to a special meeting of the Great Wheal Kitty at two o'clock, as more money was wanted, though the lode was cut, so that there was not much fear of interruption from them. I went straight to the house, and being authorised to deal for the firm, I closed both partners' bears and bought just twenty thousand for the rise. It was now half-past one o'clock, and finding that nothing was wanted at the office, I went to lunch at Mabey's, which, after this eventful morning's work, I needed much.

CHAPTER XVIII.

LUNCH, AND A DOCTOR'S WIDOW'S PRESCRIPTION.

Now, my dear "Outside Fools," if you will speculate, don't forget your lunch. If you try to save a shilling or two here, you will often lose pounds elsewhere. I was myself in business for some time, before I discovered that mind is by no means stronger than matter, unless you keep the matter nourished well.

I had supposed that the best way to keep the Evil One his proper distance was to crucify the flesh, live low, take exercise abundantly, drink water only, and work hard. If mind be stronger than matter, this should certainly be right. But this peculiar thing, this mind, which most of us exalt so foolishly, ignoring or deploring the vile body's influence, through idle longing to be more than mortal men, this curious emanation sprung from source divine (as also these vile bodies are), which, when possessed abnormally by man, so dazzles those whose healthy ample bodies keep their quiet minds well ballasted—this mind, I say, the grotesque antics and the quaint imaginings of which are called by many, "genius," has one set of ideas and arguments before a meal, and quite another after it. This is not only so with ware of common delf, such as Erasmus Pinto, or as "Outside Fools;" but it is also so with philosophic porphyry. Just give the poet potash for a week, and see what poor thin stuff he'll write. "Oh! fool am I to rid me of my bile when springtime comes," says a shrewd Roman satirist. But warm the cynic's blood with just a pint of generous wine, and you will find the germ of human feelings even in that arid breast. Fall down and worship "Intellect," not "Genius," ye "Outside Fools," and, once more, if you speculate, do not forget your lunch, or else your mind, whatever be its strength, will soon grow feeble as an idiot's.

The stomach is only a larger brain, and even now I often think with my stomach—a great deal more than is comfortable.

Now as I have already explained to my critical friend, Grammaticus, my object is, not to write anything original or sensational, but to give you value for your money, by explaining why it is you lose; and as I know that you will speculate, and cannot keep away, I will present you with a valuable prescription, which will enable you to see your bears go up and bulls go down without alarm; will give you strength to catch your broker just at the right time, to get him to do your business when caught, and to report it promptly when it's done. How often Seesaw, with his ample well-fed body, after a good lunch, would take his clients' orders in with him, stay larking in the House or dealing for himself, and then come out, and say, "I can't get on," or else *

---

* "Atria servantem postico falle clientem."

slip out another way, walk up to the office, and when the angry client did appear, say coolly, "You were gone when I came out. I did your business." Of course the business showed no profit, never once.

Oh, Seesaw was magnificent, when nicely fed ! A sound mind in sound body there was there. Yet when his body, later on, grew weak, and dragged his noble powers down, he was a wretched spectacle, looked at from broker's point of view. He could not diagnose a client at the last, much less a market, properly, and when he grew still worse would call himself a thief, and other unjust, foolish names. And then my mind, the body being right, would smile, although I pitied the old man. Grammaticus has scribbled here this note upon the manuscript,— "Old Seesaw doubtless drank."

Most learned critic, you are wrong. He was most temperate, but being mortal, as perhaps you scarcely will allow yourself to be, his health gave way, as yours and mine will surely do in time.

But to return to my prescription. It was given to me by a doctor's widow, in return for certain small but often very useful services. This doctor's widow, who was nearly forty, but whose body still made havoc with her mind at times, had two sweet children in their teens, and a nice jointure that was to expire when she did herself, and also if she took another spouse. They were good children were these two in teens, whose only aim seemed to keep their mother in sound health. And they did not do this from filial motives alone, but, as was natural, they wished to keep alive the jointure and their mother too, and still enjoy, with her society, those many comforts and that good position a nice jointure gives.

Money may be the root of all evil, but most of us at bottom like the root. Now this widow had a lively temperament, and was well enough before her husband died; but since she lost his love, she had suffered from acidity, dyspepsia, and those small ailments which prevent so many sinners from becoming saints. Well, she was doctored by the faculty for nothing, as is the custom, I believe, and of course they spent as little on her as they could, and got her well and kept her well as long as possible. 'Tis true they got no fees for all their best advice. No, not for real intelligent appreciation of their patient's constitution and peculiarities, although they got so many fees for giving pills and draughts to " Outside Fools" by rule, as though they dealt with mere machines, but still it paid them well, because this buxom widow's blooming face, the children and the jointure all conspired to spread the praises of her Galen's skill, to bring him other patients troubled with dyspepsia, who, though they had no jointure depending on their health and abstinence from married bliss, and no two children depending on the jointure, could still well afford to suffer from acidity till a good bill had been run up. As I told you, I had done this buxom widow some slight services, for which she felt some gratitude to me. Now before I knew her, whether it was from overwork, from breathing impure air, from drinking sewage or animalculæ in the London water, I know not, but brain and stomach both gave way, the seaside did no good, and all my appetite seemed gone. I went to one great man, who sagely said, " The heart is far too small for one so large" (I'm only five feet eight, and not so stout); then to another, who declared, "The brain is of abnormal size" (I always found it

much too small); and last, through Providence, I met
this doctor's widow. After a month's treatment with
her excellent remedies I was restored to the bosom of
my anxious and affectionate parents with a digestion
that an ostrich need not have despised, a heart that
did not palpitate, and a brain which, large or small,
was undisturbed by the lugubrious tones of rival
organ-grinders playing in one street. This widow
had more prescriptions than one; but this is what did
me most good, and what, I think, will suit you "Outside Fools" the best. Get one Messina lemon, squeeze,
add just one table-spoonful of water, boiled and filtered, mind, pour into that a wine-glassful of pure
Scotch whisky, drink, and bless your lucky stars.
Take this at meal-times twice a day, but never without food, and take it just as I, or rather Martha Titmass, the said widow, said it should be took. Aha!
Grammaticus, you're down upon me now. "This
vulgar broker's clerk can't write grammatically," so
runs your note. Perhaps not, but " took " is not my
word. Old Titmass wanted Martha more for warmth,
as David the young girl, than for her grammar. Go
to: this is the way with all your tribe; you strain at
gnats and swallow camels whole. And this you do
not for the public-good, but just to show your cleverness. A very simple remedy, perhaps you say this
is, dear " Outside Fools." Ah! there is the mistake.
No citron or green half-grown lemon must be used.
No fiery tavern stuff will do. It must be genuine
mountain-dew, such as the Browns or any good Scotch
family of taste would choose to drink themselves.
The lemons must be fine Messina ones. But if
you don't believe that there is need to be particular in
little points, just read what the rich parvenu told

some of Rome's great men when they came to a banquet that he gave. You'll find that your soul's welfare may depend on whether the *pâté de foie gras* you eat contain a goose's or a gander's liver in the dish. So says Grammaticus, and I am sure he knows these matters well. So take the hint, and don't laugh at my careful way of mixing widows' remedies. Now when you've taken this one month, if your secretions are not quite inhuman, or your spirits weighed down by some awful crime, you'll have a gastric juice quite ten above proof instead of one just strong enough to cope with bread and butter and beef-tea. If you are too strong, suck half a lemon in the morning; if too weak, see that you don't. That doctor's widow saved my life. Poor thing! she's gone to rest herself. *Telle est la vie.* But now to business once again.

CHAPTER XIX.

STEPHEN JOBBERSTOCK'S OPTION TURNS UP TRUMPS, AND THE HOUSE IS CHECKMATED BY DIZZY, DERBY, AND SIDONIA.

I HAD finished my lunch; each little hillock of the mucous membrane that lines the stomach was duly distilling its ten above proof gastric juice, and properly triturating a Mabey steak and fixings, thanks to the doctor's widow's prescription. I felt quite ready for my task. It was nearly three o'clock. I ran over to McLean's Telegraphic Exchange, took a glance at the tape, and saw Egypts mark sixty-two three-quarters three. As I had closed Seesaw and Turnabout's bear at a rather lower price, this was encouraging, although, of course, the news had not leaked out. I then went back to Capel Court, and seeing Gusher talking to his very foreign-looking broker, Burney Gosdoe, asked him whether any news was in. He answered evasively, as is the way of City editors,—

"I have no news; you know I think the stock ought to be bought. You will find I am right when it is too late."

By this last remark I guessed that his "sub" had sent him a wire, and in a pleasant frame of mind I returned to the office. Seesaw had not returned from his meeting; but before I had written out the contracts for signature, he came in, and I then asked permission to go out on private business.

"All right, Pinto," said he, "you can go, and I will stay in and keep the office till four o'clock, and perhaps you will then be in to see the letters posted."

I promised that I would, and went away well satisfied, for Seesaw would probably hear nothing about the fluctuations of Egyptian stock until next day, which was just what I wanted. About twenty minutes past three, therefore, away I went to watch events. The condition of the Egypt market was very peculiar. As I have already mentioned, they had been about 52½-53, but the powerful bears had closed, and among them was Deremuth, whom the inside operators, by combining, tried to catch in vain. This clever speculator, by whom the malpractices of the less reputable jobbers and brokers had been severely criticised, had made a handsome profit out of his first bear, which he closed when the stock fell down to 52½-53. But when it rose to over 62 he sold again. So did Delancey and the Baron; so did the

E

men inside. A drop of ten per cent. at least seemed imminent. The oldest hands inclined to sell; and yet I had been told that they were wrong. I was told they were all wrong. Suppose the Honorable Walter's information turned out false! He might be, after all, deceived. The thought was horrible! Just then the Paris prices came to hand. They showed a moderate rise. Delancey got a wire to buy at best. He closed his bear at once, and bought a bull of twice as much. The others followed suit, for they are not like "Outside Fools," but cut a loss at once.

You know, in days gone by, how we have heard that news was sent to England that Waterloo was lost —how Sidney Smith's "Greatest Fools in Existence" sold all their three per cents., while knaves who knew the battle was not lost, but won, bought all they could. You know how Lombards fell before the news came out of Signor Sella's convention with the government. Of course you do. Well, all at once, though only one or two could tell from whence they came, strange rumors filled the air, alarming telegrams appeared at the Lombard, the Jerusalem, the Baltic, and McLean's.

To make the "Outside Fools" think more of it, Consols, that index of the state of politics, were driven down a half per cent. Says one,—

"The Khedive's bills are all returned. I have the tip to sell."

"The Austrian troops are mobilized," another shouts.

I heard a broker say,—

"Were I not deeply in with all my clients, I would bear Egyptians till black in the face."

Black in the face he was ere long. Another broker whispered as he hurried down the Court,—

" I saw one of Sidonia's clerks just now; he says that Egypts will be quite unsaleable before the close."

I should not have imagined that so stale a trick would have taken a broker in. But he was very young. Poor fool, he sold himself!

" At sixty-two three-quarters, sell twenty Egypts," hoarsely cried a dealer in the House.

" Sell fifty at a half," another bawls.

" At sixty-two, sell twenty more," the other shouts.

Alas! poor inside fools, this time, Sidonia picks you up. He buys, so says the lying jade, a million stock, his sons a hundred thousand each. The public followed suit. In came the Paris prices good, as I have said, not bad, as thought the bears they would come in. Poor bears! their heads began to feel so sore, for in a few minutes the price had gone to 64 and tended upwards still. It still kept rising up to four o'clock and left off 65 and very strong. Though the doors were closed, Throgmorton Street was crammed by an excited crowd. Dealers, brokers, clients, runners, touts, all trying to arrange their books somehow, and almost all desiring to buy.

A few persistent, and, so to speak, constitutional bears held on, still fewer actually sold more, and called the rise insane. Insane or not, it drove more than a score jobbers and brokers into temporary insanity, and gave others such a shaking that to this day they have "Suez Canal Shares on the brain," and ofttimes scare their wives at night by waking with a start, and crying,—

" Buy Egypts, buy! Sidonia's the banker now!"

" Oh! Dizzy, how you treated us!"

When this memorable account was over, a leading member of the House wrote to the *Misleading Age*, but not this time upon the 1st of April, as before. The gist of what this jobber's luminary said was this,—

"Is it not wonderful! *we* were on the losing side,— not even were the public, who live but for *us*, so wrong as *we*—and yet I say, with pardonable pride, we *have* paid differences on three hundred millions, with but few exceptions, and for these I can find plenty of excuse. Can anything be said against men so clever and so honorable as, in adverse times like these, to pay their debts to ' Outside Fools?' From henceforth close your mouths, ye carping dolts who try to criticise our doings, for I, yes, I myself say this, and, what is more, I think it too, ' The public weal consists in floating foreign loans.' "

All that the above-mentioned wealthy and respectable jobber wrote, I, Erasmus Pinto, and the member of my firm, most gratefully endorse, there is such glorious candor in the words.

Never for years had the Stock Exchange been so shamefully taken in. No scrap of early information was given by the wire-pullers in the world of politics.

"It was," as said a leading broker, "a most snobbish piece of business, looked at from a City point of view." Among the "Outside Fools" the greatest fools had won, for they were bulls; the clever ones had lost, for they were bears. So Capital oft catches Reason in its net. Just as I left for home I spied old Stephen Jobberstock, with looks of exultation in his hanging cheeks and winy face. That lucky option had brought back the three per cent. with other seven in its train. No bull of Bashan ever looked so pleased as be. The Honorable Flora and the Lady Di. were once again in funds. How everything in this well-ordered world does some one good! The crowd dispersed at nearly six o'clock.

CHAPTER XX.

ERASMUS PINTO REASSURES THE BROKEN SPIRITS OF HIS FIRM.

> When panics come, who seems to wear
> A calm, serene, superior air,
> As though it wasn't his affair?
> My broker!
> *London Charivari.*

THE above lines would be found applicable in most cases, whether the panic be downwards or upwards; but in this memorable case of the "Egyptian bear pickling" they were altogether out of place. The next morning, full three-quarters of an hour before eleven struck, excited would-be bulls tried their level best, as City men would say, to buy, and frantic bears, with heads so sore from Dizzy's pungent brine, writhed and wriggled, trying harder still to close. To aid this pickling process, adroitly-written articles appeared in the money columns of those great and, in all other respects, honorable educators of the nation, the daily newspapers. And these insidious articles on stocks, that sullying stain upon the bright escutcheon of the "Fourth Estate," were swallowed eagerly, as usual, by the country "Outside Fools," and brought their telegrams and orders up by thousands to the market for Egyptian Bonds.

The price reached 72, which made a rise of twenty all within a fortnight's space. And what made it so very sad was this. The men inside were nearly all caught bears. Some "*Outside Fools*" had actually rushed in where "*Inside Angels*" feared to tread, and so there was the pitiable, novel, and, to Erasmus Pinto's mind, immoral spectacle of the former making profits, while the latter suffered heavy loss. The place was all demoralized. That poor young broker, friend of mine, and such a nice young man, who fain would bear Egyptians for his clients or himself, till he, or they, or both were all black in the face, I saw, with brain all wrecked, tears in his eyes, and led away by friendly hands to moan in secret silence o'er that latest scurvy Jewish trick. That other broker who went rushing down the Court, and said, "The stock will be unsaleable by night," himself was hammered in the morning when the rattle went. "Messrs. Puttit, Callit, Sellit, Buyit are unable to meet their engagements," cried the automaton official in the House, then down the fatal hammer fell. How near a shave it was with many more the Members' Oracle well knew, although he thought it quite unwise to write about that fact.

And yet ye might take heart and rest of reins, ye fallen angels, if ye would; your case is not so very bad.

Six and eightpence in the pound will do great things, and your good names are not gazetted, as those of "Outside Fools" in trade. Oh! yes, take heart! your brethren are subscribing like good men and true; you soon may start again, a goodly crop of fools is growing up. What though the foreign loan dodge is used up, your next bait can be mines. Not foreign "wild cat" mines. Oh, no, poor Emma sounded their death knell, but " *bonâ fide* British Mines" should be the cry this year. "Investors, give your capital to bring to light the iron, coal, the lead and tin your country has abundantly beneath the soil." That is the sort of trap to lay. It seems so honest and legitimate. Investing fools, ye worst of all financial fools, be not misled by these insidious words. Good mines there are, but they remain in private hands, with very rare exceptions. The best mines are English Rails, you always will have something there. But I digress. So sick were we inside that we proposed to take a holiday while yet we had some little "root of evil" left. But when Jack Bragmehearty's cheques came back with N.E. on their face, then sullen anger seized upon the House. A universal favorite was Bragmehearty with us all; so genial, upright, jolly, free was he, no canting saint, but really straight, and let in by some "Intermediate Fools," as aptly said Sir Oracle. Sidonia, Dizzy, Derby, any one and anything was blamed by turns. I could have cried myself, but had not time, nor onions ready to my hand.

As soon as I got to the office, I found Seesaw and Turnabout in a great state of excitement, as well they might be, seeing that they knew nothing about their bears being closed, and were looking forward to no pleasant pickling tub, for I had held my tongue, as yet. John Turnabout's port-winy face was blue instead of red, and never did I see the good churchwarden look so little like himself. Had he but held the plate at church with look like that, the Rev. Silvertongue Richwife's pew rents would have been sadly lessened to make up the failing Sunday offerings. The "threepenny devout" might then have worshipped undismayed, the impecunious, free and comfortable too. But, thanks to the Honorable Walter Loftus and Erasmus Pinto, no parochial disaster such as this was destined to occur. I placed the dealing book in Seesaw's hands, and pointing to the entries, simply said,—

"The bears of Egypts have been closed, and if I might suggest, without offence, the bull of twenty thousand should be sold at once, for even now the market is upon the turn. 'Sidonia buys,' say all the 'Outside Fools;' you know, dear sir, well what that means."

"Go, Turnabout, at once," said Seesaw, "sell them twenty Egypts at the best. I know not what grim joke this is, but it is right to sell, at all events, because there's not an 'Outside Fool' who does not think it right to buy. Go sell, I say."

Away went Turnabout, in silence, though he thought his partner just a little mad; and then I told my tale, but not before Nathaniel Seesaw had for full ten minutes stared in blank amazement at the entries in the dealing book, and then recovered sober sense, as one knocked down in pugilistic ring recovers consciousness to be "up smiling" just in time. When he had heard it all, he said:—

"My lad, I cannot talk of this just now; come down and dine with me to night, and we will talk the matter over then. I only trust it is no jest. Go, leave me to myself, till it is time to go. I left him to himself.

CHAPTER XXI.

THE TELEGRAPHIC CABLE OF LOVE.

IF the reader will be good enough to turn back to the latter part of chapter nine he will there find Mr. Seesaw speaking thus on the subject of food and love,—

"Now, Pinto, take my advice: if ever you feel as though you could no longer do without the love as well as the food, go boldly to the father of some nice girl who has both to bestow and say, 'Sir, I love your daughter, but she has money, and I at present have next to none'; but although I have not money, I have learnt how not to lose it, which is almost better than possessing but to lose. Tie your daughter's money fast to her, and trust them both to me.'"

This conversation kept recurring to my mind, and I secretly determined to take the old man at his word. I met him, as before, at Chalk Farm Station. When we were seated in a carriage where there was no one else, he thus began,—

"Erasmus Pinto, acts alone can suitably repay the service you have done for me to-day. The incubus which weighed my spirits down for some three years is now removed, and this is due to you. One thing I can and gladly will do for you, which is this. John Turnabout is getting gouty, and would like to give up active partnership, still keeping his money in, and taking share of profits when the panics come, and 'Outside Fools' sell all their soundest stocks to us, who then buy all we can, and borrow, beg, or steal to pay for it. Ah, 'Outside Fools,' if ye knew this, ye would not play your cards so foolishly! As we now are safe financially, you must become a member of the firm of Seesaw, Turnabout, and Pinto. I always think a firm that has three names is more respectable."

Seizing this lucky opportunity, I quoted those words of his which stand at the beginning of this chapter, and said this besides,—

"The food, I see, sir, is now pretty well secured, and I want the love as well. You are the father of the nice girl who has both love and root of evil, too, to give. Let me win and wear your daughter, if I can."

"Nothing I should like better, replied Seesaw; but that is easier said than done. What chance have you, who have only seen the girl once, when many others, who had plenty of good looks, assurance, and the root of evil, after months of idle courting, were refused? My Clara is no common miss, although she be the daughter of a licensed thief. I wish you may succeed, but never can I force the inclinations of my girl. Though I have passed my life in the pursuit of sordid gain and robbed the 'Outside Fools' of gold, I still have sense enough to see that there's no mine of wealth so lasting and so rich as woman's virgin love, and just observe, in passing, that this virgin or first love is often felt by those who never will be virgins any more,—I mean by those whose foolish parents made them marry men against their will. My daughter has escaped that fatal trap, and never shall she marry one she does not love, through act of mine."

"You will, perhaps, laugh at me, sir," I replied; "but although I have no tangible reason to hope, and although I am not so conceited as to think my looks are equal to those of the suitors who have failed, I still have hope. Ever since I saw your daughter first, I have felt as though some subtle odic or electric influence passed to and fro between us, as though an unseen telegraphic cable ran through air, and made our brains its offices at either end. The insulation of this airy cable is, like that of ocean cables, variable, and more or less disturbed by air currents, and the would-be-lovers' physical condition; but, unlike the older wheezy Anglos and the sickly new Direct, it never is quite dumb. Well, it is very odd, but ever since that day I dined with you, and Clara Seesaw's dear brown eyes looked into mine, I have seemed to have her image photographed upon my mind, to know her thoughts and acts, and live in her society. As there is no monopoly yet in the air, as there is, and may still be for a time, in the Atlantic, I imagine it to be full of these telegraphic cables of love, which are always at work, either through the half-conscious cerebration of the would-be-lovers, or their direct transmission of messages. I further hold that most men and women, to whom nature has not been niggardly and churlish of her stores, possess in their *cerebellum* a very excellent office for the transmission of these unspoken messages of love, and that when once their affinity has been proved by the first genuine message, and the insulation of their cables perfected, although not a word of love shall have been spoken by either to the other, nor even arrowy glances shot from sympathetic eyes, that a delicious secret correspondence may still be enjoyed by both, though separated by long distances. I am, of course, not speaking of those cold sterile natures, to whom has been denied the faculty of understanding the heaven that exists on earth, to whom the book of love is wholly sealed."

Among these natures I place yours, my good Grammaticus, if really you have any nature left, and not a few dry rules of art alone. Here I remarked to Mr. Seesaw,—

"I daresay you are wondering how I can have the audacity to suppose that any such cable can exist between two creatures, one of whom is as inferior to the other as a farthing rushlight to the sun. But, sir, this is the most interesting and beautiful feature in the system, if the theory be true, for at one end of the cable there may be telegraphic offices, or *Cerebella*, splendidly furnished, and at the other, a different set quite meanly-appointed, and still the cable shall have perfect insulation, and work quite well. Surely, dear Mr. Seesaw, you must have noticed how young ladies of high degree establish cables of love with their father's footman, or their music-master, whose offices may have just the right kind of furniture. And how the youthful scion of some noble house will telegraph to girls of humble birth. It is because, although there's such disparity between them in position, virtues, education, yes, and looks, in either case, the one supplies just what the other lacks. The two possess between them all the fractions of the unit, love. One lover may possess an eighth, the other seven-eighths. One fifteen-sixteenths, the other but the one-sixteenth that's left. One three-quarters, the other a quarter. One three-eighths, the other five-eighths. And often one nine-sixteenths, the other seven-sixteenths. Sometimes there is a half on either side. And in proportion as there is a disparity between the number of fractions on either side, in such proportion will the love last longer and burn more brightly, and in proportion as the number of the fractions are more nearly equal will it last a shorter time and burn more feebly while it lasts. And this is why so many marriages which seem unsuitable to those who do not know what 'fractional disparity' and telegraphic cables mean in love turn out so happily."

As I observed that Seesaw began to yawn ominously, I said no more about my cables and fractions, and he remarked, drily,—

"I trust, Pinto, you may turn out to be the exact fraction that my Clara wants, but I don't believe it is anything so common as an eighth or sixteenth. It might be a thirty-second. I am sure the girl has a good many on her side. If there be anything in that funny theory of yours, there must be half the fractions on one side and half on the other in the case of old Stephen Jobberstock and his wife, for when they are separate, they are pleasant social kind of bodies, and you can't tell which you like the best; but visit them at their own house, and you will see them fight like cat and dog. One word more. Don't try to win my Clara by telling her how you saved her old father from ruin, for although that would make her look kindly on you, gratitude is not true love. Keep your cable, or what ever you call it, clear for genuine messages, and good luck attend you in your cablegrams."

We were at Seesaw's door.

CHAPTER XXI.

HOW THE CABLES OF LOVE WORKED.—"NATURAM EXPELLAS FURCA, TAMEN USQUE RECURRET."

ONCE more we had met, once more the dear brown eyes had looked straight into mine, and I was blest.

As our telegraphic offices were both now in the same room, and the strength of the odic current had been sensibly increased by the gentle pressure of warm hands at greeting, the insulation was perfect, and messages kept flashing to and fro, from brain to brain, from office to office, while both of us sat still, conscious indeed how well our cables' code was understood by each, yet caring not to express our thoughts in feeble words.

Now, before I give my specimens of messages, I beg my lady readers to observe that Clara Seesaw was a child of nature, with a healthy proportion of natural passion and affection, and was neither afraid nor ashamed of the ideas that came into her virgin mind. Just as her simple easy-fitting dress allowed each limb to move with supple grace, so did her unconventional bringing up permit her mind to have free play. No, ladies, Clara Seesaw was not like the modern miss, who moves, in "good society," whose manners, thoughts, and dress are the elaborate production of a high-class seminary and West End architect of narrow sacks, of which the two chief features are a prominent display of femoral symmetry or want of it, and no small difficulty, in sitting down without catastrophe. I hear that petticoats are getting antiquated now (the fact is, there's no room inside the sack and they don't show good figures off enough) and that wash-leather tights are to replace the good old fashioned garment's use. No doubt these far-seeing milliners and dress-builders are looking forward to the fast approaching time when "Woman's Rights" shall all be duly recognized, when she shall wear real breeches, have her vote, shall ask a man to wed, shall be a doctor, barrister, and clergywoman, if she likes, and have a seat in parliament, while man, quite tamed, shall wear the cast-off petticoat, make pies and puddings, and nurse babies with automaton content, and be her humble slave. Ye Fates, in mercy hurry on this golden age.

Grammaticus, who dearly loves Euripides, and hates the sex, has scribbled here some notes, which I will print to show the ladies what so great a pundit thinks of them.

"Come, this is not so bad, and if the boy had written more of it, and much less twaddle about love I might have praised the manuscript, and said 'I think 'twill do for print.'

"Give up their petticoats forsooth, and take to science and wash-leather tights! In heaven's name, what next? This would have been a prodigy in Livy's time.

"Divine Euripides! how well saidst thou these words, 'Oh, Zeus, why did'st thou place these women under heaven's light, a tricksy bane to men?'"

Again,—

"I hate your clever woman. Ne'er in house of mine may woman dwell who knows more than she ought to know.

"For love breeds mischief more among your clever

dames, while simple ones are free from folly, through the smallness of their wit."

Thus raves this critical misogynist. Ah! how one genuine message flashed along one of love's cables would surprise this classic prig and set him right. But telegraphic offices must have their proper furniture.

After this digression, ladies, I apologise, and give you now the messages that passed between your humble slave, Erasmus Pinto, and Clara Seesaw.

CHAPTER XXII.

THE TELEGRAPHIC MESSAGES OF LOVE.

1. *From Erasmus Pinto's Office.*—" What a pleasant thrill went through my sympathising frame, just when I pressed your hand."
2. *From Clara Seesaw's Office.*—" How strange ! My hand appears to linger in your grasp, and fain would stay a little longer there. I never felt like this before but once." *
3. *From Erasmus Pinto's Office.*—" How delightful it would be to spend hours in your presence, gazing silently at you, as at a lovely picture."
4. *From Clara Seesaw's Office.*—" How odd. Your silence is far more interesting than all those spoken compliments, which fell so dead upon my ears."
5. *From Erasmus Pinto's Office.*—" I will sit opposite you at dinner, and those frank brown eyes of yours shall tell me whether I may hope."

---

* This must have been when I first came to dinner with Mr. Seesaw.

6. *From Clara Seesaw's Office.*—"I must say something. How strange papa will think it if he comes and finds us serious and mute, just like two statues. And yet I would much rather sit still and say nothing."

At the precise moment when we both of us felt that it would be no longer possible to keep silence Mr. Seesaw entered the room, and the odic spell was broken. His appearance was a disappointment and a relief. In a few moments we were at dinner. Clara's manner to me was gay and apparently unconstrained, though scarcely so natural as before. This I thought encouraging, for it showed that the messages had not been forgotten, and that the gaiety might be somewhat assumed. I fell in with her humor, and we kept up so lively a conversation that the worthy old gentleman, whose health was anything but good, declared that we had cheered him up, and said he wished he had us *both* to keep him in good spirits every day.

I here despatched a hasty message along my cable to inquire what Clara thought of this remark, and looking up, I met her eye, which did not, as it used to do, return my gaze with steadiness, but slightly dropped. A welcome omen was that little drop to me. I at once made up my mind that I would know my fate by word of mouth on the first opportunity.

CHAPTER XXIII.

CLARA SEESAW'S IDEAS ON LOVE.

Oh! this first love for man, if true woman conceive it,
  What a world of new hopes, of new joys, of new dreams!
How it gladdens dull life, how it makes one believe it,
  All golden and bright as to children it seems!*

DINNER was over. After the first glass of wine our host said to his daughter,—

"You must amuse Mr. Pinto, my dear, as you best can, for as this is the vicar's night for receiving pew-rents I must attend the vestry meeting. Make our guest comfortable, and don't leave him to drink his wine alone. It is a stupid and unsocial custom."

After Seesaw *père* had left we conversed for a few minutes about general topics, when, feeling that so opportune a chance ought not to be let slip, I abruptly asked my companion how it was that women often were devoted to unworthy objects of their love.

"I fear the subject is too deep for me," said Clara, with a smile; "but as it has engaged my thoughts I'll tell you what a woman thinks the cause of this, so strange to many minds. I believe that a woman loves to place her affections so to speak, but that man loves not so much from a strong desire to love some one, such as woman feels, as to be loved by some one. This strong wish to place their affections often leads women to glorify an unworthy object, and if that object be unfortunate, or meet with

---

* Lines from the unpublished poems of *Salome Pinto*, spinster, *Erasmus Pinto's* aunt.

opposition from the friends and relatives, their love grows stronger still, and they delight in making sacrifices, thinking it a duty to their love. Of course all women with more head than heart, and they are not so few, do not make this mistake. I believe it seldom happens that two lovers feel an equal amount of passion for each other, but that much more often one gives the greater portion of the love, and I incline to think the woman gives more often than receives the love. To love with worship is, to my mind, greater happiness than to be loved. And woman's nature is more fit for this than man's, whose intellect will often make him gladly take the genuine devotion of a woman and be satisfied. And, Mr. Pinto," said this charming woman, with arch look, " perhaps we often love unworthy objects, because your sex is so prolific in those sort of men."

" I fear that is too true," said I, "though it is rather sharp on us. But can you tell me why it is that so many married people seem so miserable ? "

" I believe you are laughing at me, Mr. Pinto," replied Clara, " but I will do my best to answer you. Such a priceless treasure as reciprocal love, continuing unabated after marriage, is so rare, because, if we could find it easily, the troubles of life would be almost unfelt, the duties twice as easy to perform, and we should enjoy such happiness here that we should be in danger of forgetting the bliss hereafter we are here to try and win. I was much struck with an answer a poor Irish scullery-girl, only eighteen years of age, who was leaving service to be married, made to me. ' Why, Kathleen, are you not afraid,' said I, ' of being badly off when you are married ? You should save your wages up and wait.' 'Ah, thin, Miss Clara,' she replied, 'I'm not afeard at all, for Phelim he'll bear half me sorrer, and I will get half Phelim's joy; and with our love and pratees we will git on dacintly.' Now, although poor Kathleen has probably discovered by this time that even true love burns more brightly with something added to the 'pratees,' yet that simple arithmetic, by which the sorrows were to be halved and the joys doubled, which I suppose, ought to be the case where the love is reciprocal, seems to show me the reason why such love is seldom seen in married life. If the sum worked out as Kathleen thought it would in ordinary life, the power of evil would become too weak to make this life a trial hard enough to fit us for another world. And therefore, I suppose, it was intended by a higher power that such love should not be often found, and that, when found, it should but seldom last. And this is why we see divorce courts full of applicants anxious to get rid of married ties, and why so many who do not seek legal remedy live so unhappily at home, and why, when two, more lucky than the rest, have found this love, and it would last, the husband or the wife is often suddenly withdrawn from life.

"And do you know, Mr. Pinto, that strange as Mrs. Grundy may think it for me to say to a gentleman, I believe that there are many women in love with men whom they could make happy, but that the conventional usages of society prevent this love from becoming known, because the lady cannot speak, and the gentleman, lacking perception, does not see it. Many fine natures, possessing great wealth of affection, are thus prevented by our social system from being happy themselves and conferring happiness on others, and so a great deal of love is lost to the world, although it might have been utilized in opposing the power of the Evil One, the personality of whom I don't believe, in spite of narrow-minded foolish bigots, who read the letter not the spirit of their Bible, refuse the sacrament to honest men who cannot see Satanic tails and long forked tongues, and threaten to resign their benefice, unless their lordships of the Privy Council make us all believe this Evil One to be a person such as a blind poet has described, and artists have portrayed. Oh! for a little commonsense and charity! No wonder 'Disendow' and 'Disestablish,' are the words so often heard, when we all see episcopal, ecclesiastic, and judicial elephants engaged in picking up religious pins, grave Privy Councillors discussing whether Thomas Jones, Dissenting minister, may call himself a 'Reverend' upon a tombstone, or whether only parsons of the semi-disestablished Church may have this empty privilege. Oh! Mr. Pinto, why do not these holy men, to whom we look for teaching and example, imitate their Master more, and think of creeds and '*ego*' less?

"But tell me what you think yourself about these views, for many of my sex speak of a woman in no gentle terms who dares to talk so freely on two subjects which the cant of hypocrites would say ought to be only thought of by unmarried girls, not talked about?"

CHAPTER XXIV.

ERASMUS PINTO'S REMEDY FOR THE GREAT WANT OF THE AGE.

"DEAR lady," I replied, "your views upon the second great necessity of human nature, love, food being the first, are very like my own, and I am greatly gratified to find that my ideas of woman's love are, in a measure, shared by one as lovely as yourself. About the 'personality' of the Arch Fiend I rather would not talk, but I may just observe that one of my own friends, who dubs himself 'philosopher,' says he is negative, and represents the 'Absence of the Good,' and that another, who is deeply read in ecclesiastic lore, declares there is no evidence to fix the shape, and that he always thinks a painting set with Dragon Sovereigns round, and showing by the skilful artist's brush that deadliest of hates, the 'Odium Theologicum,' would represent him in the clearest light to common minds. The Dragon Sovereigns would be the Root of Evil, and the 'Hate' the greatest enemy of Charity or Love, which, he avows, the Bible teaches, rightly understood, throughout. This Hatred, like the Evil One, walks up and down the earth, but need not surely be a person any'more than Satan need possess a human shape. But of this enough, some men delight in finding stumbling-blocks.

"How often we hear the remark, 'How women do hate one another!' I think this remark is unfair and not founded on fact. No doubt women have rather bitter feelings against those who are more than usually pretty, lovable, or attractive to men, and they would be more than mortal if they were not jealous of superior charms in society's great matrimonial race, where, even if the running spinsters all could win, there would be prizes only for every other one, for marriageable men are, I suppose, just half as numerous as running spinsters are. Besides, two-thirds of these fine prizes are but veritable blanks, to glorify whom and make an ideal of would require a pretty strong desire on the part of woman to 'place her affections,' as you aptly said.

"With regard to the defect in our social system which prevents a lady from making her love known to its unconscious object, except in Leap Year, and which deprives so many ladies and gentlemen of the chance of finding their affinities, their proper number of fractions of love in their very limited circle of acquaintances, I believe I have a remedy. It consists in the establishment of a General Matrimonial Alliance Association. Perhaps you will say, 'There are the balls, promenades, concerts and skating rinks.' The rinks are no doubt a step in the right direction; but at all these meeting-places there is too much exclusive class-feeling to prevent them becoming a national aid to matrimony. They are excellent flirting grounds for Belgravia and Mayfair, but nothing more.

"I feel sanguine that the many thousands of unmarried persons, who are willing to marry, but possessing only average attractions or a lower position than the Upper Ten are unable to meet with their affinity, will, through the agency of my projected Association, and after six months' tuition in the Odic Theory of Love, attain to their desires.

"Here is a copy of the Prospectus," said I, handing one to Clara Seesaw, who read it with some interest and amusement. I think it is important enough to have a chapter to itself.

CHAPTER XXV.

THE GENERAL MATRIMONIAL ALLIANCE ASSOCIATION (LIMITED).

INCORPORATED under the Companies' Acts 1862 and 1867.

Capital £1,000,000, in 500,000 shares of £2 each.
Payable as follows: £1 on application, 5s. on allotment.
Balance by calls of 5s. at intervals of not less than three months.

Patron:
The Queen.

Directors:
Chairman—The Right Honorable Philander Popoff.
Deputy Chairman—Lord Claudius Guinea Pig.
Major General Shoveloff, United Service Club.
The Honorable Augustus Matchem, Director of the Surplus Population Diminishing Company.
The Right Reverend Masterly Inaction, ex-Bishop of Timbuctoo.
Lieutenant General Ramskull, President of the Ladies' Dorcas and Gossip Club.
Nathaniel Seesaw, Esq., Boyfield House, Adelaide Road, and Stock Exchange.
Thomas Pinto, Esq., Chairman of the Society for the Propagation of the Odic Theory of Love.
With power to add to their number.

Bankers:
Messrs. Kiteflyer, Buckbill, and Luvibondo, Lothbury.
Architects:
Messrs. Toolong, Propemup, and Chargewell, 1, Billdinhouse Yard.
Master of the Ceremonies:
Captain Orlando Settumrite, Detached House Club.
Brokers:
Messrs. Seesaw and Turnabout, Change Alley and Stock Exchange.
Solicitors:
Messrs. Quibble and Quirke, Bedford Row.
Secretary:
Erasmus Pinto, Esq.
Temporary Offices:
361, Gresham House, old Broad Street.

PROSPECTUS:

The object of this Company is to provide eligible persons of all classes and both sexes, who desire to form matrimonial alliances, with an introduction to each other on a very much larger scale than has hitherto been possible through the ordinary channels of society.

It is an acknowledged fact that many thousands of respectable, well-educated persons, possessing sufficient means to support an affinity, are prevented by the smallness of their social circle, or insufficient time to visit, from meeting with the object required to secure them happiness in the married state.

For this purpose all that noble site has been purchased, known as Vanity Square, adjacent to the District Railway, and a large block of houses adjoining will be immediately pulled down, and buildings erected by the Company's Architects, which, the Directors believe, as regards proximity to the leading thoroughfares, and easiness of access from all parts of the Metropolis, will be unsurpassed.

The total area of the property purchased is 80,000 square feet, on which will be erected two spacious Halls: a smaller, or First Class, for those who desire to preserve that exclusiveness peculiar to the British constitution in the upper classes, and a larger, or Second Class Hall, for all those who believe in the Equality of Man and Woman's Rights and only desire to meet with their affinity irrespective of the class in which it may be found. The price of admission will be 2s. 6d. to the smaller and 1s. to the larger Hall.

It is generally admitted now by scientific men that sexual love is not promoted by equality of wealth, station, education, or even similarity of tastes, so much as by a subtle current of animal magnetism, or odic influence, which causes persons, on the sight of their affinities, to say to themselves, "I like or I love that lady or gentleman," as the case may be.

Thomas Pinto, Esq., will give a series of lectures on the Odic Theory and the working of the Telegraphic Cables of Love.

The Directors have at great expense engaged the services of Professor Archibald Magnet, M.A., F.R.S., A.S.S., who, having travelled over all parts of the globe, is acquainted with the marriage rites and customs of every race and tribe. He will deliver a series of lectures on this interesting subject.

Brokers will be attached to the Halls, who will,

for a small commission, supply full particulars respecting the position, fortune, or accomplishments of any lady or gentleman using either of the Halls.

Several first-class photographers will be attached to the Halls to supply the affinities who have been chosen by the odic influence and introduced by the brokers with *cartes de visite* of each other. Eminent doctors will also attend daily, who have devoted their whole lives to the study of nervous disorders, which, there is too much reason to believe, especially in the case of the ladies, arise from the want of an affinity, an object selected by the odic influence.

To ensure perfect privacy in the early stage of the negociations, and to prevent even the brokers from knowing the names of their clients, or the selected objects those of each other, unless voluntarily communicated, every lady or gentleman using either Hall will be presented on entering with a card on which a certain number only will be printed.

This card should be filled up with particulars of age (approximate in the case of ladies), position, circumstances or expectations, but no name or address.

Gentlemen should state whether they are bachelors or widowers, ladies whether spinsters or widows. When the cards are filled up, they should be left in one or other of the brokers' offices, and there will be given in exchange a smaller card with the correspondiug number upon it. The Directors are sanguine that, by means of these cards and the brokers' aid, not only will *bonâ fides* and privacy be ensured in the delicate early stages of the negociations, but that those disappointments will be prevented, which in ordinary society are so frequent and so disastrous, arising from ignorance of the amount of the Second Great Requisite of Love, viz., the means to keep up the magnetic current, possessed by the contracting parties. This is too often found out when the intimacy has ripened into a warm attachment, which is broken off through want of early information on the money question.

In the event of marriage, all objects, or affinities selected by the odic influence or Telegraphic Cables of Love within the Halls will be required to pay a fee of Five Guineas, if selected in the First Class, and One Guinea if selected in the Second Class Hall.

Shareholders will be entitled to profits up to ten per cent. arising from the charge for admission, fees in the event of marriage, and a small royalty on the Brokers' Commission.

After ten per cent. has been paid to the Shareholders, all profits will be set aside to establish a special fund to provide the Second Great Requisite of Love, viz., means to keep up the magnetic current, and bear the expenses attendant on matrimony.

A preference in this respect will be shown to ladies,—indeed gentlemen will be rather nominally than virtually allowed to participate.

Prizes will be given at frequent intervals to the *Ugliest* Selected objects of the Female Sex.

No married persons will be admitted into either Halls, for fear they should disturb the magnetic currents of the cables or affinities. There will be spacious galleries to both buildings, in which vocal and instrumental music of the very best kind will be performed.

Original subscribers for twenty shares will become life members of the First Class, and subscribers for ten shares life members of the Second Class Halls, and although after marriage they will not be admitted, their shares will secure them the privilege of admitting two persons free once every day.

Under all the circumstances, therefore, the Directors feel sanguine that not only will the Company prove a brilliant financial success, but that from the inauguration of this new system of "Natural Selection," by the magnetic or odic current, happy marriages will increase enormously, that wife-murder and the brutal crimes among the lower classes resulting from unhappiness in the married state will sensibly decrease, and that the bitter and unchristian temper so often engendered by ill-assorted matches among the higher and better educated classes will be succeeded by content and harmony.

It is believed that the nation will no more be scandalized by those Breach of Promise Cases, which have become a nuisance and an insult to the people's common sense. No artful hussy will be able, after this, to catch some unsophisticated honest man by a spurious and devilish magnetic current, and when he finds, before it is too late, that she, the hussy, would not make any man a good and honest wife, and draws back from the snare, to make him pay large quantities of root of evil, amid the laughter of his friends, while she, the hussy, enjoys the joke, and root of evil too. The Directors are aware that when a real lady, with gentle susceptibilities, has unfortunately, through the imperfect machinery of society, placed her affections on some unworthy object, and has been deserted by the faithless swain, she, the real lady, does not dare to face a court of law, but cherishing still in her virgin heart the ideal of her love, often pines in secret, and would sooner die than sue the fickle one for damages. The lady loses her heart, and often the power to make a second selection, while the hussy, by her artful tricks, procures a decent dowry and another swain. This Company will stay this crying ill.

Finally, the Directors call upon all the influential and the wealthy to contribute liberally to the Company's fund for providing the poorer selected objects with the Second Requisite of Love, and for giving prizes to the Ugliest Selected ladies, as by so doing they will be increasing the amount of genuine love in their country, and thereby diminishing the power of the Evil One.

All Bishops, Rectors, and Vicars with rich sinecures and fat livings have here a splendid opportunity of preventing the poor Curate from robbing his fellow-creatures of their share of love by marrying without sufficient means, or marrying for money only, to his own great harm, and they are urgently requested to give with liberal hand, for well they know that not a single sermon they can preach will ever work the same amount of good as the successful floating of this Company.

The only contract entered into is dated the 24th day of January, 1876, and is made between Messrs. Seesaw, Turnabout, and Pinto, of the one part, and the Company, of the other, whereby the leases of the premises and the erection of the Halls under the direction of the Company's Architects have been secured, and it is believed that the Halls will be open to the public by November the 1st, of the present year.

Application for shares should be made upon the

accompanying form, which, with the deposit, should be forwarded to the Bankers, Brokers, or Secretary of the Company.

January 28th, 1876.

Form of Application for Shares.

To the Directors of the General Matrimonial Alliance Association (Limited).

GENTLEMEN,—

Having paid to your Bankers the sum of ———, being £1 per share as deposit, on ——— shares, I hereby request that number may be allotted me, and I agree to accept such shares, or any less number upon the terms of the prospectus, dated Jan. 24th, 1876, and I agree to pay the calls when required.

Name in full . . . . .
Residence . . . . . .
Profession . . . . .
Date . . . . . .

Note.—Several influential gentlemen who are large holders of District Railway Stock have promised their support, and are prepared to subscribe for a large number of shares. And it is confidently believed that the greatest of all living English Ministers who has ever sacrificed himself for the people's good will join the Board, and lend his influence to make the Company's success unprecedented in the annals of Joint Stock Enterprise.

CHAPTER XXV.—(CONTINUED.)

AN OBJECT OF LOVE SELECTED BY THE ODIC OR MAGNETIC CURRENT.

"Why, Mr. Pinto," exclaimed Clara Seesaw, "if you should float such a Company, the grateful nation ought at once to make you a peer of the realm, and all the single ladies subscribe a trifle to form a handsome testimonial to the great benefactor of their sex. Suppose two million ladies subscribed a penny each, there would be over eight thousand pounds, to raise a statue in the public squares, to print engravings, and to form an annual Pinto Prize for the best essay on some matrimonial theme, besides an ample fund to buy the silver tea-equipage, or whatsoever your fair admirers might choose to offer you. Don't you think you might extend this idea of the ladies' small subscriptions, and establish in your Halls a sort of Dowry Lottery Fund. I really think this would improve the chances of your scheme. I've often heard my father say that he has lady-speculators' names upon his books, and what a splendid field these 'Dowry Lotteries' would open up for them to gratify their speculative wish, and do a public good at the same time. Why, suppose ten millions of unmarried ladies were to subscribe only five shillings each, how much would that bring in, Mr. Pinto?"

"Two million and a half, dear lady," I replied, "in sterling pounds."

"Well, say they double their subscriptions; even cooks and housemaids could afford to pay ten shillings for a chance like this. That would give five million pounds. This would enable your Directors to give as prizes one thousand dowries of one thousand pounds, two thousand of five hundred pounds, four thousand of two hundred and fifty, eight thousand of one hundred and twenty-five, and twenty thousand of fifty pounds. Thus, out of ten million lottery tickets thirty-four thousand would gain prizes varying from one thousand to fifty pounds. Perhaps you wonder why the greatest prize is only to be one thousand pounds. As the Dowry Lottery Fund is supposed to be created not for gambling purposes so much as to enable numbers of excellent women who are not as well provided with love's second great requisite to marry their selected objects, the prizes are purposely kept at a moderate figure. Do you know, Mr. Pinto, I am a little afraid that, after these dowries are distributed, a good many of your sex will suddenly discover a telegraphic cable with perfect insulation, and select their objects with unseemly haste. To provide against any mischief here, I should make it a condition that the prizes would only be paid on the marriages of the successful candidates, and as they would come to your Halls on purpose to get married, I don't think that condition would do harm."

"My dear Miss Seesaw," replied I, "this is a most valuable suggestion of yours, and I will lay it before my Directors at the earliest opportunity. You are rather satirical at our expense when you talk of a sort of indiscreet scramble for the dowried objects; but I have the utmost confidence in the unerring working of my cable theory. Sordid motives will give place to genuine love. Oh, yes, it is a grand idea, and much good will be done. Of course the prudes and prigs, a few Low Churchmen, some doctors, who will fear that the use of the Halls, just as of the skating rinks, will seriously lessen the number of their hysterical and hypochondriacal patients, and some acid old misanthropes, and fussy, narrow-minded tabbies who oppose anything and everything, will profess to be greatly shocked,* and say, 'How dreadful! How indecent! What a shameless trafficking in love! that holiest feeling of our fallen human nature! An open hunt for wives and husbands in a public place!' But all these croakers will not stop the Company's success."

"No," said Clara Seesaw, "I don't believe they will; and as I see my father is one of the Directors, I think I shall take a share or two myself. But, Mr. Pinto, don't you long to be a 'Selected Object' yourself, if it be only to illustrate the proper working of your cable theory?"

" Ah, dear lady," replied I, seizing the chance thus naïvely offered, " I have longed to be a 'Selected Object' ever since I first saw you, and, though I know that I possess a very few poor fractions of that complex whole, 'Reciprocated Love,' while you have all the rest, yet still I dare to offer you these few in hopes they may be what you lack. Oh, surely, after the delicious but unspoken conversation that we had this afternoon, I am not doomed to hear from those sweet lips that all my theory of love is vain. Oh! Clara, say, can you accept a love like mine? for on your answer hangs my happiness or misery."

Now when a direct proposal is made to a young

---

* To judge by his notes on this portion of the manuscript, Grammaticus is simply going to have a fit, and some kind friend ought at once to clap a blister on the nape of his neck.

lady, Mrs. Grundy and her amiable tribe would have her blush, say nothing, feign surprise, play her fish discreetly, or refer it to papa at once with self-possession, and an air of business-like self-possession, free from foolish sentiment, and, above all, have a keen eye for the "root of evil," the silver tea-pots, gewgaws, fixings and settings to the matrimonial life which constitute the sole ambition of so many of these adult female babies, the elaborate productions of worldly mothers, who ignore, or do not understand, anything about the magnetic current or the odic influence. With these poor little fools the man they are going to marry is the last thing thought of, except as a necessary article of furniture, and the question never enters their carefully-trained empty little heads whether they love him or not.

But Clara Seesaw did none of these things, she only said, heaven bless her for the words,—

"There can be no need, Mr. Pinto, for me to speak, for that magnetic current which you believe in so must have already made you aware whether I am indifferent to your affection. Indeed, I frankly own that from the first time that I saw you I have felt both attracted towards and interested in you, although why it was so I could not tell. It must be because we possess between us the factors necessary, as your funny theory says, to make up the complex whole of love. Is it not so?" said she, with an arch look from her soft brown eyes, each of which seemed to me as full of love as an egg is of meat, as a certain bucolic swain of my acquaintance quaintly said in praise of his lady's eyes.

My only reply to this was a passionate kiss, a real Byronic "first kiss of love." At this interesting moment Seesaw entered the room.

"Eh, Pinto," said he, "that cable of yours seems to be in good working order; and though I did imagine your theory of love to be all moonshine, I believe it now that I see my Clara has become a convert so speedily."

"My Clara" here exclaimed,—

"Oh, papa! how can you say such things?"

The papa, unmoved, replied,—

"Do you love this young man—Erasmus Pinto? for if you do, I should prefer to cut the 'Telegraphic Period' of courtship short, and see you man and wife as soon as possible."

The dear girl's face was now suffused with a deep blush, which made her look more lovely still, and throwing her arms around her father's neck, she said,—

"I fear, dear father, that it must be love. I feel so interested in this 'Cable Theory' with its 'Odic or Magnetic Influence!' Indeed, I blush to own it; but you have ever taught me to tell you all my heart, and I must avow that, whether I will or no, Erasmus Pinto's image and his name seem ever in my thoughts. I surely have lost something—I suppose it is my heart That independent spirit you so wondered at in me is gone; I am but half myself. But spare my feelings, dear papa, for surely I have said enough."

She spoke no more, but glided from the room, and I was left, the first "Selected Object" of my sex, still sitting on a chair, with feelings indescribable. Yes, I, Erasmus Pinto, with but an eighth, at most, of love's required fractions to bestow, had won the seven-eighths or more this lovely creature had to give. Yes, she who had refused all offers, good ones though they were, had chosen me, a broker's confidential clerk until to-day, and full of wily City tricks to-day, and every day. Will sceptics now laugh down this "Odic Influence," "Air Cables" with "Magnetic Currents" bearing messages of nascent love from brain to brain? Apply, before it is too late, for shares in my great Company, ye would-be Benedicts, and you, ye ladies, who would know the joys of sacrificing self to some unworthy swain, who has, like me, that eighth, or may be that sixteenth or thirty-second which your own abundant stores of love are seeking for in drawing-rooms and balls, a sickly atmosphere of artifice and sham, in which love's telegraphic cables are but seldom laid, unless it be to break—apply at once, I say.

Now if, Grammaticus, the blister has done good, and you are now yourself again, just notice this. Surely woman loves to *place* her love, and man more to be loved.

You see how Clara Seesaw, after waiting long, though richly gifted with the qualities love needs, found her affinity in me. And when she found it, how she naïvely owned that all her heart was gone, that "Pinto" was the name blent with each thought. Her love was *placed*, and she was satisfied.

But I,—observe, Grammaticus,—though much in love myself, and though I had just gained this lovely creature's heart, had feelings of two kinds.

It seemed as if I had picked up a priceless jewel which was mine to keep and guard, and that I was delighted at my luck, and vowed I'd guard it well. But then another thought entwined itself with that. Oh! what a triumph for the "Odic Influence!" I see my Company a grand success, and married bliss, increased a hundred-fold, arrayed against the Evil One.

You see I had two loves, my Clara and my theory; and love's intoxication had not narcotized my senses as it does a woman's when her love is *placed*.

Most men, Grammaticus, feel this divided love, and seek more to be loved than love. How much more happy ought a woman's love to be than ours, if it thus surrenders head with heart, and loses self in faith. Why, I declare the learned critic is asleep !

"I think," said Mr. Seesaw, "Pinto, you must excuse my girl to-night. Her symptoms are all favorable for your happiness, but she is naturally somewhat overcome. Her mother, I remember, was the same, though *I* was pretty calm, for *I* loved both her guineas and herself.

"In giving you my daughter, I consider that I amply repay the service you have done me, though it is so great. You are now a full partner in the firm of Seesaw, Turnabout, and Pinto, Clara will have ten thousand pounds of her mother's fortune, our Company, I feel convinced, will be a great success, and of course, though no promotion money will be paid, there will be pickings for a clever and experienced man.

"I don't see that you will be robbing any one of their fair share of the second great requisite of human nature, as you call love, if you both get married at once. You need not have a separate establishment, but live with me until you both are tired. Would you like the money settled on your wife or not?"

"Oh! tie it fast, dear sir, by all means," I replied. "If I had marriageable daughters and I could give them anything, it should be tied up fast enough. A woman ought to have no voice in this, for when she really loves a man she gladly gives him all she has, and thinks he cannot fail, whatever others do. That specious plea of sons-in-law, 'I want it for my business,' has brought misery to very many homes. And yet I think I should not mind a steady son-in-law investing it in a good butcher's shop or corner public-house, or even a pawnbroker's West End place. Oh! yes, these businesses are sound enough. The people must have meat to live, they will have beer and gin to narcotize their sorrows with, and they must often pledge their goods to buy the meat and drink."

"Yes, Pinto, that is true enough, and I often think that, as the world will have its beer and gin, it ought to have it sound and good.

"We brokers do some harm, no doubt; but the great capitalist who speculates and sets insidious traps does many times as much.

"The man who keeps a gin-palace or a beershop does some harm; but wholesale brewers who supply their chemical concoctions do much more. But that's no reason why one man no better than the rest should write a fierce Philippic against brokers, brewers, and those who keep a public-house. Let parliament reform the system, and the men will soon reform themselves. The great aim of parliament should be to equalise as far as can be done the temptations to do wrong that each class is subjected to.

"I am glad you prefer that Clara's money should be settled on her, for the greatest prudence cannot always guard against reverse. I should be glad if you would make your own arrangements for the wedding as soon as possible. I will engage that we shall be ready on our side. I think my health is giving way. I cannot see through 'Outside Fools' as clearly as I used to do."

"You want a little change, dear sir," said I. "Let the wedding-day be fixed as soon as ever your daughter will allow."

After three weeks of delightful correspondence by "Magnetic Telegram," and interviews at least once every day, we both were wed.

The wedding, like most others, was a trifle dull, and just a little trying to the principals.

The Honorable Walter Loftus condescended to become "best man;" the bridesmaids were, a sister of that little hundred weight of blonde humanity *née* "Baby Clarke," the Misses Lewin Seesaw, of Wheal Ivy Lodge, at Thiddlethorpe, in Lincolnshire, and Salome Pinto, my maiden aunt, the poetess, unknown to fame, who, ever young in heart, though fifty years of age, determined she would be a bridesmaid, if she never was a bride, whatever Mrs. Grundy thought.

The Reverend Silvertongue Richwife read the service most impressively; but his superior accent made the Misses Seesaw smile, and vastly gratified the poetess.

Words scarcely can describe the sort of thing this unique accent was, but if I quote the previous Sunday's text you may derive some faint idea. The text was this, "He that hath ears to hear let him hear." This, Richwife, with imposing manner, rendered thus. "He that hath yeaws to yeaw, let him yeaw."

We spent the honeymoon at Paris, where I would advise "Selected Couples" all to go when married, and I was so happy that I quite forgot my other love, the cable theory.

And now, dear "Outside Fools" who read this

book, jovial or serious, benevolent or bilious, and you most learned critic, all take heart, for this is the last of the loves of Clara Seesaw and Erasmus Pinto.

CHAPTER XXVI.

ALL ABOUT A FALL, A CORINTHIAN AND A TEA-PARTY.

WE were a happy family, Clara, her father, and I. Of course, like other families, we had many small drawbacks to contend with in the shape of dozens of elaborate circulars from speculative purchasers of so-called bankrupt stocks of silks and satins, sensational post-cards from the anti-vaccinators, tons of best Wallsend, that turned out three parts slate, and sometimes the discovery of one of those true imps of Satan, the *cimices* of Rome, the κόρεις or Κορίνθιοι of Greece—so says Grammaticus they should be called, and he appears to like the subject by his notes; but what have we to do with Rome or Greece? The animal is cosmopolitan, and no doubt sent for useful purposes. In good society it is supposed to be unknown, and writers shun all mention of the beast.

I mean, dear "Outside Fools," a bug, which sometimes is discovered in a servant's attic, sometimes snugly wrapped up in the linen from the wash. There's no severer test of bland digestion or of Christian fortitude than this. There are some people whom the creature will not bite, Grammaticus goes on to say; but he opines that moral consciousness is lost in them, and so that neither does the Evil One nor yet his tiny myrmidons waste time in trying those whose conscience is already dead.

We had a housemaid, too, who would fall down and break the things most terribly. Four times the reckless girl fell down the stairs, and spoilt our fragile property worth several pounds.

The fifth time she, as well as crockery, fell to pieces. She was a civil and hard-working girl, was Mary Shaw, but being healthy and well-made, and having too much matter for her mind, or else more heart than head, and being promised marriage, she succumbed.

We had to keep the mother, and a brace of squalling, healthy brats three weeks, replace our damaged ware, and pay the doctor's bill.

But see how well this world's affairs are ordered for the best. The neighborhood was very dull, there had not been a single bit of scandal for some time. This windfall set the tabbies' tongues a-wagging healthily once more.

"How sad for Mrs. Pinto!" said Miss Sarah Clutterbuck, with acid smile at Mrs. Deborah Debbidge's tea-party, where some dozen Christian ladies were assembled to discuss "Revivalism" and any little parish scandal, as they drank their tea.

"I never should feel safe, if I were married, with a husband and an artful hussy in the house," rejoined Keturah Smug, a lady of uncertain age; "men are so fickle, and so soft, that any clever woman can lead them as she will."

As this Keturah Smug was still a miss, we may presume that she was either not a clever woman, or had scorned all overtures from such a soft and fickle sex as ours.

"I pity Mr. Pinto more, Miss Smug," said Miss Priscilla Wilks. "Just think what might be said,

And poor old Mr. Seesaw, the churchwarden, too, and so respectable. Poor man, no pleasant task for him to hold the plate on Sunday next. The world is so uncharitable now. But I think women often have themselves to blame. I always did think Clara Seesaw was an oddity before she married, and I should not wonder if the Pintos lead a most unhappy life."

Priscilla Wilks was still upon the sunny side of forty, still had hopes, and so she felt no love for married women, who, perhaps, had robbed her of a share of human nature's second great necessity, nor did she yet think badly of our sex.

"What nonsense you are talking," said Mrs. Sana Mens, who had a husband who was neither soft nor fickle, and a healthy family, and therefore kept her common sense and just a little charity. "The girl has only been six months in Mr. Pinto's house, and is engaged to Bumblecheek, the turncock's son. I've often seen them walking out on Sunday afternoon."

This was a healthy check to slander's busy tongue, and after Mrs. Debbidge had related sundry prodigies of early and successful birth, which Mrs. Sana Mens, whose husband was a doctor, showed to be impossible, the subject was reluctantly allowed to drop, and theatres and the Revivalists were next discussed.

Said Sarah Clutterbuck to Mrs. Debbidge,—

"You don't approve of theatres, do you, dear?"

"Indeed, I don't; I think them Satan's most insidious traps."

"And so do I," said Miss Keturah Smug.

"I rather like a screaming farce," said Miss Priscilla Wilks.

"Tragedy is dying out," said Mrs. Sana Mens, "and with good reason. There is quite enough in real life. If you go to a theatre for tragedy, and find the acting bad, as it is almost sure to be, you're bored and dull, while, if it should be good, it works upon one's feelings so that one is often worse instead of better for the play. My husband always says, and he knows more than all the men besides, that if his patients went to see a comic piece or pantomime more often than they do, he should not have so many nervous people on his hands."

"But what about Revivalism?"

"I think it is divine," said Sarah Clutterbuck.

"It's too sensational for me," said Mrs. Debbidge; "I often feel quite ill when I come home."

"I think the singing lovely," said Keturah Smug; "it steals upon and soothes the senses so."

"I like the Ritualistic service better," said Priscilla Wilks; "there is so much to interest; the chasuble, the alb, the stole, the acolytes, and all their nice accessories conspire to make one feel emotional, whereas your tunes that steal upon the senses make me think more of the Christy Minstrels than the hymn's good words."

"If you had heard the playful way in which the Bartimæus episode was rendered, while, the audience worshipped little, and laughed more, you would have felt emotional," said Mrs. Sana Mens. "I don't believe in these emotions being worked upon so much. A young man who was staying in our house, and rather out of health, was brought home half delirious, declared he was converted all at once, and if my husband had not bled him well, I don't believe he would have lived. If people must be narcotized, this may do less harm than adulterated beer, but surely true religion needs more sober sense, and does not talk so flippantly of sacred themes."

Thus having said, the lady bade the company good-night.

"I hate that Mrs. Sana Mens," said all the three. "As for myself, I wonder what she wanted in such company."

"And I believe there's more in that affair at Pinto's than she will allow. Her husband is the doctor there," said Sarah Clutterbuck.

"And so do I, and I," rejoined the other two.

But let us leave these interesting spirits to themselves.

Perhaps they would have been more happy and their neighbors' reputation suffered less if they had had more faith in the goodness of humanity.

Now of all the various kinds of narcotism which poor human nature is addicted to, I believe that this faith in the goodness of human nature is productive of the most happiness.

So thought Salome Pinto, the poetess of our family, unknown to fame, who had a dream once and thought she saw a virgin, to quote her own word, "With serious beauty dower'd, clad in robes of white," who solved many doubts that perplexed her mind, and added to her happiness.

I dare say some of you, dear "Outside Fools," are sad through want of faith.

Here is part of what this virgin is supposed to have said,—

" 'Ev'n those who have thought out life's problem, and
Have found some rest in knowing that they may
Not learn aught more on this side of the grave,
Still feel an aching void, that intellect

Both loathes and trembles at for lack of sight.
The key to happiness in life is " faith."
Faith in the wrong, if honest, is not wrong,
But want of faith in all is worse than death.'
No more she said, but upwards wing'd her flight,
And left me with an undevelop'd sense
Of some great truth, half-dreaming, half-awake."

However this may be, my Clara had full faith in me, and therefore slander's busy tongue completely failed to mar our happiness.

We got poor Mary Shaw and her two healthy babes a passage to New Zealand, where an honest man who had the food and wanted love soon married her in spite of her mistake.

You see a sheep in that young land costs three half-crowns, instead of three pounds ten; and therefore population is a want and not an ill. Give up your *cimices*, Grammaticus, and help to crack this nut.

CHAPTER XXVII.

ALL ABOUT A COOK, A BATH, AND THE CONSEQUENCES.

Now when happiness so great as ours is enjoyed by mortals, it is ordained that some stroke of adverse fortune should occur to remind us that we are placed here, not only to enjoy, but to learn enough to fit us for another world. In our case a cook was selected by Providence to give us this reminder.

She was a good cook, and not a bad-looking, but an idle and a wasteful.

Nathaniel Seesaw was no niggard in his house-keeping, but if there was one thing he detested it was waste. Now in this land of fog and changeful weather, we most of us find it necessary to have a grievance, if only to keep the less tractable secretions in order, and to establish our claim to that sympathy which all expect, but few succeed in getting, because scarcely any one thinks of giving it first.

My father-in-law's grievance was, that this good cook, who was not bad-looking, and who kept up her spirits and complexion by the liberal use of a private whisky bottle, supplied from her master's stores, would persist in cutting bread in a most reckless and unscientific manner. The worthy man even gave up his toast, of which he was fond, in the hope of inducing this cook to be less wasteful. He gave up his toast in vain.

One day, when the weather was peculiarly trying to the nerves and stomach, the Evil One arranged that more crusts and odd-shaped pieces of bread should be discovered in the pantry than ever before.

My father-in-law, who was not in good health, blew up his cook in terms more plain and expressive than those which in soberer moments and better health any vicar's churchwarden, or, indeed, any Christian gentleman, would have used, and ended by telling the baggage that she must quit his service or mend her ways.

The good cook said nothing, but went on with her work and her whisky in sullen silence.

One of my father-in-law's habits was to take a hot bath on a Saturday before dinner, in which he would read his evening paper and spend at least one hour. On the Saturday succeeding this row with his cook he went to take his bath as usual.

The bath was like all other baths, except that it was heated by a large gas stove, which after a certain heat was attained, required to be turned partly off to prevent the water from becoming too hot, and that it had a heavy mahogany lid, which swung upwards on hinges, and was only prevented from falling by two catches which held it against the thin wall that separated the bath-room from the passage on the landing.

Now this good cook, who was also not bad-looking, having an analytical mind, a body excited by whisky and a soul full of revenge, had perceived that the catches which held the lid of the bath in its place were much worn.

So with that cunning which is not seldom found in the kitchen she carefully oiled these catches and then deftly balanced the edge of the lid on the middle of the tongues, so that a slight concussion on the wall would be sure to send it down upon the bath.

The vicar's churchwarden was soon after this seated safely in his bath, was placidly reading his paper, and noting with satisfaction that the stocks which he himself had sold to two clients in the morning were steadily declining, while the water, which was now almost hot enough to require the gas turning off, was preparing his cuticle for the flesh-brush and strigil, when the good-looking but evil-hearted cook, having first nerved herself with an extra dram of chemically-compounded whisky, stole up the stairs, and along the passage, and lurching suddenly against the wall just opposite the catches, sent down the heavy lid with a bang, and shut her master in a trap, as deadly as Agamemnon's proved to be, although Grammaticus affirms that his was never shut in at the top, and that hot water baths in early times were thought effeminate, and that the water was heated in a succession of caldrons on the other side of the bathroom wall instead of in the room. After executing this devilish manœuvre the cook went down below, cut up more loaves, and drank more drams.

There was no murder in her heart; she thought her master would be flurried much, and frightened not a little too, but nothing worse.

Alas! it was not so, the sudden shock brought on an apoplectic fit, for which the system was prepared no doubt before; and when, some half-hour afterwards, as no answer was returned to the repeated knocking, the door was broken open, and the lid raised up, Nathaniel Seesaw was discovered simmering, but quite unconscious of his state.

On my return from business in a happy frame of mind, having just opened correspondence with a fresh country client, whom I could charge a half commission instead of an eighth, who was a gentleman of landed property and no experience in city spiders' webs, I found my father-in-law no more, my wife quite stunned and helpless through her grief, the good cook drunk and in hysterics, the kitchen chimney all on fire, and the fire-engine just arrived. Oh! what a field for heroism was here. What would a Stoic have thought or said?

But there are times when the feelings of the human heart are too sacred to be written about, and this is one. This chapter might teach us how much we lose by giving way to temper, how dangerous it is to gratify a feeling of revenge, and how careful brewers and distillers ought to be not to mix the *Cocculus Indicus* with what they sell to good and not bad-looking cooks.

G

CHAPTER XXVIII.

A DISCOVERY.

As John Turnabout was now a gouty invalid, and Nathaniel Seesaw dead, I was virtually the sole acting partner in the firm. Besides the money settled on my wife, my father-in-law had left a balance of seven thousand pounds, most of which was of course due to my lucky rescue of the Honorable Walter Loftus from the hole in the ice, in return for which he gave me the information about Egyptian Stock. But for this, Nathaniel Seesaw would have died insolvent.

One day, as I was looking over some of his papers, I lighted on a bundle of manuscript which on examination, proved to be an account of the dealings of some of his last clients; a note was appended to the effect that he wished the matter to be printed in case it had not been before his death. As a history of these dealings will doubtless be more instructive than anything that I can write, I will simply make a copy of the manuscript for your benefit, dear " Outside Fools."

CHAPTER XXIX.

QUALMS OF CONSCIENCE FELT BY THE LATE NATHANIEL SEESAW, ESQ., ABOUT HIS BUSINESS AS A BROKER.

CAN it be right for me to keep on helping hundreds on their downward road to beggary, now that I know so well they must lose all in time?

But is it worse to be a broker than to be a barrister? Of course the lawyer's business is as full of roguery as mine, and that is why we always charge them half commission and give half on business that they bring. But the business of the barrister is thought respectable enough, and yet he often must needs try to prove the guilty innocent, by specious rhetoric, and, sometimes worse, to show that innocence is guilt.

I often wonder why a jury and a judge are not sufficient to find out the truth.

The butcher and the farmer should be honest men enough; their business does not tempt them to be otherwise; the baker and the brewer might do a great deal of good if they would sell good bread and beer.

I wonder whether I do much more harm than many lawyers, clergymen, and doctors do?

It seems as if they had their "Outside Fools" to work upon, and I had mine.

These questions are too deep for me, but really I believe an honest thinker with literary power might show that brokers are no worse than other men.

"The means to do ill deeds makes deeds ill done," says somebody, I don't know who, but he was not a fool.

We deal so with the "root of evil" that it would be wonderful if we were better than we are.

These questions all perplex me, but one thing I know, that I would gladly give up trading on the ignorant credulity of others, and feeling nothing better than a legalized thief. It is true, I do not make the clients speculate, indeed, their wish to do so creates my class.

But at what odds to them all this is done! Why need the dice be loaded so?

Just as the judge and jury could find out the truth without the aid of legal quirk or specious rhetoric, so could A buy of B or sell to him without the jobber's and the broker's aid combined. One class would be enough.

But how is this to be effected? By the aid of parliament? There's not much chance of that, I think.

I have too many Members on my books. 'Twould spoil their paying little game. You see in foreign things they sometimes hold good cards. How must it, then, be brought about? Not by the ribald assaults of defeated gamblers on our class. This does more harm than good.

The only way is for a man who knows the system to inform the public so that they may know the risks they run. But is this I, Nathaniel Seesaw, who say this? I, whose laugh at ruined "Outside Fools" would sound like crack of pistol shot before my health gave way? I, whose gaze, inscrutable and cold, could multiply the Sunday offerings. I, whom Marrywell so loved, because, as once he aptly said, "Seesaw, we're very much alike, we both have 'Outside Fools' to deal with, and we both take much more than we give. In fact, I tell you honestly," said he, "I think that any man who reads his Bible carefully, and tries to do just what it says, will gain more good than from a hundred sermons such as mine, and they are better than the average. You see we dare not try to explain the difficult and controverted passages for fear of giving offence to our superiors. And if we would explain, I do not think that many of us could." Yes, Marrywell liked me. What would he think at my thus turning traitor? What indeed! When I drank beer and generous '63 I never felt like this; my business seemed quite honorable then. But ever since I've taken fifteen grains of potash twice a day, and knocked off beer and wine, an "Outside Fool" seems more respectable than I, and my ill-gotten gains seem to weigh down my soul. It's very strange. I could prove all I thought then right by argument. And now, when I think just the opposite, I can prove still that I am right. Potash is matter, is it not? How horrible to think so little matter can affect the mind so much. Well, so it is, and to relieve my mind I must tell "Outside Fools," for whom I used to feel contempt alone, what makes them lose their money so. Oh, those Egyptians!* I could tear my hair from off my head. Had I not bought at that high price, when the Levantine usurers and Israelitish touts arranged to force the football up, that game I had so often helped to play, I had been free by now. I give largely to charities, no doubt, but the money is not really mine, nor is the motive right. It is but slavish fear and

---

* This was written before the rise in Egyptian Stocks had taken place that saved Mr. Seesaw.—*Erasmus Pinto.*

want of health. Nay, am I not a living lie, when at the church I hold the plate, and blandly beam on those who give gold pieces, while I look severely cold on those who offer threepennies. And yet those threepennies were earned more honestly than any sovereign I have dropped into the plate.

"Well, well, a broker's business may be bad, but is not that of our great Chancellor of the Exchequer that is to be, still worse—that arch-promoter who pays forty, thirty, anything you like per cent. in dividends for three or four half years, then not a cent.—who hired the venal scribes to puff his deep-laid schemes, the hollowness of which lay hid behind that stalking horse of most financial acrobats, *" Industrial Enterprise?"*

Is not our business quite as good as that of those who lend their names to float the foreign loans of countries which are in a state of semi-bankruptcy, and which will fail to pay as soon as they can get no further loans? It certainly does much less harm. They catch the real investor, we but clear the weaker speculators out.

CHAPTER XXX.

THE LATE MR. NATHANIEL SEESAW'S POSTHUMOUS VIEWS ON THE CAUSES OF SPECULATION.

It seems to me that personal vanity and that spice of conceit that is inherent in us all, which can only be lessened by education or suffering, makes men still keep betting on the turf although they know the "*talent*" nearly always win, and though they see their friends being ruined all around.

This same conceit and vanity makes speculators still play on the losing game, although they daily see other speculators lose all they have and know the odds to be so great.

Those who do not speculate, and they are daily becoming fewer, profess to wonder at this trait in human character, and often plume themselves on being free from such insanity. They are insane perhaps on other points as bad, or worse. Just as, when their friends or relatives are ill, instead of recognizing that it is the weakness common to humanity, and showing real concern and pity for the sick, some persons blame the sufferers as though they were the cause of their own suffering, and, as it were, feel a sort of secret superiority derived from others' misery: just as "each man thinks all are mortal but himself," and though it be unacknowledged in so many words, considers others to be rather foolish to be ill or die, instead of fearing lest the common lot should overtake him next; so with the "Outside Fools," each fool thinks all are fools except himself, and when a speculating friend is ruined, instead of feeling fear and learning wisdom from the case, he feels a slight contempt and often says he to himself, "Aha! why was he not like *me*." And then with some elation, he will say, "Yes, I shall be the one, perhaps the only one, to show men how to play the interesting game successfully." How sweet a thought to human vanity.

As all the world delights to live in bigger houses than it ought to live, to spend more money than it ought to spend, to boast itself to be a greater and a richer world than it is really, and, although it knows it is a lie, yet likes to act the lie, so, too, with speculative fools 'tis very sweet for one who has a hundred pounds to deal as though he had a thousand, for one who has a thousand to speculate with men who have from five to twenty thousand at command, to mix and talk with bigger men, enunciate his views to other gaping fools, to fancy he is wise, and that ere long he will be rich. Oh, yes, 'tis very sweet, and very human, very vain.

Another cause of speculation lies in this. A wide-spread wish to get rich suddenly, to find the means for increased luxury. "De'il take the hindmost," is the cry now in the race for gold. Each wants to show his neighbor how he's getting on. This breeds a general dislike to do the steady work of life. A man who is content to live on four or five per cent. is thought a dullard now, when all the world is asked to "co-operate," and tradesmen offer to return the money back one pays in bills, if one will only give them time. This "gospel of getting on" is a fine thing for financiers, for, singular to say, we always hear of those who have got on, but not a word is said of those who have succumbed in their pursuit for gold. One cannot startle others with a dazzling and a swift success, unless one runs some fearful risks. But then one does not suffer bankruptcy.

Another more insidious cause of speculation is this. The implicit trust that five out of six speculators place in the newspapers' remarks and articles on stocks and shares. The writing is so plausible, there is so much apparent truth, so much that needs a special knowledge of the subject to fairly estimate the views on it, that when some stock is made the centre of attraction by a powerful financial clique, and telegrams appear which none but those behind the scenes can contradict or verify, and when those telegrams are aided by suggestive hints thrown out in money articles, the "Outside Fool," who hears his brother fools talk loud in praise of this particular stock, or cry it down according to their paper's tone, must surely be experienced or blessed with strong views of his own and keen perception to prevent his being taken in.

The better-educated "Outside Fools," if gentlemen and optimists, have not the slightest chance of seeing through the snare.

A few learn how to estimate the value of these articles by noting how we brokers cannot help a sneer or laugh when clients draw attention to some flaming puff of stocks they wish to bull, or fierce attack on what they feel inclined to bear. But these few have perception, watch the kind of men they deal with, take notes quietly, and add up the result. Perception and an insight into human nature is the speculator's requisite, not so much logic and deep reading of the so-called merits of each stock.

That sort of instinctive power to diagnose a market well that only few possess is worth far more than reason is on 'Change.

Then, lastly, there is that cause which Pinto mentioned when examined for the vacant post of confidential clerk. I mean that need for strong excitement in this land of liver and of spleen. I am not dealing with effects but causes now, and I declare from my own large experience that till they had lost heavily, my clients all seemed better for the stimulus that speculation gave. Let doctors give their explanation of the fact. I only can suggest what I have said.

And let a doctor tell me how it is that I, Nathaniel Seesaw, who have cheated "Outside Fools" remorselessly and liked the game, am sitting here and trying to prevent a future crop of fools from losing all. Oh! this curious thing called mind. I soon should hug myself with the idea that it was pure philanthropy that prompted me to write for them.

I am afraid it is ill health and fear. Had I not made enough to live upon I never should have thought of doing this perhaps, and now I try to stop the swollen profits of my brothers in the trade. Well, Providence rules all, and if I but forget myself, I may do some good yet. The above are, in my humble opinion, the real causes of this wide-spread speculation, from which no class or creed is free. I have not seen these causes given yet in print, but this should not be wondered at.

Suppose, dear "Outside Fools," you could make money out of your own broker by a secret and elaborate machinery, the working of which he did not understand, would you explain to him what "wheel within wheel" meant, and show him how to read between the lines? No indeed.

If "Outside Fools" were brokers, they would do as brokers do. When I read virulent abuse of us, I always doubt the writer's honesty. It is so easy and so pleasant to find fault with men. It seems to place the one who finds the fault upon a vantage ground, from which he looks down with complacency on those he blames. But surely this is not the way to teach mankind.

I may be wrong, but still I cannot think that there

is all that difference between the moral excellence of men. One man may far transcend another in his usefulness of life, in dazzling genius, in science or in art, but seldom, I conceive, is there this difference in moral excellence. The very habits and the example of a man may be much better for his fellow-creatures to admire, and they may place him on a pedestal, and not be harmed themselves by doing so, although his virtues may exist in their ideas alone. But ask the man what he thinks of himself, and you should find his estimate of self is low according to his knowledge of humanity. I don't mean modesty that springs from want of blood, but modesty that's based on sober knowledge of the world we live in, and the life we live. Perhaps I am all wrong in this, I have no learning to direct me right, but what I write I feel. And what is more, I know that many brokers hold the same idea as I.

I wonder if the motive of these authors is so very pure and good? Perhaps it is profane for an unlettered business-man like me to say a word about such men who have the power, or think they have, to teach their fellow-creatures truth.

If they write books for any other purpose, such as to try and make a stir about themselves, to gain the public notice, or to gain the "root of evil," they are, to my mind, as bad as we; they often sell a spurious coin to "Outside Reading Fools" and take the genuine "root of evil" in exchange. We give the "Outside Speculating Fools" short weight. Pray, is the difference so very great. We are called names for recommending rubbish to our clients who can't tell the difference between the true and false. They sell their wondrous wares to a public who, knowing little more of the real merits of a book than speculators do of stocks, takes readily whatever views the publishers' retainers like to promulgate according to their crotchets or their whim.

My business, doubtless, makes me practical, but I can't see that men who like to attitudinize in print and freely to assail all classes but their own are any better than the class they blame, nor do I think the writings of such men do lasting good.

Assail the system, not the men, ye scribbling "Outside Fools." But if I go on prosing thus, I might as well write Richwife's sermon for next week.

But can I be Nathaniel Seesaw, and write this? Yes, so it is, and now I know the meaning of those words, "Truth is stranger than fiction."

Why, ever since that Sana Mens knocked off my beer and pint of port, and made me take that potash stuff, I have appeared to see more clearly with each dose how black a business mine has been. And, oddly, instead of seeming to be a blacker character myself with every dose, I seem to find some consolation and excuse in thinking how many other men are quite as bad, and in imagining that, were the system much improved, I should become a better man in the people's thoughts although I might be just the same.

There is one great defect in our system, beautiful and elaborate as it is. It encourages time-bargains on a large scale, offers every inducement to the client to go beyond his depth, but discourages small dealings and heavily handicaps the small speculative investor who is honest and does not wish to speculate beyond his means.

We dare not refuse point blank to deal for these clients, because they might say, "Your system is a direct encouragement to dishonesty," and 'pon my life they would not be far wrong; but we laugh at them, charge them double commission, deal at a much wider price, and put them off with various excuses. Oh, yes, when we are well we hate these sort of "Outside Fools," and even jobbers laugh and jeer at brokers who come bothering with nasty little *bonâ fide* orders for one or two hundred pounds' worth of Foreign Stocks or Rails, and even dealing in five hundreds we set our faces dead against, because we know that it takes us twice as long to clear our clients out. How often I have said to these,—

" My dear sir, deal in thousands, and I'll charge you less commission; it does make so much trouble and the dealers always give worse prices for these bits of stocks."

But I shall have that Sana Mens down on me if I don't take my medicine, so I'll rest a little while and take my fifteen grains. I'm sure if he keeps on with this another week, I shall be able to leap outside of myself and take a good and critical look, like one who gazes at a picture on the wall, or at his fellow-creatures' faults. This doubless is the way to "know thyself." I'll give that Sana Mens an extra guinea when he comes again.

CHAPTER XXXI.

ON "BEARING" AND "BULLING."

A FIRST-RATE doctor is that Sana Mens. I feel myself again. He has allowed me just a pint of Burgundy and a glass of whisky once a day. The change is wonderful. I think I frightened him a bit when I said this,—

"How is it, doctor, that one sees the truth about oneself more clearly when one's living low? It's marvellous how much your fifteen grains of potash for the last eight days has taught me."

I do believe that Sana Mens thought I was learning truth too fast, and so he said,—

"A little nervous exaltation, my dear sir; it comes from weakness; why, you have no pulse."

I did feel low, and though rather interested in my curious change of sentiments, I was not sorry to be allowed a little stimulant. You see, I never had a headache in my life before, so being ill was very strange.

And now I am again the Seesaw of old times. My waist expands, the broker's business seems all right, and I know nothing—of myself.

The crossing-sweeper bows his lowest bow, although when I was on the potash *régime* I told him never to bow more to me, for men were equal, and I should forget to tip him if he did. The rascal knew me better than myself. Equal, indeed! No sixpence would the man have got from me if he had not done what I told him not to do.

We had a very quiet day on 'Change. "No business" was the cry inside and outside too. It was a case of "dog eat dog," for we inside think we are each the keenest man, and if the public will not let us eat them up, we try to eat each other up.

Just take a look inside with me and never mind the Cerberus; he growls, but I will stop his mouth with half-a-crown. See there. All playing! So it often is. Do you hear that chorus yonder in the

Railway market? Oh! we have our wags and poets, too, inside. Just hark!

> Oh! would they like to buy cheap Caley,
> With A and B to shilly-shally?—
> > Leeroy, Leery!
>
> Oh! yes, we all should like cheap Caley,
> Call up your forces, big bears rally,—
> > Leeroy, Leery!
>
> Tip Muffin what to write to-morrow,—
> Make bulls pay stiff con : to their sorrow,—
> > Leeroy, Leery!
>
> The fruit is ripe, come shake the tree,
> Drive down the stock to thirty-three,—
> > Leeroy, Leery!
>
> The div's all right, now then we buy :
> That A and B is all my eye,—
> > Leeroy, Leery!

Now I think you had better retire, for the wags have done singing, and they can see by your interested gaze that you are a novice, and therefore they are quite ready to cry, "Fourteen hundred," and smash your Lincoln and Bennett over your eyes, and plant fish-hooks deftly in your coat-tail pockets. Hark once more. That's Dick Whiffles, who's a bull of Peru, which keeps going down more every day. He remembers the songs of his boyhood and applies them to his bull,—

> Twinkle, twinkle, little stocks,
> I must put you in the box.

It was my new client, Sir Bemmidge Bracebrook, whom I took inside, for he was dying to get a glimpse, and as the saints were most of them at lunch, I managed it, though not without some risk and ribaldry. Sir Bemmidge was rather an odd specimen of an "Outside Fool." He always said that he expected to lose; but he did not care so long as he learnt something for his loss. So I fell in with his humor, and doled out little bits of information at a high price, as I have heard that those who aped Socrates used to dole out to their pupils.

After leaving the house we went over to Birch's and had some turtle soup and cold punch, which, in spite of Sana Mens' prohibition, seemed to do one good.

On arriving at the office, I found Monsieur Emile Boulanger, of the Baltic, waiting for me, to arrange a movement in the Dover A market. Having received my instructions privately to get Dolorous George to offer fifty thousand next day, as soon as the rattle went at eleven, to offer thirty thousand myself, and give for the put of more, so as to break the market, and then to buy all that I could get up to one per cent. above the price the stock stood at before, I introduced Sir Bemmidge to M. Boulanger, and the baronet was very soon deep in an argument about the relative merits of "bulling" and "bearing."

As this is a question which, I have noticed, is often discussed by "Outside Fools," I will give the views expressed by the gentlemen themselves, and then my own on the subject. Bemmidge was a theorist, Boulanger an experienced financier, but prejudiced in favor of his class.

"A gentleman who speculates should always be a bull," said Monsieur Boulanger. "It is not only more respectable, but pays the best. You have all the capital of wealthy men to help you if you hold on long enough. I have known many bulls make money and retain it too, but all the bears I've known have been cleared out in time. I must confess I do not like a bear. It may be prejudice, but there are many more who have the prejudice. A bear is generally a pessimist, and I suspect sometimes is not a gentleman."

"I don't agree with you," said Bracebrook. "We most of us are naturally bulls. The constitutional bear of course exists, and he, perhaps, as you assert, has either no belief in human nature, or his blood is poor and thin. It seems to me that speculators lose because they follow their ideas and inclinations so, instead of acting on some principle. Now 'bearing' is quite contrary to these ideas and inclinations, and can only be learnt by speculative thought, and resisting one's natural bent. Thousands of persons who buy scarcely understand the meaning of selling what they have not got to sell. As, then, the public are, in general, the bulls, the jobbers must be bears, and as the public loses and the jobbers gain, it's better to bear stocks than bull. Besides, a hitch in politics, a warlike speech delivered by some foreign potentate or statesman, or leading politician in our government, a serious accident, a shock to credit, falling off in traffic, and those many chances of mishap, all help the bear."

"I am not good at argument," said Boulanger; "your words sound plausible enough, but all I know is that my friends who took to 'bearing' lost their money. Good day. I must be gone."

"And so must I," said Bracebrook. "Good day."

Now, my dear "Outside Fools," I'll give you my own views on "bulling" and "bearing," and as they are based on real experience, they ought to save you money, if they do not make it.

The truth is, sometimes it is best to bull, at other times to bear; but if you will have me give a preference, I choose the bull, because, as Boulanger, who is a member of the *Haute Finance*, and knows what he's about, says truly, if you hold on long enough, you will have capital come to your aid. But this will not be true if you should be a bull of stocks intrinsically bad. Your holding on or buying more will only bring you to worse grief.

It is quite true that capital is often found in direct antagonism to reason and intrinsic merit, and so often aids the bulls by working up the price beyond its value. This was done in Emma, is done every day in something that is rotten at the core.

But it is most unsafe to think from this that you may bull anything you like. The large capitalist will get his information sooner than you will, sell out his stock, sail off to other seas, and leave you high and dry upon the shore.

No, you must bull a stock that has intrinsic merit, what the Americans call a rock bottom price, and still is always fluctuating. Such are English Rails. If you bull these and keep some buying power left in the event of a heavy fall, you will soon leave the bear behind.

Perhaps you think this easy to do, if you have money. You will find it is not so.

Indian Railways are good things, are they not? How long ago is it since the papers got up quite a scare, so vague, so alarming to investors' minds, that a nice panic would have soon occurred if it had not suited some to buy their good things back.

Just so, even in English Rails. You will have your "scares," which will be carefully augmented by the interested cliques, who partly get them up to buy.

Did you feel comfortable when the "Abolition of Second Class" was introduced? Lombards are supposed to be good things. How did investors feel when that great error in a few odd millions broke upon their startled gaze? The cynic says "Investors are such fools." And so are those who lose their purses in a crowd. Suppose you heard to-morrow that the traffic returns were false and swelled by tons of private pig iron kept on running up and down the line to raise the price, and speculative cliques sold quantities of stock, would you, an "Outside Fool," keep firm, and, when the air was thick with rumor, buy a little more? Not you; you'd sell your holding, and buy back when it had risen to its former price. So that you would have been a bull of a sound stock, not gone beyond your depth, and yet lost money by your bull. But still the capitalist will always help a bull of a good stock if he will only hold on long enough.

But you will say it must be right to be a bear, as rotten stocks are forced up so. It's logical to argue so, but it's not practical.

Suppose you were a bear of Uruguay, at 60. The knowing ones behind the scenes, and there were such, finding that the public had sold heavy bears, would buy up stock, spread rumors that a loan was all arranged, that Brazil would take the country over, or any other lie, and as the stock is small, would soon put ten per cent. upon the price, clear out the frightened bears, and then, as they themselves were bears, let out a little piece of truth, and drive it down again. You would have been a bear of an unsound stock, not gone beyond your depth, and paid something too in backwardation to the bulls.

But suppose there were no backwardation, but contango. Well, my bears would only get two-thirds of what the jobber gets, even if I did not play my tricks, and would have still to pay a half commission each account they carried over. This makes all the difference. The bull of course pays more than if he were a jobber, and the same commission as the bear.

Suppose there is a tree called *Speculation*, which grows in the poorest and the richest soil alike, and bears no fruit but leaves.

The roots and trunk are capital.

The larger boughs are great financiers and the money articles.

The jobbers, brokers, directors, secretaries, and accountants, are the smaller ones.

The twigs are the few experienced speculators, with but small capital.

The leaves the "Outside Fools."

The leaves fall off and wither, but return again next spring.

The trunk stands firm upon the "Root of Evil" placed.

The storm of panics and false Rumor's breath shake off the leaves too oft before their time, and sadly bruise the smaller branches and the twigs.

The trunk grows bigger every year, the roots more widely spread.

The crop of leaves is sometimes large and sometimes small, but never wholly fails. This year it will be very small, just as on other trees some leaves hang longer than the rest.

What is the upshot then of this?

That "bulling" sound stocks is as good as "bearing" bad, and perhaps a little better, for the wealthy buy the good whenever they're depressed.

What are sound speculative stocks? The English Rails. Buy, say a fourth of what you can afford whenever the market is very flat, and when you feel the strongest wish to sell.

If a further drop ensues, buy just another fourth. But if another fall should come, buy one more fourth, and so on till you have bought all you can pay for.

The chances are that before you have bought your second or third fourth, there will have been a rally then you ought to sell and wait to buy again.

Don't borrow of your bankers with less margin, than fifty per cent. You will make more by observing this precaution and be nearly safe.

But if you be a pessimist, and think that "all tends to deteriorate," why, sell a bear of some bad stock.

What are bad speculative stocks? The Foreign Stocks. But which? Ah! there you almost put me in a fix. Let us see. What with Turkey and Peru, Spain and Mexico, Honduras and Costa Rica, Paraguay and Uruguay, I scarcely know which way to turn.

Some eager "Outside Fool" says, "Uruguay."

If only a few more thought so, and backed their opinion strongly, we should soon have a good rise. The stock is much too small to bear.

"Egyptian," then another cries.

Nathaniel Seesaw would prefer to give for put and

call, and now is looking out for an "Outside Fool" to take the money. I may be prejudiced, but nearly all good bears seem gone.

"Russian," cries an excited "Outside Fool," triumphantly.

What! how about the carrying over day? And how about the coming loan? Would you, a wretched sprat, contend against leviathans?

I do not say the stock is not fifteen per cent. too dear, but that is no use alone.

Well, surely Anglos? Yes, I think you might sell one small bit of Anglos, if you have a friend who has a ship at your command, and you can bring yourself to foul the rival line; and, further, if you think you're strong enough to wait till some other company gets fairly started, and the Cable Ring is broken up. Well, "bearing" prospects don't look very bright, do they? nor "bulling" either, for a little man.

Take this to heart, dear "Outside Fools." Whatever you elect to do, collectively you cannot win, for we must live well, and out of you. Your consolation must be this. A few may win, and you *may* be one of those few. If you don't think you *may* be one of those, I do not pity you. You've learnt what few learn all their lives, and it should make you more content.

But don't you think these foreign loans a good investment for that surplus capital that springs from prosperous years? It would tend to raise the price of labor in other countries, and so act indirectly on our own.

In theory I do, but not in practice, when I see such countries as Bolivia, which is by no means the poorest and the least honest, receiving so small a portion of the loan subscribed ostensibly for her. Well, could not the public supply the funds less a commission of a half cent to the financier?

No respectable financier would lend his name to any foreign loan unless he had large pickings from the same. This is the power of capital.

Then try a financier who does not take enough to be called respectable.

The public would not subscribe enough to float the loan.

Now, then, red-hot reformers, what will you do next?

Let the nation know a little more of these financial tricks.

Well, something may be done, no doubt, by that; but education of all kinds is very slowly gained, and where each fool thinks he is not a fool, although his brother is, you'll have no easy task.

"Black-hearted traitor!" are the words I seem to hear from brother-brokers in the house. You've cheated "Outside Fools" as much as any of us have, and more than most, and now you turn against your friends when you've enough to live upon.

My dear old friends, it does seem shabby, I allow, but I begin to think with Tyndall, that we're all *automata*. I never thought so till I took that nasty potash Sana Mens gave me. Now don't be angry with a poor old man who has not long to live, whose conscience or whose liver troubles him so much. The "Outside Fools" won't learn as quickly as you seem to think, and surely men who know the power of money as well as you can give some two or three poor devils fifty pounds a-piece to show what empty stuff old Seesaw wrote, and how it was well known that he was just a little touched. It is an insult to suppose you can't do this.

And really, my dear brothers, you would not quite like old England to become a byword of financial folly, and the "*working man*" to raise a cry and pull the building down about your ears. You know what said the chairman at the meeting of Honduras bondholders in October last, how poor mechanics held these worthless I O U's, and how the savings of several humble households had been scraped together to purchase single bonds. You really must steer clear of working men—and clearer still of lions shaking dewdrops from their bristling manes. Be warned in time.

Why not form powerful syndicates to place the shares in the Great Matrimonial Company which Nathaniel Seesaw and Erasmus Pinto are about to float?

Approach, ye noble barons, acrobatic jugglers of finance, we can afford you a good bonus on each share ye place, and yet do good to all our shareholders.

Here is the proper outlet for the capital of prosperous years. A sum not far short of the national debt is sunk in foreign loans, of which no small amount comes from the clergymen, the widows, and the spinsters of our "merrie" isle of cant, and trade, and fog. And of these many millions, pray, how much is sound? and if it be, how long will it keep so? I have not reckoned France and the United States, nor even Italy and Portugal, Brazil and Chili, no, nor yet the Argentine Republic, although some of these, though good, are very high. No wonder that the parsons' sermons are so poor, the girls with those Satanic dragon sovereigns sought so for. Just think, ye magnates of finance! Had you not wanted huge commissions for your hocus-pocus tricks, how many pillars of the church would have had minds left free for holy speculative thought —not those distracting thoughts of Bs. and Cs., Egyptians and Perus. The Evil One must have picked out those Moslem Bs. and Cs. with their seductive nine per cent. on seventy to eighty pounds, according to the market price, besides the chance of being paid at par, to catch the good apostles with. Ah, if the bishops saw my books, they'd wonder how it is that these good men have such a fancy for the stocks of infidels and for your "Wild Cat" mines. 1 never had a bishop as a client yet, but I was told to-day, and by a clergyman, that a Colonial bishop had put five hundred pounds into Ben Hoax's Co-operating Bank to get eighteen per cent. paid monthly. He paid a small subscription with a Hoax's cheque, which was refused, and that alarmed his reverence, but he was just too late.

Wake up, ye great ones on the bench episcopal. Bring all the stores of your ecclesiastical learning forth to show your weaker brethren that the personality of Satan is there seen wherever eight or nine or ten per cent. is offered by Mahometans to Christian dogs. Eight hundred millions is a noble sum. Suppose one half alone is lost! How many women of your congregations might have had a husband now and been blessed with large families? Four hundred millions! Four hundred thousand *surplus* ladies (I did not invent the term), might have been happy with selected objects of their love, and with a thousand pounds apiece. Ah, how much married bliss have ye financiers destroyed! Yes, now I know what "root of evil" means. Before I took that medicine of Sana Mens, I always in my heart supposed that money was the root and source of good, not ill. Haste, then, ye magnates of finance, loan-mongers, jobbers, bankers, brokers, robbers, runners, touts, and guinea-pigs, subscribe for shares, combine, form syndicates to spread co-operative married bliss, and save your sordid souls. Make haste, I say, the list will soon be closed.

And you, ye greedy "Outside Fools," who bring your savings to Co-operating Credit Banks, take shares in this association to increase the fund of married love. The cables are unerring in their choice, and cure so many female ills. You'll have a handsome dividend, get all your daughters, sisters, cousins, and their friends wed to their true "affinities," and then you'll feel that happiness which springs from having done what's right, and being paid for it besides. I'm sure I've felt a better man since I have been director of this noble Company. Erasmus Pinto surely is no common man. I take great pride in him and Clara, for they show the cable theory to be correct. They both are practical, yet brimful of romance. That Pinto has the rare kaleidoscopic sort of mind that never is the same, yet makes its changes with some kind of rhythm, and keeps its balance well. No wonder Clara loves him so. We all like change. Yes, there it is. And then my Clara is so very natural, and yet so fond of speculative thought that he can always find an interested listener in her. If all the "Objects" should get on as well as they, the devil won't have half his former power.

To think of making money by a Joint-stock Company, and making it for shareholders and self as well, and doing good to thousands both in body, mind, and purse. I feel elated. But this will not do. I shall have Sana Mens here with his fifteen grains. The only bargains that I've done to-day are these. I bought fifteen Wheal Peevishes for two housekeepers and a footman, and sold ten Egypts for Sir Bemmidge Bracebrook. He sold upon the morning telegrams, and thought none knew the news before himself. He's getting on quite nicely with his theories. Well, well, he can afford to pay, and judging from the airs of the kitchen dignities, I should not think they've seen much suffering. We will teach them some. A broker's office is a little stronger castle than the master of a house can hope to have.

There was a little governess with honest face (her father had once been my client), who came into the office in the morning, and said,—

Would I invest six hundred pounds,—for that was all she had to live upon, besides her salary,—in something safe, that paid not less than ten per cent. She said she heard her father say, " He always got that interest."

"If so, why was he not a richer man," thought I. Poor little thing! I bought her some South-Western Railway that a client had to sell, charged him a half per cent. commission, and a jobber's margin of another one, and put it down to her at the real market price, and charged no brokerage.

Nathaniel Seesaw, how much changed you are! There was a time when you'd have thought that you were fit for Hanwell had you acted thus. The girl,

I swear, your worships, looked both pale and ill, and was not pretty in the least. I'll shut my desk and go off home, or I shall have that Sana Mens here with his fifteen grains again, and he quite frightens me. I seem to see myself so clearly after his prescriptions have been taken. It vexes and distresses me to think that mind can't govern matter better than it does with me. Perhaps I am peculiar. I'll ask him next time that he comes.

CHAPTER XXXII.

A DOCTOR'S VIEW OF THE RIGHTS OF PROPERTY.

How well the Company is getting on. The applications are fast pouring in; I had more than two thousand letters yesterday from single ladies, amorous bachelors, and eminent divines, couched in approving terms, and some enclosing cheques; but one was full of fierce abuse, penned by a doctor who inquired if I meant to rob him of his largest and best paying class of patients, the nervous invalids. I gave the rest to Clara to amuse her; this one I will read to you, dear " Outside Fools,"—

TODMORDEN LODGE.
7, SPINSTER'S ROAD.

" SIR,—

" You seem to have a very hazy idea of property. Perhaps this need not be wondered at, as you style yourself a broker. But I would just remind you that if married women, close on sixty years of age, get twenty-one days' hard labor, and men get three weeks for stealing turnips valued at threepence, while the Home Secretary sees no reason to remit the six months' imprisonment to which the man who stole ten Hastings cabbages was lately sentenced, surely financing charlatans like you will not be allowed to rob me of my nervous-patient property, worth many thousand turnips, ay, and many times ten thousand cabbages.

"I would have you know that I am at present in correspondence with Lord Derby and Mr. Disraeli, on this very important infringement of the sacred rights of property, and I await their answers with impatience. Judging from the damages awarded by British juries to impecunious females who are represented by their counsel to have lost what they never possessed, I feel sanguine that the most substantial damages will be awarded me, if indeed it be not a case for imprisonment without a fine.

"I am, sir,
"Your's faithfully,
"TRISTRAM TARBOX, M.D., M.C.S."
"To Nathaniel Seesaw, Esq., Director of the Matrimonial Alliance Association (Limited).
"*Jan. 28th*, 1876.

Good lack! this man of pills and potions has quaint notions about property. What does he mean? Well, I daresay these nervous patients are real property. Everything is getting so unsettled in this age. What with these magnetizing agents that deprive one of autonomy, and make us moral slaves, these cloudy *Automatic Theories* that, to a common mind like mine, seem to grant indulgences for any crime, I shall not know whether I'm a man or a machine, that eats and drinks, and sleeps and wakes, and goes to church and prays, and in the city cheats and swindles just because he cannot help himself. I like that Tyndall, though I've never seen the man. But, Allah! what a talent! Why, he'll prove that wrong is right and right is wrong, if he goes on at such a pace. Ah, me! my Company is nothing to his theories. Why, with a dozen particles of dust he can make skies. But surely, Mr. Tristram Tarbox, your ideas of penalties for crimes are wrong.

"It is a sin to steal a pin"—a heinous sin to steal three pennyworth of turnip-property.

It did not seem so wrong to pluck just one geranium. But yet the fourteen days were well deserved, and the four years of comfortable supervision would have very likely done some good. What better educated people than myself, with finer sympathies, would call a tendency to *kleptomania* was in the child, or else the hue and cry raised by the newspapers, all about this pretty injured innocent, have turned its *automatic kleptomania* into thieving of a very common kind, and made it steal a new cloth jacket, and, more odd, made one of its most staunch supporters take the jacket with an automatic readiness which should be very interesting to philosophers. No, the Spalding magistrates were not so wrong, and harm instead of good has sprung from those sensational philippics against members of that bench.

Ye men who write the matter in these "admirable daily papers," as John Bright most justly called them but the other day, ye should be very careful how ye use your power. Ye are the educators of the British nation, and when aught is wrong ye should attack the system, not the man.

A magistrate who sentences a man to six months' prison work and fare for stealing a few cabbages but represents the feelings of the men of property who live around. He only executes the law, and often is a most kind-hearted man.

Ye should explain the merits of stipendiary magistracy, and not abuse odd persons here and there. You would not then hear in the rural districts this remark so often, "The papers do more harm than good,"—"they tell a pack of lies,"—"they set one class against another so." The latest target is the sellers of cock-robins for the ladies' hats. A robin is a happy, harmless innocent, that suffers fearfully in death. A mackerel or elephant 'tis right enough to kill in sport, and no one need regard their sufferings. They are not happy, harmless innocents. Women are as cruel as they're vain, some cynic says, and care no more for a cock-robin's pangs than for a jilted suitor's broken heart. Well, I agree with Sana Mens, who talks good sense on most things, and not least on this.

He says, "My dear sir, it's all sentiment, and all this sentiment springs from our great luxury. A man likes shooting elephants. His vanity is flattered to think that he can kill so large a brute. His health improves with the strong exercise, and so he thinks it right. Just so with the fox-hunter, and they both are right. Why, sir, if this enfeebling luxury goes on much longer, we shall never dare to hang a man, whatever crimes he may have done." .

Let these would-be philanthropists relieve the silent sufferings of their own poor instead of whining morbidly over the deaths of partridges and robins, mackerel and grebes. I have a patient now who is sinking into a consumption because she cannot bear to eat a piece of beef and mutton, and she always says that sheep and cows look at her with reproachful eyes. I told her she might safely take cod-liver oil, for it did not come from the live cod's liver, but the refuse of the dead mixed with all sorts of curious things.

What do these wise men know about cock-robins' happiness and harmlessness and innocence? And what do cynics know of women's cruelty? My daughter Mary wears a cloak trimmed with the grebe. Just ask the parish poor what they think of her cruelty, Diogenes? She would not hurt a fly, I scarcely think she'd kill a flea. And when you talk of happiness, I think a bug would lose as large a share as any grebe or robin would. The joy of biting the highest class of animated beings in this world, and then becoming suddenly invisible, must be supreme. At least, so says my wife, and we are one. Why don't the papers call upon the highest ladies in the land to use their influence, and stop the purchase of these birds?

They could do more in one short week to cure the ill, if ill it be, than all the letters of indignant fussy people, whose aim seems to be to make out that *they* have finer feelings than the rest, that *they* are not such brutes, whatever others are.

But perhaps the papers write for "Outside Fools," and care no more for them than we do for our ruined client's loss. I should not like to think that true, though it would make Nathaniel Seesaw seem a better man.

Excuse me, Mr. Tristram Tarbox, I had quite forgotten you.

"It is a sin to steal a pin." No doubt. Extremes will meet, they say. Let vice be on a grander scale, and change its name. There is a feather in financial caps more costly than the plumage of ten thousand grebes and robins. It is gained by robbing widows, orphans, poor professional men of their hard earnings under the specious and ensnaring titles of *Investment* and *Industrial Enterprise*. It seems a brighter feather in the caps of magnates of finance to gain their millions by heading the prospectuses of foreign loans with their great names, although they know full well that but for those great names not one investor would be trapped.

But the gayest of all plumage and the costliest of feathers are worn by those who in this "merrie" land of ours make it possible to spend more than the total value of a so-called property to gain collusive aid from men whose names and high position weigh well with the public, and can influence subscriptions for the shares. Yet, when Co-operative Credit Banks are started by the small financial acrobat, whose honesty is quite as great, although there is less money in his till, and when he promises, poor imitative ape, eighteen per cent. per month, the same as lovely Emma promised to her luckless shareholders, then the papers' indignation is aroused, short is the road to Newgate then. And yet what is the difference? The one has nothing, and the others much. That's all.

But what can Tristram Tarbox mean? Aha! I see it now. He has just opened shop, and has his "Outside Fools" to catch. Not half a bad idea that corresponding with Lord Derby and the premier. A very cheap advertisement. Of course he knows that they will burn his letters, probably unread. No matter, he will write to the right sort of papers with his grievance (I should say advertisement), and they will gladly print. Yes, we do live in an age of advertising now. Some enterprising quack, I hear, has sent round circulars to all the farmers in the country and the butchers in the towns, and offered them most liberal terms if they will brand their grazing flocks and herds with the name and price of his great "Heal-all," and print the same upon the carcases and joints of sheep and beasts when killed. 'Tis an original idea. Oh, yes, it is an advertising age. I thank you, Mr. Tristram Tarbox, for the hint, and I will write myself by the next post to Mr. Disraeli, to say that my great Matrimonial Alliance Association has so seized upon the public mind that thousands of my shareholders and correspondents think he really ought to set the jail-birds free, to see if they can find their true "affinities" within the Halls; I say the Halls, for true love levels all, and a convicted felon might find his affinity in the first-class Hall as well as in the second-class. And if he only could find that *affinity*, such is the power of love, he would turn out a useful member of society, that hydra-headed beast, so whimsical and difficult to please. How many convicts in the colonies, where food is cheap, have risen to respectability, and legislate for those who never broke laws yet!

CHAPTER XXXIII.

A BROKER'S IDEA OF A GENTLEMAN AND A SNOB.

To my thinking, a speculative gentleman is one who has money to lose, and loses cheerfully—who is delighted at a little piece of luck, and makes that compensate for many a heavy loss—who always thinks of next account when once pay-day is past, and wipes all past scores from his mind—an open jovial sort of man, a merry tosspot, fond of a good joke, at peace both with himself and all the world while yet his money lasts—who listens well to all his broker says,—not to advice, no, that is wrong, but what he lets fall in a casual sort of way—who don't remember when you contradict yourself twice in a week, or, if you have a headache or a cold, twice in a day, in your remarks about a stock—who never quarrels with contangoes, backwardations, brokerage, or dealing price, but stands it like a lamb, because he thinks it is the thing to do, although he has a dim idea that his broker takes care of himself. A nice high-stomached fellow, whose "changing spirits rise and fall," of course, but rise more often than they fall—a vain conceited fop, nursed in the lap of luxury, we brokers dearly love. A self-willed, stiff-necked, empty-headed noodle, with a handle to his name and a good balance at his bankers, is our joy. A prig, a theorist, a man of one idea, we take to kindly, though we chuckle and feel better, yes, much better, as we clean such out. All these are speculative gentlemen. Secretaries and accountants, we must allow, are gentlemen, but there is little picking to be got from these. They are the parasites on speculation's tree. I speak not of the great financiers, directors of large companies, and those who own the money columns of the papers in which they deal out daily *pabulum* to hungry "Outside Frols." They are the nobility of speculation, and they rule us as they please. We rather fear than love these men; they often bring us loss as well as brokerage. A lawyer is too much like us to be exactly a speculative gentleman. We try few tricks with him.

All tradesmen with a *bonâ fide* business, such as tavern-keepers, butchers, pawnbrokers, jewellers, and those who by their puffs of bankrupt silks and other goods half ruin little honest men who have not capital to catch the "Outside Buying Fools," are gentlemen with us.

Our country gentlemen are mostly made up of the rectors, vicars, doctors, tutors, who are all nice wellbred targets for our telegrams.

But the prince of all our gentlemen is one who has a large estate in land—who, like so many other human beings, thinking something else is wanted to complete his happiness, or bitten by that melancholic love of change of which we all have some small spice, embraces speculation simply for excitement, backs his opinion with true gambler's wilfulness, and feels grim pleasure in the market's ups and downs. These are born aristocrats, the kings of speculative kings, and if a broker does not put forth all his genius, his deepest knowledge of humanity, to make things pleasant for those noble patrons of his trade, he is a scurvy mongrel, a slow addlepate, a charlatan who does not know the difference between a gentleman and snob. How often have I grieved to take a cheque on settling day from such as these. I mean how often I have seemed to grieve.

Young brokers, take your gentlemen to drink with you as often as they're in the mood. A glass of good dry sherry, on a dull damp day, will give the speculator courage for the strife. Talk loud in praise of Bacchus; but let claret be *your* strongest drink. Discreetly send a brace of early partridges, a pound or two of hothouse grapes, when they are very scarce, an English pine, some grouse, or salmon caught in Scotland's rivers— not in Norway, mind—a fine stag turkey, if it's Christmas time, or any other seasonable gift, to your best clients, when the speculative gadfly does not freely bite. These slight attentions tell with broker's gentlemen. Each present has some brilliant possibilities attached to it. If you have clients who are not in good society, but are in business, and well off, good honest bees with honey in substantial hives, then ask them down to see you at your house, and dine them well, make them at home, give them good wine and good cigars. Think nothing of the extra cost. They'll vow you are a right good fellow, bring more fish into your net, and your preserves will be well stocked. These honest bees will listen to your sage remarks about the stocks, will buzz about you cheerfully, fly off to speculative gardens hinted at by you; and, in their clumsy efforts to extract some honey from the prickly flowers, will bruise and tear their wings, to your great gain. 'Tis well to call your gentlemen aside, to whisper confidentially while their friends are standing by, to buttonhole them in the courts—this makes each one important in his fellows' eyes; and human nature wonderfully likes to be thought something of. Philosophers and other learned men may know that reputation is a shallow sort of thing, and oft depends on what some half a dozen friends or enemies may think of one; but brokers do not deal with such, but with all sorts of very human "Outside Fools." Don't treat your clients just according to the orders that they give, but think how long they probably will deal with you, look at their expectations, friends, connections, and temperament. I've known a broker lose some steady paying clients by devoting too much time to one or two, who gave themselves great airs, dealt in large quantities of stock at once, and then defaulted suddenly. This is a barbarous mistake, and shows the raw and inexperienced hand, whose knowledge of his fellow-creatures is but slight. Don't sneer or laugh at any folly that your clients may commit, if other "Outside Fools" are standing by. And never tell the reasons why this one or that lost all he had. You may say with advantage this,—

"I never saw a man have such bad luck."

This sort of spurious sympathy will often tell. You see we all are so dependent on each other when it comes to facts. Talk loud in praise of chance, this will prevent the gamblers seeing what great fools they are. 'You may call a man a rogue sometimes without insulting him so such; but never may you call him "fool," and still remain his friend. Send wires freely to the country bees, except when very favorable movements in their stocks have taken place. Then wait a while, to see if it will not pass off. We have our duties to the House as well as to our clients, and self-preservation is the first great natural law. No broker in his senses should allow a client to make money in a soda water rise. That is the jobbers' perquisite. But if your client be a bull, and the rise has nearly all been lost, I should advise you then to wire, for the client might reply, "*Sell at the best.*" Oh, how I love those words, "Sell at the best." Suppose he wires to buy or sell at some fixed limit, you can play around the limit with your usual skill, assisted by a jobbing friend. You might sometimes do this, but you must know your man. I mean, if he's a bull, and there has been a sudden rise, and your own judgment thinks that it won't last, sell for yourself the same amount, then wire to say, " There is a sudden rise in A, B, C. No cause assigned. The market flat. Reply." Suppose the client should reply, "Sell at the best." You then can buy his stock yourself and close a bear at the full market turn. It might sometimes go wrong; but with your telegrams and logic you would soon come right. Send price lists out at night. It keeps up clients' interest. But be judicious in your sending out price lists. Give prominence to stocks you wish your clients to deal in.

Sometimes it is quite clear that a certain stock will rise. All know it in the House. The object then of course is to clear all the "Outside Fools" out of their bulls; because we don't require the aid of "Fools" to help a stock up that we know will rise. It is to take stocks off our hands that will not rise for which we want these "Fools."

For instance, we'll suppose "cheap Calcy," as the singing wags called it, has now been bought. You have some clients who are bulls, and who do not attend. Report each little rise in that stock with alacrity. Forget to wire if it rise decidedly. I had a client who stuck to his stock, and would not close. The order had been given, "Squeeze out—the dividend is good." I squeezed, but this one stuck; and so I wrote to say that the contango would be very heavy, and that he had better close for this account and buy for next. He trusted me, and sold for this. I waited till the stock had risen one per cent., then wired to say that it had slipped away from me, what should I do? "Buy at the best," was the reply. I bought (it was carrying over day, when clever brokers can do what they like with prices) at just $\frac{5}{8}$ above the market price. And so I saved the House one and five-eighths, at all events. I wrote at night to say that I was wrong, and said I hoped my client would accept apologies. He did, for I was dealing with a broker's gentleman. Young brokers, take the hint. For our greatest gentlemen often deal like this.

They bull the rotten stocks, close in the smallest panic instead of buying more, then buy the same when they have risen to the same old price; and if they ever bear, which is not often, they assail the very strongest stocks, like English rails. This is the constant way of dealing with our ideal gentlemen.

A speculative snob is this, according to Nathaniel Seesaw's view. A client who has learnt the system thoroughly, one who knows a broker like a book—who, though he is a bee with honey, will not let that honey go. A wretched pessimist, who dares to sell the rotten property of others as a bear and be a bull of sound securities. A man who will not listen to our views, who don't believe in money articles, who will not go beyond his depth, who checks the prices that we bring him out, and often deals with two brokers at once to see how competition works, and how their statements and their prices look when they're compared. A man who does not take his own opinions unless checked by averages and fact, who don't believe in tips, not even if Sidonia's clerks should give the tip. A sober, serious beast, who never takes a glass of wine except at meals—an oddity, who is not vain, and who is no automaton—a beast who cuts a loss before it grows, who does not let a profit run too far, who leaves no limits in or out of the House, and grumbles if we charge an eighth too much or make an error in the price. You will not often meet with such a pest, but if you do, laugh at his views, snub all his theories, cheat him in the price, have rows, don't budge an inch, say, "Nothing doing," "Not a chance," "I do not know," to all inquiries, and in short, do anything except refuse point blank to deal. If this don't drive him off to other offices, resign yourself; you're being punished for your sins. A friend of mine had such a client for ten months, but luckily he caught a pleurisy and passed.

And now, dear "Outside Fools," that you may learn more pleasantly these various ways of operating on the Stock Exchange, I will relate to you a true account of what my latest clients did, and tell you how and why they lost their money so.

And if you recognise a friend, a brother, or yourselves, don't be surprised, you are all very much alike.

CHAPTER XXXIV.

THE HISTORY OF OCTAVIUS MARMADUKE BUBCHOOK, EX-M.P. FOR ROTTENBORO'.

OCTAVIUS MARMADUKE BUBCHOOK, Esq., styled himself a ship-broker, and resided, as so many vulgar plutocrats elect to do now-a-days, in a pretentious house at Brighton. He had been in a large way of business in Liverpool, but finding his affairs were getting in a very queer state, and that trade was more likely to be worse than better, he settled twenty thousand pounds upon his wife just in time to prevent his creditors from touching it, and, as soon as he could legally, went through the court. Having lost not only his business at Liverpool, but his seat for Rottenboro', he came to London, the place for all true genius, brought with him his good wife and the twenty thousand pounds which should have gone to pay his creditors, and opened an office once more as a ship-broker. His true style was "ship-knacker," and a clerk whom he had turned away was heard to hint at sundry strange machines which he had spied in a dark room, and guessed to be infernal engines ready to be sent on voyages, when the insurance made it worth his while to get rid of some surplus human life, and gain for himself many turnips' worth of property. As this clerk had been dismissed, no one thought much of his hints, but this one ugly fact remained. Such wonderful fatality attended this ship-knacker's ships that the underwriters grew afraid of them, and asked much larger premiums. These he would willingly have paid. But luckily, Mr. Plimsoll, to his eternal credit as a man, forgot that in the House of Commons, where man is a fighting animal and, with few exceptions, cares as much for party and for place as for philanthropy, etiquette must not be set aside, though sailors' lives be lost the while, and as a consequence of this appeal, a temporary Merchant Shipping Bill was passed, and Bubchook's occupation was too dangerous to last. So he turned to speculation as a business, but still kept his office on, to give a more respectable appearance to the thing.

This ex-M.P. for Rottenboro' was a curious-looking man. His complexion was a sickly yellow, not the yellow that belongs so often to the nervo-bilious constitution, but to the lymphatic, semi-vegetable sort of being, whose vital force seems insufficient to completely energize the frame. His features were all negative, except the eyes, and no keen or electric glances ever shot from them. I scarcely think I can describe his eyes. If ever you have seen a hippopotamus with body all submerged, except a portion of the head and all the eye, which gazes at you watchfully, and yet you cannot tell what the expression means, you may have some idea of Bubchook's eye. It was not shifty, did not drop before your gaze, but seemed to look up almost through the upper lid half at you and half past you. You felt the man's eye had you in its gaze, and yet when you looked up it did not seem to have. His manner was indifferent and listless, his figure tall and loose and gaunt. You might have been for months in the same house with him, and never known him any better than before. His ships were just like other ships, except that you might easily have knocked a hole in most of them as large as any cannon-ball.

Yet, strange as it may seem, this man was very sensitive. If you had brought to him a robin or a grebe, in all the throes of death, its little frame convulsed, the fatal film obscuring its pretty interesting eyes, just now so bright and clear, he would have turned quite ill through sympathetic pity for the creature's sufferings, and lost his appetite for food, and even shed an automatic tear or two. He often fainted at the sight of blood, yet when a ship went down with all on board, he took the insurance money quietly without a thought or pang, and ate his dinner like a Christian gentleman. He never saw the upturned faces of the drowning sailors, or their limbs all bruised and shattered in his broken sleep. He never either dreamt or thought of them. He was a good husband, a kind father, and went to church with regular respectability.

And he belonged to a society of cynics, who had so little love for man that they constructed deftly-made machines, which, packed away like other merchandise, exploded at a given time, and sank the ship and all beneath the waves.

What! say you, a miscreant like this shed tears to see a robin die! This wretch, a husband and a father, and a member of our church! He faint at the sight of blood! It is impossible! He must be mad!

You are mistaken, it is true enough. I had some business to arrange with him before he died, and he confessed it all to me. Perhaps you say it was delirium. Well, hear what Sana Mens says of these extraordinary crimes that shock society.

CHAPTER XXXV.

DR. SANA MENS' VIEWS OF EXTRAORDINARY CRIMES.

HE first says that there are not so many of these crimes now as there used to be. And then he says that man is better educated and more civilized, but not much changed in heart.

But though this is the case, society objects to face this fact, so lowering to human vanity.

A long-continued peace and modern luxury, the less natural and less simple way of living, and the overgrowth of population, coupled with the unhealthy check to passions which a prudent man cannot afford to gratify, has sapped the nation's strength and energy, developed morbid sensitiveness, and a sickly sentimentalism. We shudder at the thought of war, of bloodshed, and the taking human life away for any crime. And yet our bitterness of feeling to one another is as great, and were it not for legal check, and better knowledge of the consequences, it would often end in crime.

We ought to hang all such wretches as Bubchook, not try to bring them in insane, because their act would seem to prove that man is not much better than he was. Society says education has improved the human heart. Then why do clergymen of different sects hate one another so. Their Bible tells them charity, not fierce intolerance, should be their guide.

"My doxy's orthodoxy, yours is heterodoxy," is the cry that has so sorely shaken men's belief and brought the church so near to "Disestablishment."

Men feel inclined to say this crime of Bubchook's is insanity.

And pray, when rectors advertise to say that they reject the "desecrated title *Reverend*," because a Wesleyan has gained the power to write this awful sacerdotal term upon a dead man's tomb, ought not society to call fanatic ignorance like this "insanity."

Indeed, I do not think that crimes like Bubchook's do the same amount of harm. They are so very rare.

Thus argued Dr. Sana Mens; but I don't understand these things.

I know there's great injustice in the world. We brokers, and the jobbers, too, get all the blame whereas the real ship-knackers of finance insure their rotten vessels, and make profits by their foundering.

Like Bubchook, they are sensitive, and would not like to see a robin killed. But they are not disturbed when poor investors lose their all in loans which their great names have helped to float; and, luckily for them, there is no Plimsoll yet to spoil their business so. There's so much jobbing in the parliament itself. "The government would have enough to do if it tried to take care of all its fools," said some shrewd man not long ago. Of course it would. It spends some of the nation's money in protecting fools from losing purses in the streets; but when it comes to bigger thieves, who steal enough to be respectable, it owns that it is powerless. Just so with all the bankrupts, when they fail for large enough amounts.

Of course it is. The jobbers in the government could easily outvote or buy non-jobbers members' votes as the city cliques buy off a rival company, or pack a meeting to secure their ends.

Man is a fighting animal, and nowhere more than when he gets into a pulpit or is sent to parliament by "Outside Fools."

I'm sure Nathaniel Seesaw would fight better for his party than his country, and for sect at least as well as church.

CHAPTER XXXVI.

OCTAVIUS MARMADUKE BUBCHOOK, ESQ., BECOMES A BULL OF PERU.

But I forget the ex-M.P. for Rottenboro; you want to know his dealings with myself before he came to grief and died.

It happened that Commander Cookson issued his report upon the guano of Peru about this time. Bubchook remembered Peruvian sixes at eighty-four, and as he failed to see that this so-called report was really nothing but a few "I am tolds" strung together without any really trustworthy evidence gained from an exhaustive survey of the stock by independent English agents, he chose this dirty stock, with all its dirty tricks, to bull, bought forty-thousand sixes at an average price of seventy-two, and thirty thousand fives at sixty-one, and as the banks had not yet put a black mark against the rubbish, he took it up and borrowed money on it, leaving but a margin of just ten per cent.

Now, as most speculators in Perus have found out to their cost, this valuable stock is so extremely lively, and the price depends so much upon the way in which the cliques behind the scenes elect to pull the strings, so much upon what that mercurial Paris market is about, that trying to hit the fluctuations right is just as difficult as picking up spilt quicksilver upon a smooth surface with your hand, or catching brokers when they play at hide and seek, although, meantime, your stocks are dancing up and down like bears upon a hot brick floor. Many of my clients have dealt in Perus, a few at times made profits, but I had but one who did not lose on balance, and he hit it right first time, and died of heart disease before he had another deal. The stock had been much higher than it was when Bubchook bought; and as the old investors had received their money back in dividends, they did not sell, or if they did, the least collusive telegram or story of a fresh discovery of dirt was quite enough to make them buy again. This fact made it impossible for "Outside Fools" to do much good as bears, for as soon as they had sold, the stock jumped up, and in rushed the old bulls, and sometimes new ones in their train. If this was not enough to make the others close their bears, out came some rumor that a survey of the whole guano beds was going to be soon made—that more had been discovered—that negotiations for some loan were coming on. Then as the cliques who knew the truth (and there were such, more shame to them for acting with their knowledge as they did) bought large amounts of stock, the bears who then remembered the high prices that had ruled were frightened into closing, mostly at the highest point. The cliques sold out their bulls upon this artificial rise, and then a contradiction of the rumors came, and "Outside Bulls" were punished in their turn, and as the market looked like going worse, these "Outside Bulls" all sold, and once again the cliques bought stock, and fresh mendacious tales were spread about.

All the movements in Peruvian trash since Bubchook bought until this present time have been produced by variations of this simple but dishonest game.

But, says some "Outside Fool," "You should have been persistent in your plan, and not been frightened into buying back your bear or selling out your bull."

Now, my good sir, if you alone thought this, and acted on it, you would find it right; but, singular to say, when anything is mathematically plain in stocks, so many do the same, that it becomes worth while for capital to show how little use is reason in a fight against its power.

Capital must win whatever it elects to do, with money articles at it's command, and so long as you will think that all your losses come from your own folly, or because you deal in this way or in that. It's nothing of the kind. The pieces on the chessboard are all moved according to a pre-determined plan, of which we get some hints inside, while you get none. Suppose the public as a body bought the soundest stocks, and nothing else, we then should buy the rotten ones and have the money articles with us, and you would buy the rotten stocks when City editors had proved conclusively how cheap they were and how a stock, though sound, was dangerous to buy at such a price.

Suppose the public, as till now they have preferred to do, still buy the rotten stocks, we then shall buy

I

the sound, and when they have bought all they can, we then shall bear the very stocks they're loaded with, and all our organs will turn round and say, "It serves them right to buy such rubbish at so high a price."

You know we jobbers are supposed to gain a living by the market turn, and brokers by commission, and in theory we do not speculate; but even you, dear "Outside Fools," do not believe that this is so. We could get a good living so; but just as women who are beautiful and vain, and cannot tell the limit of their power, strive hard to catch a noble or prince, and let the worthy swain of humbler station go, so we strive hard to pick the biggest plums that "Outside Fools" may offer us, and not one broker in a hundred knows what brilliant possibilities may not be his, in the great lottery of "Outside Fools." I tell you candidly that we should all feel happier if our power was more limited and definite; just as a woman does when ruled with strong firm hand.

We never know when we have done our best to catch the largest fish, or when we've broiled enough the ones we have already caught.

A woman cannot know if she has done her best until she's wed, and then she's bound to try to get the upper hand. But if she finds a mate who keeps her in her proper place, she then is more contented, for she has the conscious pride of having done her best, and feels more happy, "now that her domain is well defined and limited." And we should feel more happy if our power to cheat were circumscribed, for really this roach-fishing is no easy task; there are so many fine ones in the swims all waiting to be caught, and when the fish are on the feed it makes our arms ache terribly to pull them out. The "Outside Fools" are just like fish—all bite together —take a gentle one day and a worm the next. For them we catch the early worms. Oh, yes! Just now the weather's very bad for fishing; the large pike have made such havoc with the fish that they are frightened and keep in the weeds; there are some pike that weigh some forty pounds, but there's no angler yet been born that can get hold of them. They do us harm as well as kill the roach most wantonly. We get the blame, and run the risk of being caught ourselves; they keep safe in their muddy holes.

We're rather puzzled now to find attractive baits; but if no new ones can be got, it won't be long before the old are swallowed greedily.

But I assure you this is true. I mean that all our honest members, and they are at least as ten to one are praying that they may no longer be exposed to such temptations, but that what their power and duties are may be more clearly known and definite.

Men, like myself and Turnabout, would rather have things as they are; but I am vastly changed since Sana Mens has doctored me, and sometimes think I'm getting ominously good.

It may be conscience, liver, or I may be one of those *automata*, but anyhow, I feel more comfortable, and that ought to be the truest test.

I beg your pardon, Mr. Bubchook, I had quite forgotten you. Excuse an old man's moralizing, my dear "Outside Fools." You might learn something from it, if you would.

Now when this philanthropic ex-M.P. had bought his South American Dirt, it did rise nearly two per cent. He, knowing not the way in which the dice were cogged, and being quite as greedy and as foolish as most speculators are, who when a market rises think it will not cease to rise, and when it falls think there will be no limit to the fall, refused to take a profit, and so missed his chance. Perus don't dwindle —as a rule they *flop*, to use a City term. They don't go up by eighths, but jump by halves, and ones, and often more. Not even could Commander Cookson's "*I am tolds*" keep up the stock. Parisian shopkeepers' puffs had not the weight they used to have. The farmers, who, though not accomplished in the Riggers' tricks, are shrewd and practical, and do their country much more good than millionaires, whose fortunes have not come from trade or industry, but all from robbing England of her gold, and giving portions of the plunder, sometimes large and sometimes small, to countries most of which are bankrupt, while the rest depend upon the name of their financiers, who when they think the orange has been squeezed enough for their good names will hand it over to some lesser lights, who can afford to do more dirty work, and so it goes on to the end. Is any one to blame for this? Not much. Your ignorance, ye "Outside Fools," makes all this juggling last. But hold. You cannot help your ignorance. Why? Because you read, with very few exceptions, interested lies. What is the cure, then? Legislation never will do much, however honestly it try. No; all you want, dear "Outside Fools," is better knowledge of the thousand ways and means that capital, when in such hands, adopts to catch its victims with. In your case "ignorance is vice," and Dr. Sana Mens declares it is in most. Wake up, then, do your duty, learn and save yourselves.

But let us go back to our Bubchook and our Dirt. The next event was a complete *exposé* of this half-breed's country's real financial state by the *Economist*; all honor be to it, though it's too cold and cautious to be cared for much by speculating men.

Fierce was the rage of baffled touts and money-mongers then. It was a very pretty war. Not one where "Outside Fools" held all the Bonds. By no means so. Some very high-class "Firms" had touched this pitch, and most of it stuck to their fingers still. The worthy ex-M.P. for Rottenboro' tried his best to catch the quicksilver, but, like the rest, he failed.

In vain adulterators tried to sell wares half as good at one-tenth less in price.

In vain the syndicates worked hard to place some of the last enormous loan by buying millions of the stock and giving calls for more. They could not sell sufficient to recoup their loss each time, and so they got the aid of foreign lies.

And then the banks refused to lend upon the stock, although they might as well have lent. The oblong bits of paper which made many Collie-kites to fly were worse than "Penniless Peru."

Bubchook had sold his six per cents. ere this at 63, and fives at 51, and with his intermediate deals the account stood thus:—

CHAPTER XXXVII.

O. M. BUBCHOOK, ESQ., IN ACCOUNT WITH MESSRS. SEESAW AND TURNABOUT.

Cr.	£	s.	d.	Dr.	£	s.	d.
Bought—				Sold—			
40,000 Peruvian 6 per cents. at 72 28,800		0	0	40,000 Peruvian 6 per cents. at 63 25,200		0	0
Com. $\frac{1}{8}$th per cent	50	0	0				
$\frac{1}{16}$th com. for sale of above.	25	0	0				
30,000 Peruvian 5 per cents. at 61 18,300		0	0	30,000 Peruvian 5 per cents. at 51 15,300		0	0
Com. $\frac{1}{8}$th per ct.	37	10	0				
$\frac{1}{16}$th com. for sale of above.	18	15	0	Balance carried down	6,731	5	0
	47,231	5	0		47,231	5	0
To balance carried down	6,731	5	0	By cheque......	6,731	5	0

Pro Messrs. Seesaw and Turnabout.

ERASMUS PINTO.

THIS account, although it was not really made out in the above form, as the stock was purchased some time before it was sold again, will show the reader clearly that Octavius Marmaduke Bubchook, Esq., ex-M.P. for 'Rottenboro,' had lost to our firm £6,731 5s. Add to this £1,750 17s. 6d. for his vain attempts to catch the quicksilver, and £460 7s. 6d. for bank charges, and the amount will be £8,942 10s.

Many brokers only charge a sixteenth commission

for speculative dealings in foreign stocks, and yet they charge a quarter per cent., or even more, on Rails; but we always charged an eighth and often a quarter on foreign, and by doing so we think we did some little good by discouraging the dealing in such rotten stocks.

Why does not government charge heavy duty on these I O U's, and much less on the English Rails? Free trade is certainly in some respects a dubious sort of thing. If it were not for those stamps and fees, there would be three times the amount of dealing in the home securities. For some time after this I did not see Bubchook; but as he still had rather more than eleven thousand pounds to lose, I imagined that he had given speculation up and now was living on the interest. I quite expected that he would return again. They always do until they've nothing left. Before we leave Peru I must just say a little more. When the "ship-knacker" had done dealing in the stock the syndicates and the loan-mongering firms who were stuck with the Bonds chose "*Contract*" as the next watchword.

The Paris "Riggers" tried the "*Pocket Order*" dodge, and sought to make their losses up out of dull "*perfide Albion*" by buying on the London Stock Exchange, and sending private telegrams that an important contract was then being signed, then selling all they bought and bears besides and suddenly discovering a hitch.

Talk of Nathaniel Seesaw's robberies, forsooth! or of Erasmus Pinto's tricks!

They never in their happiest moods could reach the fancy-flights of those artistic highwaymen.

Then all at once negotiations for this wonderful

"*Contract*" were rudely broken off, a panic fall took place, the fives were driven down to twenty-four.

It was said openly in Lima that some persons of great eminence had formed a *Speculative Ring*, and meant to drive the bonds down to fifteen, then call a meeting hurriedly, and offer the poor holders of the stock half dividends secured on a "*Nitrate Loan.*" A London firm was mentioned as the agent of this precious scheme.

And what strikes me as very odd is this. No words of blame are bad enough for men like Pinto and myself; but not a word of indignation do we hear against the want of faith in public men—nay, a corrupt official is looked on with envious eye, as one who has such splendid chance of filling his own pockets at the public cost.

Well, out of evil some good comes. This Bubchook had received a salutary check, and, as I thought, he soon came back again.

CHAPTER XXXVIII.

OCTAVIUS MARMADUKE BUBCHOOK, ESQ., BECOMES A BEAR OF NORTH BRITISH RAILWAY STOCK.

PERU had done its work not badly, but North British was the stock that Providence selected to avenge the sailors sunk beneath the waters in our M.P.'s rotten ships.

This interesting stock for two years previous had paid no dividend, but had just then declared a dividend of one and a half per cent. The year before it had been down to 58, but had now risen to 77. The "Daniels of Finance" wrote articles on the "North British Rig, so-called investors and shareholders, calculators and observers who knew about as much of the real merits of the stock as a baby-girl six months of age does of a skating rink, or flirting ground, did hire themselves a space wherein to ventilate their sapient views each week that came, and these wild views the "Outside Fools" of "bearish" turn devoured greedily. It was affirmed with confidence by those who lead their readers by the nose that it was much too high, would soon be back at the old price, and cease to pay a dividend as it had done before. These prophecies caught the ship-knacker's eye, and up he came one morning early to my office and told me that he had found a perfect mine of wealth, a virgin lode, that no "outsiders" had yet worked. Said he,—

"Of course the jobbers sell the stuff and laugh well in their sleeves at those who buy at such a price. This is my bear," continued he, "and I will pay out money till it does come right. A stock at 77, paying only one and a half per cent., which shrewd men say was never fairly earned, or else was earned through some exceptional cause, must be the proper thing to bear. Besides," said this delighted would-be bear, "I have a friend called Jonathan MacBrewin, who declares that he is told that many thousand tons of pig iron and other weighty goods are owned by some large bulls, who keep them running up and down the road at their own charges, to increase the traffic, and that though it costs them much, the rise has paid them hitherto. He further says that this game cannot last, and that the knowing ones are selling bears because they know that the collapse will be severe when it does come."

I here remarked,—

"You must not act on all you hear; the wheel within the wheel is often not so easy to perceive. Your man, MacBrewin, certainly is one who knows his way about. But I have friends in Scotland, and not one word have I heard of this. It's very strange. I wonder if MacBrewin's information is correct?"

"Correct!" said he, "look here, he dined with Kippered Herring yesterday. Now, will that do?"

"Aha!" said I, "you don't say so? Well now I'll hold my tongue, my dear Mr. Bubchook, you know more than I do myself."

Now wasn't he a fool to believe such tales? This bit of flattery struck home, and hugging the sweet thought that he, an "Outside Fool," knew more than his own broker, he told me to sell 5,000 at the best. It happened that I had received a letter from a canny Scot in Glasgow, with whom I had done some business, advising me that a large syndicate was being formed to buy North British, and that the rise would be both great and lasting too.

So as I thought this canny Scot was quite as likely to be right as was MacBrewin of the pig iron, and as I felt myself a humble instrument selected to avenge the sailors who had been blown up or drowned, I thought I'd take the book myself and buy of Bubchook all he liked to sell.

I recommend young brokers not to put a jobber's name upon the contracts, if they're not compelled. It leaves them a much better chance of making a great *coup* themselves. Of course it could be done, if names were given; but half the profits would go then to the jobber who was a sharer in the game. And so I sold for Bubchook to myself 5,000 British at $77\frac{1}{2}$. In April next the stock sprang up to $84\frac{3}{4}$.

I sold 5,000 more at 84. Observe that all the sales will be to me, although my client knew it not. Well, there's no harm in that. Some parcels of political gunpowder exploded then, and down the stock fell to 82. It rose a quarter, and as I wanted him to make a profit at the first, I with some trouble made him close the last at $82\frac{1}{2}$. This showed a profit of £75. In May the stock went up to nearly 87; but before it reached that price Bubchook had sold 5,000 more at 85.

More detonations on the continent drove down the price to 81. He bought none back, for sapient calculations proved that two per cent. was all the dividend that could be paid, and you may well be sure Nathaniel Seesaw did not urge him to buy back. Oh, no, he rather comforted the fool with now and then a wise remark, a knowing look, a meaning shoulder-shrug. We brokers are like some more modern poets: critics find deep meaning in their commonest ideas, a meaning sometimes never thought of by the poet's self. Just so our clients act. If I should put my finger gravely to my nose and wink, I do believe some fools would find a rise or fall in something meant by it. Young brokers, these remarks will sometimes pay you well, but hang a little mystery around your words, and say as I did then, "I don't much like the British market's look. The buying there is very weak. I rather think there'll be a split. The bulls will have to pay next time. Is it not a swindle this great rise? I'll tell you what—if dealers all refused to carry over, I should not be much surprised." But if your stock of phrases should be all used up, take refuge in an instinct, and observe sagaciously, " Well, I've no reason but I don't feel right about the stock somehow." In June up went North British to 90½, but business took my client out of town, and so he did not sell. It fell again to nearly 83. And as he thought the rig was broken up, a view that I did not oppose, he sold 5,000 more at 83.

The rise was rapid now, and in July the price was 97 and a fraction more. He sold 5,000 once again at 97. It fell to 95, and this time Bubchook closed, and made a profit of one hundred pounds. Now after he had closed and made this hundred pounds, down went this lively stock to nearly 89. Mad with himself at having closed too soon, he sold 5,000 more at 89¼. This was the bears' last chance to close. In August, to the horror of the Calculators, Lectors, Joltheads and Scrutators, and the bears in general, there was declared a dividend of four per cent. Up sprang this jolly railroad stock to 105½. As, though their heads were very sore, some few bears still were found to vow that four per cent. could never have been fairly earned, my British fool sold yet 5,000 more at 104⅞. And he was right, for down it fell to 100¾. And now, as he was undecided in his mind, I thought of those poor sailors, and I played another little broker's trump. With an inquiring, somewhat puzzled air, that played around a very human, open-looking face, I said to him,—

"What would you do? I have an order here to sell ten British for a man, who, singular to say, is nearly always right. His information is so good. I can give you the turn in five, if you would like to buy."

"It's clear enough what you should do," said he. "Why, sell of course for him, and sell a bear yourself. I won't buy five, not I—I'd sell some more, if not so deeply in. I'll bet you a new hat your man is right."

I did not take the bet, for I was making thousands of new hats, but I said this,—

"Well, I daresay my man is right, but this North British frightens me, and I should take a profit now if I were you."

I should not have said this had I not seen how much he thought of my fine telegram to sell.

"I'll take my profit when it's bigger," said this "Outside Fool."

Now, ye young brokers, just attend. I did not give advice. You never must do that. Indeed, I asked advice. Do that as often as you please. And yet it was Nathaniel Seesaw who put off the wavering Bubchook from closing his last bear, which showed a profit then. Did I not positively say to him, "If I were you, I'd take a profit now?"

Give your advice by gesture or by look, by quoting other people's views, producing other clients' orders, telegrams, and countless little ways which any quick and imitative mind will soon pick up. But without vanity I tell you this. It is not every one who can attain to Seesaw's nearly perfect way. If you come near it, you will make your mark on 'Change.

Yes, this is how the broker who has genius works. No class of men should understand the likes and the dislikes, the tempers, constitution, hobby-horses, and the frailties of his fellow men so well as brokers should, unless it be the doctors, for their case is something like our own. But for the dunces there were none of us.

Why 'pon my conscience, I have had pig-headed "Outside Fools" to whom I had but just to say, "Be sure you don't buy this," "Sell anything but that," and I had then a market ready to my hand in them.

Then work away, my youthful hearties, study human nature well, and you'll grow rich, and when you hear Nathaniel Seesaw's name take off your hats.

We left North British at 100¾. A few days saw it up to 105⅞. Bubchook was laid up with an influenza cold, and at those trying times, you know, philosophers are rather puzzled in the head, much more than are the "Outside Fools."

I did not bother the poor man with telegrams, and as he kept expecting me to wire, he did not wire himself or write while he was taking gruel in the house. The stock rushed up to 108. This cured his cold, and up he came. It fell an eighth that morning, and he sold 5,000 more, to me of course, at 107¾.

CHAPTER XXXIX.

THE HISTORY OF MR. AND MRS. SILAS SNOAD, AND DR. SANA MENS' VIEWS ON TEETOTALERS.

Now, see how little things work out the ends of Providence. This Bubchook had a married sister. She had made up her mind to marry, asked or not, and found at last her true "affinity" in Silas Snoad, a burly publican, with jovial honest face and Herculean frame, who sold whatever beer was sent to him by the great brewers who were owners of the tavern which he kept in Toppletipplers Road. His conscience never troubled him; no qualms had he about the effect of *Cocculus Indicus;* of chemistry he knew no more than his great toe.

He drank his beer himself and whisky, too. They suited him, they brought him money, flesh and strength, and as the customers were plenty at the bar, and seldom dull or sad, he thought they must be suited too.

This Silas Snoad was a good honest fool, who did not see below the surface far, and had those strong convictions that a narrow mind so often has.

I should not think he saw one hundredth part as far through a brick wall as those who wage the whisky war and the Good Templars see. I wonder what *their* form of narcotism is. Some kind we all indulge in, though we know it not, says Dr. Sana Mens.

I dined with him last night, and here is what he thinks.

Their "narcotism" may consist in the proud thought that *they* by *their* example may drag into Paradise unnumbered drunken fools who have not signed the "pledge."

This is a pleasant and a high-class sort of narcotism.

But, says Sana Mens, these good hot-gospellers of cold water are mistaken if they think that an abstaining fool is so much better than a fool who drinks a glass or two.

One takes his glass and thinks himself no better than another man. The other whose secretions, maybe, will not harmonize with alcohol in any form or shape, ofttimes drinks copious draughts of *Ego* wine, then poses as the savior of a lost degraded class.

Yes! there are many subtle forms of mental drunkenness.

If there be any whose sole motive is to benefit their fellow-creatures by these whisky wars, loud praises of cold water, tea, and ginger-beer, I honor them, says Sana Mens.

But still I call on them to sift their motives well, to see with diligence if there should be some slight narcotic in this abstinence.

The devil is so very deep, he often prompts what we suppose to be our purest acts.

As soon as we can see ourselves as others see us, we shall all, both those who drink and those who don't, be ready for a better world. Well, as you're really earnest in this cause, and no class-feeling underlies your acts, just see if these few hints of mine will help you on at all.

CHAPTER XL.

DR. SANA MENS ON THE USE OF THE WONDERFUL WORDS $MH\Delta EN\ A\Gamma AN$.

First buy yourselves new banners for processions. Have worked on these banners in large letters those Greek words, the sum of all philosophy, $MH\Delta EN\ A\Gamma AN$.

Send placards with these golden words upon them to each tavern in the land, and fine all those who do not hang them in the bar a good round sum.

Send to the universities for lecturers to show the esoteric meaning of these noble words to "Outside Fools" and "Inside Rogues."

Let each child learn them with its A B C. They are not Tupper's words. Teetotalers, call on the clergy of your parishes to sermonize upon these godlike words, to illustrate their hidden wisdom every Sabbath Day with all that learning, logical ability, and eloquence for which our church is justly famed.

Ye bishops, rectors, vicars, and all lesser lights, call on teetotalers to dive into the secret meaning of these words and see if haply any may pursue one virtue till it end in vice.

"What, Greek?" said I, aghast, to Sana Mens. "Why not use the vernacular?"

"Now, Seesaw, this is scarcely worthy of your knowledge of the world," said he. "Have you not noticed how those great philanthropists who spend their lives in seeking panaceas for the human frame choose rather names from other languages to give their sovereign remedies. Sometimes the name is half from Latin, half from Greek. They know that few would buy their nostrums but for their fine names."

"You're right," said I. "It's so in City matters too. If I had advertised a bank, and styled it thus, '*The bank that promises to pay eighteen per cent.*' not one flat-fish should I have caught, much less have hooked a live Colonial Bishop, and five hundred pounds. You're quite right, Sana Mens, there is a great deal in a name."

Once make men wonder, then they will let you explain.

Nil admirari, rightly understood, is true philosophy. But neither tosspots nor teetotalers are true philosophers.

Ye soldiers of the whisky war, attend. Form in procession, let your banners, with the golden words inscribed on them, float in the wind; let "Mother Stewart" and a choir of spotless virgins pass along the streets of all our towns and chant their *MHΔEN AΓAN* as they go.

CHAPTER XLI.

DR. SANA MENS GIVES FURTHER VALUABLE ADVICE HOW TO IMPROVE THE QUALITY OF TEA AND REDUCE THE PRICE OF MEAT.

This is the first great step, but there are other minor ones.

Let teetotalers, Good Templars, whisky warriors, and all who shudder at the name of Bacchus, pray Sir Wilfrid Lawson to induce the government to send some ships of war to catch some leading Chinese Mandarins and bring them here to keep as hostages till they have made their heathen countrymen send cargoes of real tea for all teetotalers to drink instead of poisoned filth. It is not beer and gin alone that leads to crime. What we call tea has much to answer for.

Next let this glorious, self-abnegating band still further worry Parliament, until amended legislation brings us ample stores of foreign meat.

Get *bonâ fide* tenants rights for those who raise or graze our stock at home.

Though this be done, rest not teetotalers.

Subscribe, and form co-operative stores to sell good meat half price.

Next rid us of those selfish pessimists, the middlemen, who play their hanky-panky tricks with meat, as jobbers in the Stock Exchange with "Outside Fools."

Erect a pillory, or good old-fashioned stocks, in all the public squares, regale consumers' angry gaze with living portraits of "Forestallers," wealthy "Carcass Butchers," men who go to meet the droves and buy up with their "root of evil" all the best, to make an artificial scarcity. Stick three "Slink Butchers" in the pillory, and feed them with the putrid stuff they would have Britons eat.

Then send your agents to the Pampas of America, New Zealand, and Australia, to all those distant grazing grounds and sheep walks where the sheep are valued only for their wool and fat, kill, freeze, or aërate, and heaven be with you in the noble work. Cheap meat will bring more love and charity than thousands of Philippics against beer.

CHAPTER XLII.

HOW TO PREVENT THE PLAGUE AND CHECK THE OVERGROWTH OF POPULATION.

You must next arrest all the directors of the water companies and make them drink nothing but unboiled water, supplied by their own companies for six months, and if after that time they are alive, and not suffering from low fever or any zymotic disease, release them on a promise that they will attend your processions and meetings to show how water-drinking directors look, and to dissipate the wide-spread fear of plague that is about.

Then if the government will force the brewers and distillers to produce a genuine inartistic beverage, and let the chemicals alone, and if by this time all the parsons and professors have explained to "Outside Fools" what the words $MH\Delta EN$ $ATAN$ mean, the glorious teetotal band, the whisky warriors, and "Mother Stewart" will have rest. The world will not be far off from its end or the millennium.

One more suggestion to a paternal government.

Until the price of meat be just half what it is, let the Lord Chamberlain, or any other great official who may have a truly philanthropic heart, create an anti-population fund, to give rewards to married people with the smallest families, to send to all poor curates and the newly-wed in general these noble words of wisdom, printed well and neatly framed, that they may hang them up where they can read them day and night.

"Money" is the root of evil, so we say; but in old countries such as this is, "over-population" quite as much deserves the name. And thus said Dr. Sàna Mens.

CHAPTER XLIII.

THE EXCELLENT AND MYSTERIOUS INVESTMENT OF MR.
SILAS SNOAD, AND WHAT EFFECT THE WANT OF A
NARCOTIZER HAD UPON A CABMAN.

But where did we leave Silas Snoad? Oh, I remember now, we left him at his bar in Toppletipplers Road.

He had saved money, had this publican, and he was fond of boasting of the interest he got; and often he would say that men were fools to be contented with a paltry four or five per cent. But never would he tell a soul what Eldorado he had found. This grieved and vexed his better half. She coaxed, caressed, shed tears, blew up her Silas well, tried to provoke him by declaring that he had some other love, or sent his money to the Carlists' aid, or to the Pope of Rome; but all in vain. She might as well have tried to make a dead ass bray. Then having done her very best, she felt relieved and satisfied, as every honest woman ought to do.

One day, late in the afternoon, a cabman was returning from the top of Haystock Hill, that hill that cabmen hate. He had nearly carried safely to their destination two Revivalistic fares, who weighed between them nine and twenty stones, of whom one was so heavy with sensational ecclesiastic lore or carnal fat that he fell through the bottom of the cab, and for a little space walked on the ground, and helped to draw the vehicle, as Wombwell's elephant would draw his caravan. The other blew poor cabby up in tones most secular and commonplace.

Two miles had Jehu driven within three yards, his cab was broken, and he got a shilling for his fare, and, more, was threatened with a summons for his cruelty to animals. Now Mrs. Artful Dodger had just summoned him the week before, and as the distance proved to be one yard less than the miles required, he lost his case, and did not feel much appetite for law. And so, with anger in his heart, he pocketed his shilling, muttered curses, and drove off. He had no bottom in the cab, and so he got no fares. The day was close, and not a drop of beer or glass of grog had cabby tasted all that day. So every yard he drove his anger grew and boiled within.

He reached the Toppletipplers Road, and Silas Snoad, who had been into town to see about his Eldorado, was then coming home. He was more than a little narcotized. He did not walk quite straight, although he thought he did. The cabman would have been the better for his usual soothing pipe and glass. They neither of them knew what MHΔEN AΓAN meant. The cabman saw that Silas Snoad was most unsteady in his gait. Perhaps the burly figure of the publican brought back to his excited mind the fat ecclesiastic fares who broke the bottom of his cab. Perhaps the devil said,—

"It's not your fault if he runs in your way, fools should beware. And if an accident should happen, it will change your present anger into something else. You know the body seldom has two pains at once; a change of passion is delightful to the mind. If one has laughed too much, there is a luxury in tears. If man and wife fall out, if you say but a word against the one or the other, they will turn on you and feel relieved. So with intestine disturbances in states and civil wars: sometimes invasion is the only thing that brings them to an end."

What was the cause? Decide, ye Metaphysical, Original, Doctoral, Magisterial, Tropological, Episcopal, Enunciatory, and Dialectic Fools.

Sages, Joltheads, and wise Jobbernols, come to my aid, for, as I live, it gravels me. Ye captious and sophistical, soritic, catechetic, pedagogical, and critical wiseacres, fight it out among yourselves. It is not worth so many words.

One thing is certain, that this cabman all at once put on that unconcerned and stolid look that draymen and van-drivers often have, which if your peripatetic fool should disregard, the chances are he'll find himself run over in a trice. These draymen and cab-drivers, like the magistrates, know the true worth of human life.

Well, Silas Snoad came lurching on, and cabby did not pull the rein, or shout or stop, but let the horse knock down the man. The horse recovered instantly, the man's head struck upon the curbstone, and in a few moments he was dead.

Another instance of the effects of drunkenness, say the teetotalers.

But how about the cabman's rage? And the Revivalistic fares of such great weight who put him in a rage by kicking out the bottom of the cab? And what if he had smoked his pipe as usual and drank his daily glass of grog?

Well, pundits, have it as you please; first motives are not easy things for man to find. Take "*Ne quid nimis*" as your motto, and you won't go very wrong, and think as well as possible of all your fellow-fools.

But I must to my tale. Great consternation was

there at the Goat and Compasses. Poor Mrs. Snoad went off into hysterics, cried and laughed, and laughed and cried, till she was quite worn out.

A curious form of narcotism is hysterics, but a very useful one sometimes to feeble minds, who do not understand what sort of life this is, and might give way beneath the load of misery, but for hysterics or—yes, whisky warriors—a glass of grog.

But grief is not my subject. Let us suppose the shock is somewhat over, and that Mrs. Snoad feels nearly as she felt before.

CHAPTER XLIV.

THE DISCOVERY OF MR. SILAS SNOAD'S MYSTERIOUS INVESTMEMT.

"I wonder how I'm left," thought she. "Now I shall know the secret of his Eldorado, and high interest."

She had not seen her brother Octavius for many years. Indeed, the Bubchook family had cut her ever since she found her true "affinity" in Snoad, and glorified him with her love. But times were changed. She was a widow now. Who knows, a widow perhaps well left. She might find yet another true "affinity," one higher in the social scale. She had seen the beer narcotic overmuch. Her nature yearned for something more refined. It was but the reaction, but that she did not know. So she wrote a letter to her brother thus:—

"THE GOAT AND COMPASSES, TOPPLETIPPLERS ROAD.

"My Dear Octavius,—

"I am in great trouble. My husband is dead. I wish you would come and see me, if it is only for a short time, as his affairs are in confusion, and I have at present no idea how they are arranged. He was always talking about the high interest he got for his investment, but I do not even know what the investment is. I hope you will forget the past and come.

"Your affectionate sister,
"DOROTHY SNOAD.
"Oct. 2nd, 1875."

Now Dr. Sana Mens affirms that the most sober, sedate, the most mathematically-minded, at the bottom rather like a little mystery. To many it is another form of the various narcotisms, and a delightful hobby-horse. The more difficult to solve, the more delightful is the mystery. The moment it is solved, we have to look out for another, for nothing is more true than this, τὸ ἀπὸν ἀεὶ θαυμαστόν ἐστι.

Bubchook was attracted by this mystery, and much as he desired to watch North British closely, he resolved to go and see what money Silas Snoad had left his wife. There might be something to be got. A loan, at all events, thought he, and that would come in useful, till the bear came right.

He went and was treated to the best the Goat and Compasses could give, and that was not so bad. The two hunted and rummaged with industrious zeal, but found no will nor any clue to the investment mystery.

At last on an old bill file they discovered some accounts between Silas Snoad, Esq., and Messrs. Bullbait and Bearpickle, of Size Lane, which showed a purchase of ten thousand Honduras at 79½. Nothing but this purchase-note could be found.

K

CHAPTER XLV.

THE WONDERFUL SHIPS THAT WERE TO SAIL ACROSS THE LAND ON WHEELS.

The next morning Bubchook went to call on Messrs. Bullbait and Bearpickle, at their office in Size Lane, Trucklebury. Having stated his business, he was shown into the partners' private room. He asked whether they remembered the transaction. They did perfectly well. The gentleman wanted high interest. Did they know of any Bonds? They did. In fact they had kept Mr. Silas Snoad's Bonds for him from the first and collected the dividends.

"Had no idea Mr. Snoad was dead," said Bullbait, with bland and deferential air. "Very sad affair that failure of the Great Ship Loan, to transport vessels of enormous tonnage from sea to sea on wheels, yes, sir, on iron wheels and rails. Ah! there was true financial genius."

"Yes," chimed in Bearpickle, "and the loan would have been floated but for this. They were penny wise and pound foolish. Had the great financier's bribe been big enough, had money been more freely given to touts and scribblers, it would have been a grand success. No scheme has ever seized my fancy so. Huge ships, their sails all set, and steam up too, careering on the iron path at fifty miles an hour. Why, sir, the man who first originated that idea deserves a statue quite as much as he who made the first steam-engine, or discovered circulation of the blood."

"Of course the country promptly avenged this insult to its credit and its enterprise, and stopped its dividends. I think the country was quite right, don't you, Bullbait?"

"Most certainly," said he. "Unfortunate for Mr. Snoad, that is, I beg your pardon, sir, his wife. What is the price now of the stock? My clerk shall run and see."

He ran and saw, and said the price was nominally 2-4, but nothing doing in the stock. This was the mystery. No wonder the poor man dare not inform his wife. Especially when the dividends and all the boasted rate of interest—were stopped. He had eight thousand pounds. His 10,000 so-called stock was nominally worth £200 now.

Bubchook was taken quite aback. He quite forgot his sister, and thought only of himself. While he was poring over books and papers at the Goat and Compasses, rummaging and ferreting, North British had slipped up to 110½.

CHAPTER XLVI.

THE RISE IN NORTH BRITISH CONTINUES.

THE ex-M.P. still tried to put a bold face on the matter, still vowed that he would sell as long as the rise might last. But brokers like Nathaniel Seesaw are not children. I could see the man was frightened now, and as he told me all about the Honduras affair, and I could see that money was not very plentiful, I thought it time to draw the rein, to put him off, in fact do anything but quarrel with the man. I felt it would not do for him to sell when the top was nearly reached, and as a flaming article came out that week about the line, I was a little bit afraid that it would fall. Somehow these articles are so unfortunate. They almost always come out just too late.

That very morning I received a letter from a Glasgow dealing friend, who knew the moves, and as I sent him business, he sometimes gave a hint to me. I'll give it to you.

21 Riggers' Road, Glasgow.

My Dear Seesaw,—

"There is nothing much doing in our market. New Caledonian shares are worth looking after. They are so light to hold in event of anything going wrong, and are much cheaper than the old stock, to say nothing of carrying over. There is still some good buying of British, though the market seems hesitating. They say 120, and then a relapse; but don't sell a bear on the drop. The same party are going to put the stock on a level with the Midland, and then offer to make terms. If you have any clients who can afford to lose, keep them in as bears, it will help the market. You could take the book yourself and so keep the money in the House. But if you want to get any out, do so, for I certainly believe that if politics keep right, the stock will soon be at 130, and I know the traffics are meant to be good.

"Yours very truly,

"Alexander McWheedle."

This was a lucky chance. I could show Bubchook this if other arts should fail. Despair makes human nature obstinate sometimes.

Before the evening of that day the stock had risen to $113\frac{1}{4}$. Next morning, about ten o'clock, my bear came in. His head was very sore. With bland and sympathizing look I took him into my own private room, my little fly-trap, as I called it to myself, and shut the door. Ah me! how many flies had I shut in that little room!

If ever in the course of my whole life I felt my bosom swell with the pride of conscious merit, it was then, when I saw my Bubchook, as it were a fish, so nearly gasping on the bank, his money coming fast, into my till, the blown up sailors well avenged.

"Dear sir," said I to him, "your losses in Peru were large, but these will be much larger, I'm afraid. I can assure you these repeated losses weigh upon my mind; although of course a broker can't advise. It always seems to me when clients lose, as if I were myself to blame. My partner is now getting old, and I shall give this speculative business up, and look up the investing clients more. I really thought with all your perseverance and your pluck you would have made this bear come right. But though I can't advise, I really must not see you being ruined thus.

Said Bubchook,—

"I believe this is the highest point the stock will reach."

"How many times we have thought so, dear sir. Has it ever struck you how much will pay 5 per cent. upon this stock? Or how much stock there is?"

"Not I," said he; "I don't believe in figures; I am told they always lead one wrong"

"I know 'Outsiders' always argue so; but we do pay attention to the figures, and in this case I will tell you why. There is only about 3,800,000 of the stock. £160,000 pays rather more than 4 per cent. per annum on the ordinary stock. After 4 per cent. has been paid, the Edinburgh and Glasgow takes 1 per cent. more than the ordinary North British, as it is a preferred ordinary stock. But about 62,000 would give one per cent. more dividend both to the ordinary North British and the Edinburgh and Glasgow.

"Now it takes more than £1,500,000 to pay a 5 per cent. dividend on the ordinary stock of the London and North-Western, so that a child may see that when times are bad a stock like North British must suffer very quickly, and benefit quite as quickly when they are good. And more, as the stock is so small, and a good deal of it held in little parcels by people who have a free pass, which in bad times may be regarded as a sort of dividend, and as some trustees hold for persons now dead who bought at higher prices, there is every temptation for a large capitalist to force it up even beyond its proper price, but next to no inducement to sell it until it has reached the highest point attainable.

"What you want to know is this. Is it near its highest point? Has it good times to look to in the immediate future? I must confess I think it has. I have received a letter from a very keen dealer in Glasgow, who seems to think it will go much better.

CHAPTER XLVII.

THE MISTAKEN VIEWS OF OUTSIDE SPECULATORS.—MR. OCTAVIUS MARMADUKE BUBCHOOK CLOSES HIS BEAR.

"Most outside speculators, my dear Mr. Bubchook, make this mistake. If a stock has been low for years and paid no dividend, or if, as in this case, the price has often been much in advance of the actual dividend and apparent prospects, they say at once, 'Oh! it is a rig,' and sell a bear. The reason why the price has been so much in advance of the dividend is that the holder knew that when the good time came it would be very good.

"You gentlemen outside generally have an imaginary range of fluctuation for each stock you deal in, and you form that idea from the past fluctuations you have known. This sort of experience is often very delusive.

"What you ought to do is, not to look behind, but keep your head in front; try to diagnose the prospects of the next half-year when papers are informing you of this; form a fair estimate yourself of what the probabilities are of a further rise or fall; look at the amount of stock, the wealth and the stability of those who hold the shares—to any expected events which are likely to benefit the line in the immediate future, as in the case of this North British, the completion of the Tay Bridge, the accession of traffic soon to come from the extension of the Midland to Carlisle.

"Then buy yourself a little stock (not 5,000 at a time) when markets are all flat. As for selling what you have not got, I don't much think you'll ever do any good with that unless you are a jobber in the House, or a director who can sell his own stock, take the contango, and not deliver at all, but buy back when it suits. A splendid business is done so. There are plenty of ways of avoiding the director's name appearing on a contract note. As for those traffic-books, don't trust too much to them. The traffic returns are not made closely by the companies, and if you draw your dividend conclusions thence you won't be often right. Because it is not meant you should. They're like the tape, they help us more than you."

"But can you trust your information?" said my man to me. "I see too late that mine was but a snare."

And then I read to him the portion of McWheedle's letter that referred to the North British stock.

The ex-M.P. for Rottenboro', after reading this letter, turned a trifle pale. Although an "Outside Fool," he knew that when one thief writes to another confidentially he does not tell his brother lies. The pallor was succeeded by a scowl of most malignant hate and rage, and hoarse with passion, Bubchook cried,—

"Ten thousand curses on the riggers and their tricks. This loss has hit me very hard."

"I thought as much," said I unto myself. "The lemon's nearly squeezed quite dry. I should not mind a quarrel now."

"Well, I suppose that I *must* close," said he. "Go buy them back; and do your best, for goodness' sake."

The stock had glided up to 119. Was not that Providence? With heart as light as that of swain who goes to meet his lady-love, I hurried off to close my Bubchook's bear. I bought the British back at just $\frac{3}{8}$ more than the market price, for was he not too much excited to correct the price? and was I not an instrument of Providence? and had he not lost all he had to lose? There was no answering these arguments. Like one half frantic Bubchook rushed away. Of course the stock went back; it always does when large bears close. How is it that the jobbers know so well your means, your temper, and what pressure you require, dear "Outside Fools," to make you act? They never see you. No, but very often they see us. If we don't speak, we have masonic signs.

CHAPTER XLVIII.

THE PROFITS AND LOSSES OF O. M. BUBCHOOK, ESQ., AND HOW HE SOLD HIS LOMBARD SHARES.

I CANNOT give you my client Bubchook's accounts made out in broker's form. There are so many to make out.

The total loss and profit will be quite enough, and the commission is included in the price. No income tax is taken from the dividend. It's not worth while to be so mathematical.

O. M. Bubchook, Esq., in account with Messrs. Seesaw and Turnabout.

1. Sold 5,000 North British Railway at $77\frac{1}{2}$
   Bought ditto . . . 119
   Difference £2,075 0
2. Sold 5,000 ditto at . . 84
   Bought ditto . . . $82\frac{1}{2}$
   Profit . £75 0
3. Sold 5,000 ditto at . . 85
   Bought ditto . . . 119
   Difference £1,700 0
4. Sold 5,000 ditto at . . 83
   Bought ditto . . . 119
   Difference £1,800 0
5. Sold 5,000 ditto at . . 97
   Bought ditto . . . 95

K*

	Profit	£100 0
6. Sold 5,000 ditto at	. .	89¼
Bought ditto .	. .	119
	Difference	£1,487 10
7. Sold 5,000 ditto at	. .	104⅞
Bought ditto .	. .	119
	Difference	£706 5
8. Sold 5,000 ditto at	. .	107¾
Bought ditto .	. .	119
	Difference	£562 10

An average of ⅜ contango was received by my client, from which has to be deducted my ⅛ or half commission for carrying over. No contango is reckoned on the two bargains closed at a profit, as they were not carried over.

His profits were therefore these:—

¼ contango on 30,000 stock, amounting to £75 each account for seven months—£1,050.

Seventy-five pounds from closing the second bear.

One hundred pounds from closing the fifth bear.

With your permission, dear "Outside Fools," I will substitute the word "differences" for "losses." Our committee does not like the word "loss." It is startling to the clients.

		£	s.
Total differences	. . .	2,075	0
" "	. . .	1,700	0
" "	. . .	1,800	0
" "	. . .	1,487	10
" "	. . .	706	5
		562	10

Include £600 for half-year's dividend at 4
per cent., which of course a bear must
pay 600 0
                                        ━━━━━━
                                        8,931 5
Include the previous loss in Peru . . 6,731 5
                                        ━━━━━━
                                        15,662 10

So that of the £20,000 which he possessed at first through defrauding his creditors, there was left £4,337 10s. Of this, however, he had lost £1,750 in Lombard Obligations, so that all he had was £2,587 10s. for himself and wife to live upon. Another broker told me of this Lombard episode. He held a thousand Obligations, and as I was out of town he went to Straddle and Cover, of Shoe Horse Lane, in great alarm, on that memorable morning when the great *Misleading Age*, with its most wonderful arithmetic, so startled all investors in these Lombard Obligations and shares. They told him if the article were true that they would drop to 5 or 6. So this ship-knacker, like so many much more honest folk, was frightened out at 8⅝, the very lowest price. Well done! Messrs. Straddle and Cover! Not so bad for you.

Then thought I to myself, "How very odd. The lowest price was on the morning when this article came out, not when the nation had had time to read and think and sell. There must have been some knowing bears, for on the article and momentary fall the buying was so very good."

Said I to Pinto, when I read that article,—

"Ah, Pinto! what a pity all this blunder is so wasted here. If I were a Leviathan and you the scribe how nicely we could work. I should have gone to you and said, "These Lombards are now nearly low enough. They are good stuff, especially the Obligations. They'll stand a bang. There's a great quantity of those same Obligations, Mr. Pinto, is there not? A very great, a dangerous quantity. Let's see, I have a cheque for you. I trust no fool will think of writing down those Obligations. 'Twould be a pity, for investors are such fools."

Then Pinto would have taken up his cheque, and I my hat; next day he would have written, on his *own responsibility*, observe, an article confusing figures to the tune of many millions. While the panic was still on, I should step in and buy, and so would Pinto, just to keep the market up, you know, for fear investors should be ruined quite. And so the tree would have been shaken well by accident, and we should have picked up much fruit. What a pity in this case the men were such philanthropists.

This banging of good stocks, that lately has come into vogue, is not so dangerous as puffing rotten ones, though more pernicious in effect. In the one case, many greedy "Fools" learnt that high interest means bad security. But in this latter, real investors who are sober, honest people are knocked out for interested rogues to buy. Learn, "Outside Fools," that bearing down the good with big men's aid is quite as easy and as profitable as puffing bad to sell. Oh, what fun to be a City editor! How soon would Pinto's salary of seven or eight hundred pounds have grown into three or four thousand pounds a year!

Now, as I was an honest thief, dear "Outside

Fools," and not ashamed of it, these were my thoughts, and these were Pinto's, too.

But I must caution you, dear "Outside Fools," that strange coincidences will oft occur, and that although this article was soon corrected, which correction brought a further rise (when I and Pinto should have sold had we been principals), it was no doubt but a coincidence, and don't believe that City editors can bear to live in such good style, and pay with cheques *sub rosâ* sent. I never will believe such calumnies. That Paraguay affair has no effect on me. Avaunt! with your dark hints, you are a pessimist. I cannot bear your tribe. You can pull down, but you all build up nothing else instead.

CHAPTER XLIX.

THE MORAL OF MR. BUBCHOOK'S HISTORY AND DEATH, WITH MRS. BUBCHOOK'S CURIOUS REMARKS.

YE "Outside Fools," first get to know the sort of stock you're dealing in. Study the chances for a rise or fall. But if the rise or fall be caused by money articles, buy more if you're a bull, sell more if you're a bear. The chances are recovery will ensue, even if it does not last. That's how the jobbers act inside. Just cast an eye over the monthly fluctuations in our English Rails for some three years and strike the average. You'll find a part of the fall is almost always recovered in the same month, and so a portion of a rise is lost. What business have you to suppose for a penny or for threepence you can buy such information as will make you money upon 'Change? Have more faith in yourselves and in hard work.

I did not see Octavius after this, but when I was at Brighton once, I called to ask him how he was, and this is what I learnt. He had gone to his account. Some time before I called, he came home in a hansom cab. The horse had glanders, and gave him the same in milder form. The doctor said a change would do him good. They did not like this strange complaint, it's so infectious; so he went to see some friends in Lancashire. I quite forget the place. He caught the foot-and-mouth disease. Don't laugh, ye "Outside Fools." It is a fact. The air conveyed it to the cows; the cows conveyed it to their milk; the milk conveyed it to Bubchook. His own wife told me so. Poor lady, she is of Revivalistic turn of mind, and does not seem to think the glory of the woman is *her* hair,—or something else's,—for woman's extra hair is got from funny sources now. Soon after I had called, she came into the room with capless head, which seemed more like a bladder of lard than anything besides. This hairless lady quaintly said to me, with air severe and frosty tone,—

"It behoves us all to ponder these things well. The cows' milk is the instrument ordained to check man's pride, and stay the surplus population's growth, and maybe it will spread into a plague. I hope you're ready, if these times should come," said she.

I said good morning to this awful creature, whose head, though like a bladder of lard outside, was filled with things quite different within, and I was glad to get away. That woman's words and look spoilt my digestion for a month.

Now, what's the moral of this tale?

1. Don't bear improving properties.
2. Don't bear a stock that's small, and, better still, don't bear at all.
3. Don't try to blow up sailors in a rotten ship, for they will be avenged.
4. Don't sell good stocks when you have read the money articles, but keep an average of these same articles' effect on price.
5. Don't ride in hansom cabs without examining the horse.
6. Don't drink bad milk, you'd better far drink beer.

CHAPTER L.

DR. SANA MENS' REMARKS ON HEALTH, HAPPINESS, AND RELIGION.

My doctor, Sana Mens, whom Mrs. Bubchook forced me to attend again, says this about the plague idea.

If poor, don't wed too soon, or if you do, keep *MHΔEN AΓAN* hung up in your rooms both night and day. Wash well, drain well, don't over-eat or over-drink, look to your ventilation, boil and filter all the water that you drink, try hard to break that secret league that is so often formed between the dust-contractor and the vestry-man, for if you don't the plague won't stop at milk, nor yet at foot and month. A little more morality would do no harm. More healthy exercise and less three volume trashy novel narcotism is wanted much.

Now if, dear "Outside Fools," you can see even in a plague the presence of a wise *necessity*, if you can recognise that fact, to one who deeply thinks, so comforting, that man is but a worm compared with what our God can make, and doubtless has already made—if you can see that the good of the *greatest number* is the aim and purpose of whatever happens here, and that the few must bow to that, don't waste your money on this book, you are no " Outside Fool." Or if your heart is very large, and you are filled with pity for your fellow-creatures' sufferings, which day by day increase, as hungry babies faster come, and butchers still charge more and more, give up your fuming and your fretting, your attitudinizing and grimacing, your whisky-warring and your idle preaching, your fatal gospel of "*get on at any price*," and use your surplus energy to think out some grand plan to cheapen meat, or stay the swelling army of invading babes. Give up your shallow and conceited strictures upon this or that form of narcotic which poor human nature and, God knows how often, human misery requires.

Sincere fanatics are themselves but narcotized with false enthusiasm. Gough's eloquent appeals and Father Matthew's earnestness made men a little struck and stupefied with fresh narcotic for a time, but only till the new excitement wore away.

Good men will often narcotize themselves with an enthusiastic hope of saving souls by thousands at a time.

This fond enthusiasm will make them push one Scripture rule too far, and fewer souls will in the end be saved, not more. Sensational dramatic preachers, whose own text is this, "*Man's nature will have something startling, something new*," do harm, not good, by working on secretions so and overbalancing the reason of their audience.

Christ ought to be their model, not an actor on the stage.

The old crusaders were but drunk with fierce fanaticism, and the fighting instincts of robust rough health.

The infidel still holds Jerusalem. The revenue from drink increases every year. We ought to pause before we say, " My little sect's views are not right for me alone, but also right for all these millions who hold different views."

Wherever there is education there is tolerance. Men ever will suspect, and they are mostly right, that with these fierce invectives, this rash zeal and straining after novelty in the religious world, there's blent a wish to pose before an audience, as being better than the rest.

The devil has no stronger fort, and none so difficult to take as Castle EGO is.

Is it not harder to have faith and keep on working quietly and calmly than to blindly grasp at some sensational ideal—to drink some sweet imaginative anodyne, which is to lull your intellect and take you in a kind of moral stupefaction up to heaven.

Try this narcotic, it is very safe.

Identify yourself with some pursuit that does a little good, or does as little harm as possible.

Believe that happiness is where you are, wherever that may be. Lose thought of self in your pursuit, no matter whether it be sweeping chimneys out or writing poetry.

Get drunk with this narcotic, and you'll be as happy as a man is meant to be upon this earth.

It is what other people think you ought to think and speak and do that makes so many miserable. Yes, many more than pain or want or real grief.

I like this Sana Mens' idea of cheapening meat, there is so much romance connected with cheap butcher's meat. Yes, practical romance and not Quixotic castles in the air.

This cursed competition is invading 'Change, though we are all protected so.

'Tis " Dog eat Dog " at least thrice in the week. Ask any broker, he will tell you so.

CHAPTER LI.

THE CURIOUS HISTORY OF A CLERICAL GUINEA PIG.

THE Rev. Josiah Fetchem was what is termed, somewhat irreverently to my mind, a *Clerical Guinea Pig*. Now I opine, your Worships and your Reverences, that this term implies a sort of moveable pillar of the Church, who for a guinea or more will hold forth, argue, and dispute upon any orthodox subject, in any pulpit for any other stationary pillar of the Church.

Now as an "Outside Lay Fool" myself, I should have imagined these Guinea Pigs to have been gentlemen, not only more versed in the ways of the world from moving about more than their stationary clerical brethren among their fellow-creatures, but also more charitable, and more free from that high-stomached conceit which is so liable to environ a man and imprison his better judgment and understanding when he vegetates in the narrow though sacred precincts of a country rectory or vicarage. I speak not, your Worships and your Reverences, of the great towns, for there a man's angularities and eccentricities, his hobby-horses, and his prejudices get so knocked about and attenuated, so rubbed out of the man, that very often you would scarcely know him from a common layman, except that he so frequently wears the same livery as a footman, always excepting the calves, for in that particular no doubt your Worships will be ready to allow that Jeames is *facile princeps*. But your Reverences must be well aware that in the country it is generally very different. The parson is often there a sort of petty prince. He is not only the repository of religious knowledge, but the representative of the magisterial power. It is an event if he take a drive round the parish; it is also an event if he stop at home. An intimate clerical friend of mine, whose acquaintance I first made through some dealing in East Lovell Mining shares, by name St. John Thoresthorpe, who is the Vicar of Great Gedneydake-cum-Sutterby le Marsh, in Huntingshire, has often declared to me that he sometimes feels uncomfortable because of the great responsibilities connected with his vicarial dominion, for he affirms that, should he be so unfortunate as to have an attack of bilious colic, or an influenza cold, the whole parish would be straightway seriously alarmed; while if Samuel Stubble has a dispute with William Thatch, or if Susannah Twitch should fall out with Jane Hodge about the veriest trifle, he is sure to be appealed to to settle the difference. This vicar of Great Gedneydake-cum-Sutterby le

Marsh is a parson of the old school. He likes his glass of port, and his rubber at whist, is a good shot even now at seventy years of age, and has only just given up fox-hunting. And it is precisely because he is this sort of man and possesses a kind heart and liberal hand that he has gained that autocratic power, the responsibilities of which he seems so afraid of. St. John Thorestherpe has an ample bow window to his vicarage, and to his person too, and preaches a better sermon than I have often heard your Worships and your Reverences do in town. This vicar is an excellent illustration of the *Mens Sana in Corpore Sano*, and even rustics are quick enough to perceive any truth worth picking up when it is to be found in their neighborhood. My friend really thinks that he is no better than the villagers, as a man, and acts on his belief, and that is the key to his influence over the parishioners. I myself, when visiting once, heard a farm laborer say to another, " Whoy, Bill, ower St. John be more loike a Wesleyun or a Baptest than a Church parson, he be so free with a man loike." Yes, your Worships and your Reverences, it is this geniality of manner and easiness of access that brings the Wesleyans and Baptists so many proselytes. I fear there are but few country parishes that have an "ower St. John" to teach the simple folk so much by showing them how little difference there is 'twixt man and man, and by this modest excellence and ready sympathy to prop a tottering Church, so split up into rival creeds as ours is, unhappily. Too often in the agricultural districts the word "Rector" means no more than *a great scholard or receiver of great tithes*, and many of the humbler parishioners never come into the clerical presence except at church, a marriage, christening, or a burial.

When such is the attitude of men who receive from one to two thousand a year, and even more sometimes, when the whole parish often does not contain more souls than pounds it brings into the rectorial or vicarial coffers, what wonder that a self-supporting Church should find support among the thoughtful part of the community? What wonder, when fanatic zealots, for a creed which they themselves and not their Bible limits so, insult our common-sense and decency by offering Dissent the burial of suicides and murderers, that men say, "*Disestablish such a Church?*" When landlords will not let their farms to tenants who support Dissent—when zeal makes working men forge tickets to control the sense of meetings held by other sects—when clergymen are not content with simply *not* electing female teachers duly qualified to a Board School, but must hurl texts of Scripture at the applicant, and publish their grim jokes in papers of the day, where is religious liberty? Observe, your Worships and your Reverences, these few besotted bigots, for I trust they are not numerous, bring sullying stains upon your cloth that charity alone can wash away. Can texts of Scripture not be found to fling at any sect? But what have I to do with this? Let me return to my Josiah.

CHAPTER LII.

SHOWING HOW TO CATCH AN OLD MAN IN THE MATRIMONIAL NET.

UNLIKE many more worthy Guinea Pigs, the Rev. Josiah Fetchem had means of his own; for he had by his smooth fresh face and oily tongue so bewitched or bewizarded an aged maiden lady that she left him all she had, to the great disgust of her relations, who vainly tried to get the will set aside upon the plea of her insanity.

In the case of these strange wills and grotesque legacies, where does insanity begin ?

I often think the devil is well served in this respect by the English law.

Some poor old man in feeble health and with fast-failing faculties is snapped up by a keen professional whose power to scent a widower with money is simply wonderful. It would not matter if the hussy with her full-blown venal charms cared for her aged swain, but next to never is it so.

A very different *rôle* she has to play.

She must first make the old man think himself neglected by his relatives. This is the best card that she has to play. Then she should narcotize him by insidious winning smiles that may mean all or nothing, and pay him small attentions, thoughtfully arranged. The contrast will be sure to tell if those at home neglect the same. She should profess to have discovered that her aged swain is delicate, and would do well to choose some fancied malady that's interesting and respectable, for there is much in that.

Avoid disease below the belt. Prefer the lungs. It's better form in good society.

Let her profess warm friendship for the daughters of the house, if there be any; but when they're away, she then may damn them with faint praise, or dexterously vilify by innuendo and by hint. It's wonderful how much more powerful to harm this sort of praise and these vague hints are found to be than open blame. The poison churns and works within the hearer's thoughts, like yeast in bread, while open censure startles and ofttimes develops feelings of downright antagonism. Man is a fighting animal, and if you say,—

"Yes, black *is* black," and emphasize the *is*, he'll feel inclined to say, "It isn't, it is white to me sometimes."

So, then, you hunters after widowers, be bland and gentle in your manners, as Nathaniel Seesaw always is to pigeons which he shortly means to pluck. Let nothing put you out of temper, wear a happy, infantine, and placid look. You'd be surprised how this serenity of temper and face will soothe and charm an old swain's mind, when his digestion's weak, or when there is acidity about the frame, or just a twinge or two of gout. Act thus, and you will soon become a necessary piece of furniture. Next grow a trifle distant, come more seldom to his house. He soon will ask the reason of this change. Then, with that air of fearless candor, and that child-like innocence which, whether in the private house or broker's office, the true artist can assume at will, appear to show him all your heart. Say with a graceful sigh,—

"Ah, me, I fear I cannot trust myself. In spite

of the disparity in years, our tastes are so congenial, our dispositions are so similar."

If this be not enough, let fall vague hints about the neighbors' tattle, and imply that even now you are a little compromised. If there be one small spark of generous feeling in the old man's bosom, if the merest phantom of an amatory thought lurk there, your fish will soon lie gasping on the bank. And even if no spark be kindled in that arid breast, the fear of damages will do the trick. Your aged lover will have not forgotten all those pleasant little "*Artful Hussy Episodes*," which even now-a-days divert us in our daily papers so. Then throw your arms around the old man's neck—you really must—his blood is poor—and vow you love his children as himself. I swear that as I give you this advice, I feel as though a client waited for my operating and artistic touch.

There, Madam, take these golden hints, and, if you don't catch some old doting swain, who's longing to be narcotized with your quack Senile Soothing Syrup, never will Nathaniel Seesaw read a client's thoughts again. Madam, you are my friend. We always love those whom we've done a favor to, 'tis those we owe one to we shun. I have conferred a favor upon you; I take a pride in your success; good-bye, good luck.

And when you've caught a fish, then think of me and my advice.

"And serve the old fool right," I think you said, dear sir?

Ah! that's uncharitable, and shows an ignorance of human nature too. I cannot see it so. The man is not to blame. Poor soul! He thinks it will be good for all, and means quite right.

Why should not one who has not long to live try to obtain what *may* prove to be happiness? Why not indeed? "Because it harms his family," you say. He does not think it will. But, then, he ought to think it will. Ah! now you're in reforming Fools' Utopian land. I leave you there to dream. My dear sir, you will very likely be laid gasping on the bank yourself. Why, had I not my Clara and her husband living in the house with me, although I know the wiles so well, I very likely should be hooked myself.

But somebody must be to blame. No, not some*body*, but some*thing*. In all these cases self-sufficient fools split on this rock They blame the person not the thing. The huntress only follows what's her natural game, although she hunts sometimes in a nasty narrow-minded sort of way. It is the law, dear "Outside Fools," that is at fault. It gives the man the power to make himself an ass. It gives the woman the power to turn the children out of doors. In this respect in France they manage better than we English do. Reform the law. Just so on 'Change. Reform the system, don't attack the men. We brokers shall feel grateful to the man who finds a way to circumscribe our power to cheat. We shall have less temptation then. I'm sure we have too much as things are now, and if a man can stand against it, he deserves a higher place than any "Outside Fool." Have you not noticed how a broker always tells his clients when he has a chance to keep away? We have, say "Outside Fools;" but then he knows we can't. There's room for thought in that reply, dear "Outside Fools."

CHAPTER LIII.

THE FAVORITE FORM IN WHICH THE EVIL ONE TEMPTS HOLY MEN TO SPECULATE.

Now although, by his great physical recommendations, our Guinea Pig had not only obtained, but, in spite of the relatives of the deceased lady, maintained his legal right to enjoy and spend as he elected the sum of six thousand pounds sterling, yet not disliking the change of scene and pulpit connected with his vocation, and, considering rectorial and vicarial deference a thing not to be lightly esteemed, he determined to remain a Guinea Pig.

It is a singular fact, to which I would draw the attention of your lordships of the bench episcopal, that when Satan wishes to tempt a holy man to speculate, he almost always takes a British or a Foreign Mine, or else a Mahometan Bond as the instrument of his unholy plan.

Now, your lordships, it is notorious that if a bishop, rector, or vicar were requested to explain, sermonize upon, or denounce from their pulpit the *increasing evils of speculation,* and the peculiar seductions of mammon in this wise, they would each and all be sadly at a *nonplus,* through an almost total ignorance of the subject; nay, there exists among these apostles an almost universal, and, to the laity, an incomprehensible disposition to plead that *money* is too low and base a subject for the greatness of ecclesiastical wisdom to concern itself with. And yet this money is the root of all evil, and most good. And further, I would pray your Lordships to observe that the enemies of the Church do assert that this position is neither logical nor tenable, for that in all matters connected with this so base and despicable a thing termed *money*, the apostles, luminaries, pillars and other officiating members of the Church do possess and display on all fit and suitable occasions a most commendable intelligence respecting the accurate value of this same base " money."

And that, therefore, in the present schismatic and dangerously zymotic condition of the Church, when malicious persons are ever waiting to discover a flaw in the so nearly invulnerable armor of the great generals and Captains of the Christian army of the Church militant, it is to be much deplored that your Lordships and Reverences have unwisely taken shelter under this assumed ecclesiastical or ecclesiastico-philosophical disdain of money.

Again. Some captious spirits have alleged that it is upon record that although our transatlantic cousins have, of late years, in that generous and self-denying spirit for which they are so justly famed, presented to the British public a series of magnificent investment prizes, and that although the magnates of finance have, in a true spirit of self-abnegation and philanthropy, allowed the public to participate freely in their gigantic usurious undertakings with Mahometan and Moslem countries, yet that it is upon record that not one single pastoral or letter has been addressed by your Lordships to your clergy either drawing attention to the vast advantages—or, with the superior wisdom and decision for which your Lordships are so remarkable, pointing out any disadvantages connected with these dazzling and gigantic schemes, prizes, and undertakings.

And these same captious spirits do further allege that, paradoxical as it may appear, although your Lordships, and their Reverences, following the example of your Lordships, have shown this singular reticence and indifference with regard to your congregations' welfare on these important matters, yet that your clergy have shown a more than lively personal interest in the above-mentioned philanthropic operations, and have contributed in no small degree to float, support, and maintain the credit of the countries who have so nobly afforded them the chance of lending their base money to such holy usurers at so high a rate of interest. To a liberal mind it should doubtless appear to be a commendable and Christian proceeding to secure from these lost Mahometans this same high rate, and had the security continued to be undoubted I should not have ventured to address your Lordships on so wide and difficult a theme. But seeing that, from the many opportunities afforded by my position as one who continually comes into such close contact with this filthy lucre, I well know how severe the losses are that have been recently sustained by your Lordships' clergy as well as by their congregations, through their ignorance of the whole subject of investment and the properties of the root of all evil, which ignorance is increased by your ecclesiastico-philosphical indifference to the same all-important subjects, I should certainly be failing in my duty if I did not humbly, and with all that deference due from an *Outside Lay Fool* to an *Inside Clerical Apostle*, place before you certain suggestions which my brother brokers and jobbers all fully endorse, as being serviceable to yourselves, and your clergy in particular, and to the religious community in general.

CHAPTER LIV.

CERTAIN VALUABLE SUGGESTIONS OFFERED BY NATHANIEL SEESAW, ESQ., THE REPRESENTATIVE OF THE BROKERS AND JOBBERS OF THE STOCK EXCHANGE, TO THE BISHOPS AND CLERGY OF GREAT BRITAIN.

WE, the brokers and jobbers of the London Stock Exchange, through our authorized representative, Nathaniel Seesaw, Esq., suggest that your Lordships do memorialize the Universities of Oxford, Cambridge, London, Dublin, and any others you may think advisable, and pray their chancellors and vice-chancellors, their fellows and ,professors, to contribute liberally to the founding and establishing of professional chairs, to the end that all under-graduates specially and the outer world generally may derive from the professors' learned lectures and lucubrations a full and exhaustive account of the direct and indirect causes of speculation, the theoretical and practical working of the " *Root of all Evil*," especially when possessed in a quiet abnormal quantity by the great magnets of finance. For, your Lordships and Reverences, we, the brokers and jobbers of the London Stock Exchange, have observed with regret and indignation that certain Radical reformers do basely insinuate that these universities, the great storehouses and sources of all learning of any practical utility, shelter and maintain within their august and time-honored walls in luxury and conservative comfort numerous pundits, who have no more idea of what is meant by a bull or a bear, or a put or a call, than Tristram Shandy's Uncle Toby had of the meaning conveyed by the phrase, "*The right or the wrong end of a woman.*"

And that although they exhibit this philosophical ignorance of or indifference to money, still they declare that there is more "Root of Evil" possessed by these national institutions than they know how to put to a proper and productive use.

Now, if your Lordships and your Reverences condescend to adopt our suggestions, the mouths of these slanderous detractors will be stopped for very shame, when they behold how the learned lecturers and professors do argue, dispute, discuss, elucidate, and explain, respecting the uses and abuses of "money," and how through their noble efforts reason is once more enabled to become victorious over the wiles and snares, the tricks and chicaneries of "Aggregated Capital" in financial hands.

And we would further respectfully suggest that the vernacular be substituted for that semi-barbarous and monkish Latin which designates many of your proceedings at the universities, and prevents them being easily understood by those who, like ourselves, have not been fortunate enough to have received the inestimable boon of a university education. For that those of us who have a smattering of Latin feel persuaded that Cicero himself— we beg your worships' pardon, *Kikero*—would have been ashamed to adopt such Latin, in the same degree as we are ashamed when we are compelled, through the thin attendance of " Outside Fools," to have recourse to that barbarous " Canine Cannibalism," in plain English, the objectionable proceeding of "*Dog eating Dog.*" Your Lordships, Worships, and Reverences, we respectfully offer these suggestions through our accredited agent and spokesman, Nathaniel Seesaw, and we are your humble servants, the brokers and jobbers of the Stock Exchange.

CHAPTER LV.

THE REVEREND JOSIAH FETCHEM MEETS WITH A CERTAIN DEFERENCE FROM THE RECTORS AND VICARS, WHICH IS A SORT OF PARADOX.

Now, my dear " Outside Lay Fools," although there exists at present among the luminaries of the Church this contempt—well, no, contempt is not the word. I should say this philosophical appreciation, the Kikeronian " Despicientia," of money—yet, paradoxical as it may seem to shallow minds, this Guinea Pig of ours, who now possessed three hundred pounds a year from money invested in mortgages on house property or ground rents, from the very date of that possession, and not before, was treated with a certain deference, or, if your Reverences prefer it, with a certain sympathetic attention from both Rectors and Vicars, which less fortunate Guinea Pigs, who had nothing but their hebdomadal guineas to live upon, sighed for, but in vain. Human nature is full of paradoxes, and if that same Kikero had studied human nature more, and cribbed less from the Greek philosophers, his Paradoxes would have been better

worth reading than they are. But Kikero was a
conceited egotist, and therefore it is difficult to learn
much from him.

A critical friend of mine, facetiously named "Opsimathes," although he was so advanced in learning at an early age, here observes, with that caustic irritability peculiar to the "*Grammaticas tribus*," "Why, what the dickens have brokers to do with Kikero and the Greek philosophers?"

My dear Opsimathes, it does seem rather out of place, I grant you, for a broker to have a smattering of Latin, and to know the alphabet in Greek. But it is no more odd than for so great a critic's name to be on contracts for the purchase of Wheal Mary Annes, or for the speculative sale of Egypt '73. I'll bet you a new hat (we always bet new hats on 'Change) Opsimathes, that you don't know so much of any stock you like to name as I of Greek or Latin, and yet it's next to nothing that I know."

Josiah Fetchem liked this deference from his superiors, and argued thus unto himself,—

"Suppose I had ten thousand pounds instead of six. Their Reverences would like me all that better, and who knows, if I take care not to adopt any decided religious views, but dexterously wait until I see what views the biggest men may hold and then adopt their views, I may become a greater man myself. The motto of a Guinea Pig, and many others, too, should now-a-days be this—I *temporise and learn from bigger men.*"

Now your Lordships, Worships, and Reverences, I pray you to observe that if these Rectors and Vicars had not changed their manner towards their Guinea Pig when he came into possession of his three hundred pounds a year, he would have been a happy Guinea Pig, and would not have tried to make it five. They were the first to start him on the downward path. And when a brother parson told him that he held a hundred shares in the far-famed Van Lead Mine, which only cost him £4 10s. per share, he was completely given over to the Evil One. But let us now look some years back.

CHAPTER LVI.

HOW JOSIAH FETCHEM MADE AN INVESTMENT IN THE CELEBRATED EMMA MINE, WITH AN ACCOUNT OF DR. SANA MENS' VIEWS ON THE GOODNESS OF HUMAN NATURE.

In eighteen hundred and seventy-one, when the long-suffering and ill-used British public were recovering from that panic which in '66 and the succeeding years made a clean sweep of all the joint stock companies, the Overends, the Credit Fonciers, the rotten banks, the grand financing bubbles, and industrial enterprise, so called, through which so many thousands of investors come to ruin, the "Outside Fools" were dazzled and bewildered with the wonderful prospectus of the far-famed Emma mine, which, both in liberality of promises and influential names upon the Board, has never been surpassed.

This famous mine was there described as half a mile in length, and was declared to be producing seven hundred thousand pounds a year. Americans, so philanthropic, yet so keen, had actually sold this priceless treasure to their transatlantic cousins for a million pounds, not so much more than one year's earnings would come to. Kind American hearts! 'Twas some set off for Alabama claims.

Ye pessimists, don't talk of human nature being bad. A man who did not love his fellow-creatures much would have kept all this treasure to himself, and could he not have eaten all the cake himself, he would have choked with trying, and not shared it with his fellow fools.

Opsimathes says here,—

"'Twill serve the fools quite right, suppose it should turn out a hoax."

What fools? How wise these critics are after the event. How they can pick out flaws in books that do not sell at all, and find out merits in them when the "Outside Fools" have bought.

I never heard you say a word against this celebrated mine, Opsimathes, when the prospectus first came out. But now that its fair fame is sullied by foul slander's breath, now that the honorable men who worked so for the public good are worried by the disappointed, greedy, and ungrateful shareholders, now that eighteen per cent. paid monthly is just for a little space delayed (it surely will not be for long), Opsimathes can join the hue and cry, and feel his liver better for the fling. This is indeed contemptible. We are getting to a pretty pass in journalism now. Down from the Queen herself, no one is safe. The *person*, not the *system*, is the modern object of attack. Well, where there's no ability to scribble anything but coarse abuse, what can one look for else?

Look here, Opsimathes, if you had warned the public when the mine was first brought out, you should have been my "Cleverest Outside Fool." I would have put you on a moral pedestal, against my rule. But pray, when four Americans of very high position, presidents of banks and railroads, senators, ambassadors, assisted by three members of the British Parliament, and two more gentlemen of social rank, all joined in recommending us to buy, shall we call poor Josiah Fetchem fool because he thought with such great names he must be safe? You may —I never will.

"But," say the optimists, "the idea is too preposterous, too shocking to our faith in human nature, that we cannot think these men intended to deceive. One might as well suppose the only difference between a high and low position to be this, one gives a man much greater opportunities to cheat."

Upon the other side, the pessimists triumphantly exclaim,—

"It proves that man is bad at heart."

And now, dear "Outside Fools," as this is no slight matter to decide, I'd rather tell you what my doctor, Sana Mens, thinks of it all, for he has thought as much as most and what he says he really thinks; and, more, he knows that he, as well as you, is but an "Outside Fool."

He says,—

Both sides are partly wrong. Man is not bad at heart, for if he were, the bad would ultimately swamp the good in spite of legal check. Until you show conclusively that there are *more* bad men than good, you have no right to be a pessimist. And in your estimate of man, you ought to take your specimens more from those countries where both food and love are plentiful and easily obtained; not from old countries, where a turnip is almost as valuable as a life.

"Bring *nil admirari* to your aid, if you would estimate your fellow-man aright. Those words I render by '*a calm philosophy.*'

"Suppose *one* rogue were to concoct a scheme such as this Emma Eldorado seemed to be, can you not well imagine that he might deceive the others by his artifice ? Was theirs not rather carelessness than wilful fraud ? and was not even he led wrong by *aggregated money's* baneful influence ?

"I'll tell you how it is. There are pernicious systems in finance, professions, trade, and everything in life. The custom of these systems gradually pushes men still further on the path of wrong, each quoting what the other safely did, until at last one just a little worse and bolder than the rest sets in a blaze the smouldering flame, and is a scape-goat for the system's flaws.

"Whenever 'a great crime,' as it is called, is brought before the world, we hear these words, ' How horrible!' 'How shocking!' 'What a miscreant!' ' Can this be done by civilized, by educated man ? ' Now all these phrases are immoral in effect.

" If you could analyse each speaker's inmost thoughts, you probably would find a secret satisfaction blended with the horror which he seems to feel.

" Each, often unacknowledged to himself, thinks, ' Ah ! I'm not so bad as that man is,' and each superlative ejaculation of disgust and horror seems to make him more removed from such a miscreant, as he would say.

" Let God decide upon man's moral guilt, not men like us, dear 'Outside Fools.'

" What say you then, shall we let criminals go

free? By no means so. Society has laws and claims which must be carefully observed. Hang criminals that should be hung. Flog those that should be flogged. Don't let this modern luxury sap all your mental vigor so that you both shrink with horror at the *name* of what you term *these shocking crimes!* and also shrink from punishing the same.

"There are things worse than death. But do not argue that your fellow man is bad at heart because society must punish criminals whose moral guilt no man on earth can accurately weigh. Instead of hugging to your heart the fond idea that you are not so bad or better than your fellow men, work hard to give your mite of imformation to the general store. Attack the system, ye reformers and enthusiasts, and not the man.

"And recollect that education must be slow. There is no revolutionizing things on earth. Spasmodic efforts in the cause of virtue often end in vice.

"I strenuously hold that human nature is not shown to be depraved by cases such as Overend's, or Collie's, or the Emma Mine. In all these cases, the old theory that '*ignorance is vice*,' applies to most involved.

"Because some two or three great juggling scamps, who have so much temptation through their money that they hardly can do right, lay artful plans to drag in men who are well-meaning in the main, —because financiers, with long experience in the muddy ways of usury, have drawn the savings of the nation to supply the vicious means for their extravagance and luxury—because investors, through their greed and ignorance, have thrown too great temptation in directors' way—because, I say, if one man chose to lend his name, a loan of many millions could be floated in a day for Russian Railways that can only pay for warlike purposes as yet—because if he but said the word, even ten per cent. could be put upon the value of a Spanish Bond, it does not follow that the men who have this power are not good men; but it does follow that the gulls should learn the snares, that legislators with clear sight and a stern sense of honor, like Sir Henry James, should take this burning question thoroughly in hand, and that the power of aggregated capital should henceforth be more widely known. Let none be able to buy up the press. This is the real source of ill. While ruined gamblers are inveighing against men on 'Change, stung by the senseless smart of loss, the first cause lurks unseen and to unnumbered thousands quite unknown. Yes, let the public think more deeply, let the papers write more fully on this most important money theme—upon the way the pieces are all moved in speculation's game of chess.

"Enthusiasts, and fools, and hypocrites, and all who have it not, may talk against this money as they please, but few mean what they say, and who pays heed to them?

"A man who says, 'I care not for this *money*, all I want is meat and drink,' is more a fool than a philosopher. Suppose he have no means to buy his meat and drink?

"Go to—just take a red-hot Radical. Give him a small estate. He'll turn Conservative before he has enjoyed it many months. No doubt this money is the root of evil, but it is the source of good as well. It is most dangerous when aggregated in the hands of those who use it to consume, to lend at usury, and not produce or trade as our best merchants do. Wake up, ye 'Outside Fools,' and learn, give up your greed of gain, you can yourselves curtail this power of money if ye will. Dig out the accursed *Ego* from your hearts. 'Tis that which makes each fool say to himself while rushing onwards in the race for gold, ' De'il take the hindmost, I shall not be last.'

" And one word more. There is more happiness in the *fallentis semita vitae*, the quiet life unnoticed by the world, than in the glitter and the tinsel of the finest palaces. How many does that Gospel of ' *Get on, by fair means if you can, if not, get on by any means you can*,' bring to their physical and moral death !"

" I always listen to what Sana Mens may say, because I think his motives are quite right. But as, dear 'Outside Fools,' I am a broker, you will not expect that I myself should have so high a standard of what's right. For education is a gradual thing. I may improve in time. Indeed I think I have improved since Dr. Sana Mens attended me."

What think you of those dummy shares, not the debentures, in the once famous Mineral Hill? A ten pound share, of which one could not prove the real existence, sold at six, seven, or eight premium, if flat-fish could be found to buy. If flat-fish had but tried to sell, they would have found no market then at all.

What of the celebrated Russia Copper, which deceived a member of that veteran firm whose name was good enough before to turn a hole into a mine? When Washoe, Washoe, was the cry on 'Change, did cautious Starwise know the mill was all those miles away, that silver bars were few and far between?

When those small stores of Taquarilian gold, left where they were so nicely to be found, and bring abundant interest to few from many's ignorance, did none of us on 'Change know how the game was being played? What if there be some gold in other Brazil mines? The best horse does not always win upon the turf, nor yet on 'Change. Learn more, and then you will lose less. But Emma waits for us.

The shares were very flat just after the allotment letters were sent out. Some arch-promoter doubtless thought it would be well to take a little profit then. Besides this flattering, the market was a very clever piece of jugglery. Sharp speculators who did not believe these flowery promises, and thought they saw through a gigantic hoax, sold bears, and so played into the ensnarers' hands. For well they knew that bears must close some time, and that if they got up an artificial rise the "Outside Fools" would buy, and so come to their aid. And so they bought up quantities of shares, and very likely, you, dear reader, helped their little game. So Emma rallied from her drop. The Christmas circular came out, in which all timid bulls were positively told *that great pains had been taken to check all the statements made in the prospectus, and that the directors now declared those statements to be true.* In April, 1872, in spite of circulars and this directors' narcotizing faith, one third of this rich cake was still in their own hands, their hearts were stirred by a deep philanthropic wave (a gradual improvement in the mine produced the wave), and all entreated sleepy " Outside Fools " to take this third—but at a premium. The shares of twenty pounds had risen now to over 29. Josiah could resist no more, and purchased fifty Emma shares at twenty-nine pounds ten per share. The great men's creatures put in motion all their wonderful machinery by which our nation has lost many million pounds, and by loud blatant bidding, with audacious jobbers' aid, by giving calls for more by tips, and touts, and circulars, the bears were pickled and strung up, the price was raised to this 32. Josiah Fetchem, silly fool, thought he had found on earth a little speculative Paradise, and some time after this he startled some good people by his wandering thoughts. But more of this anon.

CHAPTER LVII.

A DESCRIPTION OF GREAT WHOPPLIDDE-IN-THE-FEN AND OF THE RECTOR, THE REV. JEDEDIAH TRING.

Josiah Fetchem often went to take the duty for the rector at Great Whopplidde-in-the-Fen. You don't know Whopplidde-in-the-Fen. You must be, then, yourself unknown. It is in Clayshire, not so far from where the Pintos used to dwell. A very primitive and priggish little place it is. Quite different to Gedneydake-cum-Sutterby le Marsh, where my friend "ower St. John Thoresthorpe" resides. The parish is a scattered one, and large, the glebe is rich, and there are just about one thousand souls, of which eight hundred are day laborers or cottagers with families. The rector's living is worth just eleven hundred pounds a year, and though advanced in age, and rather dropsical, he did not keep a curate, but got chronic help from our Guinea Pig, whenever he could not get through the duty by himself. This rector, styled the Rev. Jedediah Tring, was a narrow-minded, ample-bodied bookish sort of man, who read and wrote works on divinity alone, and, like so many more, did not perceive that all the education that can possibly be got elsewhere should be acquired so, and then applied to sacred subjects, and thus make them comprehensible to common minds. If a congregation be already safe, what need of explanation and instruction in the gospel truths? If most of them require teaching and are somewhat slow to learn, shall clergymen say, simply, "This is true, believe or disbelieve, and nothing else?" Or should they rather try to suit their language to the capabilities of those who hear—to illustrate from ordinary life—from what their congregations understand? Let those who know decide. 'Tis not for me to say. The more abstruse a thing you make religion out to be, the fewer hearts you'll touch. The teaching of some parsons would imply that one is saved or lost already; but this surely cannot be with the great bulk of men, and those are they whom parsons have to try and win. It's not the staunch believers in his creed the clergyman must try to please; the danger there is lest they should rely too much upon a creed's narcotic influence. The unconverted and indifferent should be the ones a working parson tries to bring into the fold.

CHAPTER LVIII.

A DESCRIPTION OF MISS LOUISA PANTOSNIFFLE'S CURIOUS DRESS, AND OF MADAME EMMA LA FARGUE, WITH OTHER GREAT WHOPPLIDIANS.

WE have accounted for eight hundred of the Whoppliddians. The remainder were thus made up. The rector, his wife, and Miss Louisa Pantosniffle, who was a companion to the rector's wife, and acted as a housekeeper as well. She was a Londoner, and dressed in quite the newest style, the narrowest of sheaths, with wonderful cockscomb behind. Her *tête* of hair was quite unique, and what was false did not match that which was her own.

Now as Louisa Pantosniffle was both plump and short, the effect of this strange narrow sack upon her figure was more curious than elegant.

It was as though you had inserted a short alderman in a long common sack, and left the head alone exposed. His figure would be sure to make itself be seen, and so did hers. But ignorance is bliss sometimes, they say, and really this appeared to be a case in which it was. Louisa Pantosniffle knew it was the fashion, the Whoppliddians heard that it was, and as they had no sense of the ridiculous, all thought it right.

Poor girl, she could not help it if she was full five-and-thirty inches round the waist, although she really should have taken now and then a side-glance in the glass.

If one great lady and a score of west-end milliners should say that fig-leaves had come in again for summer dress, I dare be sworn you'd find no stint of wearers for the dress. And why? It's not the fault of women in the middle class; they do not set the fashion—they adopt it when it's set.

Rank has its privileges and its duties too. If ladies of the highest rank would set their sisters of a lower grade a different example, we should soon be rid of these indecent and bizarre disfigurements of female forms. The milliners of course keep changing to make trade.

Then there was Dr. Miggs, with bright though pock-marked face. He knew a great deal more of human nature than his art, and so he got on well, and was an acquisition in the place. His daughters were long, light, untidy girls, who dearly loved the style of book that now goes down so well. Main incidents—a country barn, a murder, and a mystery. As fixings to this dainty dish there should be added just a spice of bigamy, adultery, and a smart description of the *demi-semi-monde*.

Oh yes, this sort of narcotism is much sought after in our towns and villages. Whose fault is it? 'Tis yours, ye "Outside Fools" who read. Yes, yours, ye mothers, who don't stop such trash from coming near your homes. You often read the books yourselves. Opinions may be wrong, but facts cannot tell lies. The sale lists show the sort of book that sells. Forsooth, if some one slanders people high enough, there need be nothing else to palm it off upon the public taste.

Such narcotism must indeed be bad for girls and boys, if not for men and women grown. And who's to blame? The system in the trade. Why, any fool may write three volumes of the most pernicious twaddle, call it by a taking name, and all the circulalating libraries will buy one copy each, which they get something over half the price. A few flat-fish, with too much money and but little brains, give thirty-one and sixpence for these sort of books. As there are about five hundred of these libraries that take one copy of whatever may be brought out in their own pet form, there's not much fear of loss, for this five hundred just repays the cost. But for this system often not a dozen copies of these so-called novels would be sold. Why don't the critics tell you " Outside Fools " all this ? Whose business is it if it is not theirs ? But let that pass, and turn we now to Whopplidde-in-the-Fen again. There was a lawyer and his newly-married wife; but they were just like other people, so we do not care for them. There were the Wigginses, three tabbies, whose old father had been in the liquor trade, and left them comfortably off. Then there was Captain Dudman, who was in the coastguard service, a thin prim-whiskered sort of man, who spent his leisure time in staring through a telescope, or walking miles and miles with aimless energy. Then there were half a score bluff, honest tenant farmers, and the usual tradesmen to be found in any place. But there was one more person with whom my story has to do. Madame Emma La Fargue was a widow, and a distant relation of Dr. Miggs. Her husband died before she settled at Great Whopplidde-in-the-Fen. She was a partial mystery; she always seemed to have sufficient means, though none knew whence the money came. Dr. Miggs must have known within ten years how old she was; but any stranger, I feel sure, could not have guessed within a score. She had mysterious little boxes come at times from Paris, but none knew what it was that they contained. Her maid was never allowed to help her to undress, and seldom saw her till she came down stairs. Her manner was reserved, but the Whoppliddians got used to her ways and liked her well enough. To look at her figure and bust you might have taken her for a married woman about forty, and then at times, when her features were at rest, she looked as though she might be sixty-five. This Madame Emma La Fargue professed to like Josiah Fetchem very much, and made Louisa Pantosniffle jealous of her influence. She had learnt ways of flirting while in France that were unknown to the untutured girls at Whopplidde-in-the-Fen. The Reverend Josiah paid attention to both ladies, but in a mild Platonic sort of way. You may imagine that his chronic visits were looked forward to with interest.

In person our Guinea Pig was not unlike a turtle raised on its hind legs. His complexion, men would have declared must have been copied from the lobster boiled; the ladies said no doubt it was the sun in travelling about. Josiah's skin was very tight. He looked as though he had been stuffed by steam, a sort of animated sausage filled by powerful hydraulic pressure till the merest trifle extra must have made it burst. The knowledge that he had three hundred pounds a year did not detract from our Josiah's charms. Oh, what a funny narcotizer Cupid is! Louisa Pantosniffle told her *confidante*, Miss Laura Miggs, that Fetchem was her idea of a cherubin. I wonder what this lady thought of Satan's personality.

CHAPTER LIX.

HOW THE GREAT WHOPPLIDDIANS DETERMINED THAT THE REVEREND JOSIAH FETCHEM SHOULD MARRY ONE OF THE LADIES OF THEIR PARISH, AND HOW BETS WERE ARRANGED ABOUT THE EVENT.

Now the great Whoppliddians had quite made up their minds that the Reverend Josiah must take one of their ladies as a wife. They had no doubt but that he would do so. And, your Worships and Reverences, do observe how that man is a gambling animal by nature, and reflect that if the Stock Exchange were pulled down to-morrow, he would still find means of gambling. Just as, from the peer to the coachman, everyone has a trifle on the result of what the Japanese ambassadors not inaptly termed "the *Great God Darbee*," so there were few of the Great Whoppliddians who had not backed according to their means the two favorites for the matrimonial event. Even the ladies had gloves depending on the issue. The odds were slightly in favor of Miss Louisa Pantosniffle, no doubt more because she occupied that "coign of vantage," the rectory itself, where the Whoppliddians' Benedict that was to be, ate, drank, and slept all through his stay. And this is no despicable advantage, this being in the same house with the man you want to marry. If there be the least *scintilla* of "affinity" in his composition, if he possess but a thirty-second or only an attenuated sixty-fourth of the necessary fractions of the unit of love, it must indeed be *gaucherie* that fails to successfully fan the same into a flame. I remember that Erasmus Pinto told several amatory applicants for shares in our great Matrimonial Alliance Association that if a cable could not be laid in half an hour at most between two persons of opposite sex in either of his halls, the parties might at once return home, quite satisfied that their "affinity" was not to be found that day. But of course there are drawbacks in a rectory; there is not quite the same freedom, as in the matrimonial halls, the same directness of purpose cannot be evinced, but a certain finesse and masking of batteries is often necessary from the obstructiveness of crass ordinary Grundyites, who take a malicious pleasure in seeing that the course of courtship is as rugged as it can be made.

I had a striking proof of the inestimable value of these Matrimonial Halls, from an incident that occurred the last time I was staying at the house of that excellent old-fashioned parson, St. John Thoresthorpe, of Great Gedneydake-cum-Sutterby le Marsh. He thought that it would promote a good understanding among the parishioners if he invited them indiscriminately to large Dorcas meetings, held in the evening, at which the ladies worked articles of clothing for the poor, and the gentlemen read to or decorously flirted with the ladies as they worked. I happened to be present when the first meeting was held, and, as will happen with English folk, there was a certain stiffness and awkwardness among the members of the large party assembled that threatened to mar the object in view, which was to make each class more cordial to each other class. As soon as St. John perceived this stiff reserve, he determined that it should be remedied, and hit upon an original expedient. The parsonage was a large old-fashioned building, full of holes, and cupboards, and corners, and dark attics. He at once, gifted with that infections cheeriness of manner and voice that some few privileged beings possess, proposed a game of hide and seek (not broker's hide and seek, dear "Outside Fools") in the parsonage itself, divided the parties himself, and conducted them to cover. Barbarous as this will doubtless seem to the languid clerical swell with a lisp, or the august dignitary who could scarcely survive such a desecration of his reverend person as hide and seek might bring, it answered admirably in our case, and the result was eminently satisfactory, for the ice of reserve was completely thawed by the free interchange of ideas, developed by the darkness so favorable to lay a cable in, and by the numerous convenient crannies of St. John's old house. It is on record that three couples were asked in church within a month after this happy idea had struck my worthy friend St. John. The reason no doubt was that the masculine portion of the party discovered in this one game of hide and seek that, after all, the Miss Chillies of the Grange had much the same inclinations and feelings at bottom as Jane Ruche, the village dress-maker, or merry little Emily Snart, the nursery governess, while the ladies were pleased to find that Captain Dragoman, who looked the swell all over, and Anthony Nowers, the young undergraduate staying at the parsonage, were quite as good at a game of romp in the dark as any boys let loose from schools. You may depend upon it that human nature is pretty much the same in the prince and the peasant, only the higher you go the less human nature you can afford to show, because all may be gained by acting and artifice, and all lost by candor and sincerity. Well, as I said above, among the great Whopplid-

M

dians the odds were rather in favor of Louisa Pantosniffle. On the other hand, a tenant farmer named Becuda Smales, alluding to the other favorite, Madame Emma La Fargue, said quaintly,—

"Our foreign madam has such ways o' looking at a chap as makes him think o' things."

This was the state of matters at the last visit of our Guinea Pig.

CHAPTER LX.

A DESCRIPTION OF CHURCH MUSIC AT GREAT WHOPPLIDDE-IN-THE-FEN, THE PARISH CLERK, AND THE RECTOR'S FAVORITE THEOLOGICAL WORKS.

THE church of St. Mary's was one of those old-fashioned Gothic buildings, still so often to be seen in country parishes. But if the church itself was old-fashioned, the church music was much more so. The absence of an organ was supplied by Captain Dudman, who operated on the violin; Becuda Smales, the above-mentioned farmer, who played the clarionet; Dr. Miggs, whose fancy was the ophicleide; and Mr. Barloe Healey, grocer, whose instrument was the bassoon. The parish clerk was quite a curiosity; his Christian name was Gad. His father had been sexton many years. The first year of his married life his wife had twins. The next she had also twins. The first arrival pleased the good man much. The second startled him, and being well read in Scripture lore, old Nathan Vessey said sententiously, "'A troop cometh.' The next arrival I shall christen *Gad*. Yes, be they twins or even triplets next time, they shall all be christened Gad." However, the next arrival was neither twins or triplets, but the normal unit, and Gad, in spite of clerical remonstrance, was the name the boy was christened by. When Gad became a youth, he cleaned the boots and shoes, and worked in the kitchen garden at the rectory. As time went on, he married Kitty Perke, the rector's housemaid, and became the coachman, living in a house close by the church, and when the parish clerk went to his rest, Gad Vessey was elected in his place.

This coachman-clerk was a curious original. His sanctimonious whine was wonderful. The only wonder is that Gad should have been born with such a tone. Had one not known his antecedents, one must have supposed the accent to be the result of evangelical instruction in some superior training school.

Here are some samples of Gad Vessey's renderings of passages in holy writ.

"He was alien to his mother's children" became this, "*He was a lion to his mother's children.*" "The great leviathan of the waters," with some deep poetic meaning he described as "*The great lieutenant of the waters.*" "Conies" he changed into "*kionies*" "Sennacherib," with reckless versatility, he rendered as if "*snatchacrab.*" But why go on? I've said enough to point the moral of my tale, and there is nothing written here, ye "Outside Fools," that has not some more meaning than to make you laugh. And if you think that this is fiction you're mistaken; it is fact, for fiction on these sacred matters is not pleasant to my mind. Gad Vessey's childlike confidence that what he said was right was most refreshing to behold. I feel convinced that he would soon have risen to fame, had but the manager of one of the new travelling companies to teach religion, and make people shake their sides with laughter at the actor's serio-comic style once heard him give some specimen of his abilities. No language can describe the man's "Amen." There was in it a strange *farrago* of hypocrisy, self-righteousness, resignation, pity for the lost. There was a sermon in Gad's rendering of that one word. But let us hope these scandals are fast passing into the limbo of oblivion. It's time they did.

The village boys sat in the middle aisle, and every now and then, when not engaged in struggling with his verbal enemies, with swift and stealthy movement, Gad would reach out a long stick kept in the desk in which he sat, and deal a stunning rap upon the pate of some unruly irreligious imp, whose thick head rang again. This mostly happened during the prayers.

Gad's master, as I said before, was a bookish man, who knew no more the way to deal with unconverted men than does a pig; indeed, he might have been defunct for all the good the parish got from him. Scarcely ever was he seen outside the rectory, and when at home he shut himself within his study, just as if the people and the place were quite beneath so great a man.

This pleased Dissent, which daily throve, and a new chapel had been lately built and some tradespeople left the church for it, for, as they said, the rector never spoke to them, nor noticed them at all, Dissenters certainly are wise to mingle with their people so. Thus at Great Whopplidde-in-the-Fen while the Reverend (I choose to call him so, although I don't belong to the Dissenters' sect) Winsole Easy was visiting the sick, and working hard to save, if not in the right way, yet with right will, the Reverend Jedediah Tring, forgetful of his flock, forgetful of his coachman-clerk, who wanted teaching English so, and heedless of the Reverend Winsole Easy's onward march, was poring over musty treatises, such as the learned *Misanthropicus Malignus* wrote, "*De Odio Theogorum Inter Se*," or such as that distinguished light of ancient days, *Blitomammas Bekkeselenus*, gave the unenlightened world, to wit, that ponderous tome that treats, "περὶ τῆς τοῦ Θεοῦ μόνης Ορθοδοξίας," or the more modern publications of Grammaticus Micrologoumenus on the "Divine Right of Creeds," or his very exhaustive and learned disquisition intituled, "*Caulium et Vitae Mendicorum Esurientium Comparatio*," and other valuable works, the best of which, to my thinking, is that well-known treatise on the "*Increasing Value of Turnips as Property*," which has lately so attracted the attention of the learned men. How could you in reason expect a man engaged in studying the noble works of these great pundits to devote his priceless time to correct the pronunciation of a coachman-clerk, to shaking hands with baker's or a grocer's wife, or check the insinuating progress of ridiculous irreverend Dissent.

CHAPTER LXI.

AN ACCOUNT OF THE CREED HELD BY THE RECTOR OF GREAT WHOPPLIDDE-IN-THE-FEN, AND HIS VIEWS ON THE TITLE "REVEREND."

THE Reverend Jedediah Tring's own creed was a sort of eclectic *farrago*, extracted from the creeds of the narrowest and most ascetic theologians, and it remorselessly consigned to perdition all those millions of impious heretics who allow that it is possible for any man, woman, or child to be saved, even if they do not hold strictly by one exact form of belief or ritual.

The reverend rector's creed, on the contrary, required that every man, woman, or child (the infants so to do through their duly appointed sponsors) should believe literally and in the strictest sense, without any evasion—so-called liberal interpretation of the spirit, or other damnable subterfuge of modern days—every word in both the Old and New Testament, that they should have expressed such belief openly in the presence of witnesses, and have been baptized according to the strict directions of the rubric, and that all infants who have come into the world and suddenly died before the rite of baptism has been performed are lost eternally. This worthy rector's creed further required professing Christians to believe it to be an heretical and apostate act entirely beyond Divine forgiveness to bury or inter in consecrated ground the body of any nonconformist or schismatic, for that such act doth not only imperil the immortal soul of those who bury or inter, but in all likelihood disturbs and desecrates the bodies of those true members of the church in proximity to whom the body of the said heretic or schismatic may be laid.

And, further, that the profane desecration of the holy and apostolic title *Reverend*, which is the rightful property of the orthodox alone, is a crime in a much greater degree, inasmuch as it doth tend, by the wide application of the title, to impair the veneration felt for, and, so to speak, the glorification of the person of those elect few on whose holy shoulders alone has fallen the mantle of the great apostle of the early church.

Now, was it likely that the Reverend Jedediah Tring, who held a creed like this, should care for simple Great Whoppliddian folk, or for the verbal acrobatic feats of Gad, his coachman-clerk, or for the vulgar doings of irreverend Dissent?

CHAPTER LXII.

THE REVEREND JOSIAH FETCHEM ARRIVES AT THE RECTORY OF GREAT WHOPPLIDDE-IN-THE-FEN WITH EMMA ON THE BRAIN—THE CRAVING FOR MYSTERY A PRIME CAUSE OF SPECULATION, THE SUCCESS OF QUACK MEDICINES.—THE DANGER OF THE STOCK AND SHARE LIST.

Now just at the time when our Guinea Pig bought his Emma shares, the rector had another attack of gout, and summoned him to do the duty as before, and further invited him to stay a week or a fortnight at the rectory. Josiah, who was in the city, telegraphed to say that he would reach Great Whopplidde in time for Sunday's services. Miss Pantosniffle donned, or, rather, I should say, was inserted, in her tightest, smartest, gayest, silken sheath, and rumor said that Madame Emma La Fargue had been shut closely in her room all Saturday forenoon with those mysterious boxes that came at times from Paris to her house.

On Saturday Josiah reached the rectory in time for tea. They did not dine late there, but generally at two o'clock. He was in spirits, as I dare say some of you, dear "Outside Fools," were when you made your first small profit upon 'Change, and thought what stupids brokers must all be to deal for clients when they might deal for themselves. Josiah left his Emma shares at 32, and looking firm. Alas! Satanic dragon sovereigns narcotized his holy mind. Be charitable, "Outside Fools." Poor human nature's very weak, whatever interested cant may say, and one small favorite weakness is that each fool thinks he's not so weak as any other fool.

Louisa Pantosniffle smirked and smiled upon *her* Fetchem, as she fondly thought, but he was unaccountably *distrait*. Poor fellow, he had Emma on the brain, and sadly missed his *Evening Standard* at Great Whopplidde-in-the-Fen.

Yes, very sweet to speculative human minds is the perusal of the stock and share list twice and sometimes thrice a day. Perhaps you don't see why. It's this. There always is a mystery that hovers round the ever-fluctuating prices of your bulls and bears. A speculator never feels that dull and leaden calm which many suffer from who know not what is meant by dealing for account. No *ennui* troubles speculators' minds. But just be careful, "Outside Country Fools," how ye devour the prices of that share list. We have funny ways of cooking it sometimes. I am desired to tell you this, for our honest members cannot bear the plan that holds. They call it nothing but a swindling trap. You clever "Outside Fools," would you not think that if you looked at nothing but the *business done* you must be safe? Of course you would think so. What innocence! Suppose we have some wares that do not sell, collusive bargains can be nominally made, and then reported in the "*Business done*," and this so-called official list investors act upon, because they have no other guide. The dealers give the prices for this list themselves, and their own interest of course induces them to suit the prices to their books. And so the price is quoted higher than it ought to be when we desire to sell, and lower than it ought to be when we desire to buy. But you may say, some would see through the trick and do the opposite. How many, pray? Of course we cannot nip an inclination in the bud. Oh, no! I know there's scarcely one Outsider whom old Seesaw could not indirectly urge to buy or put him off—induce to sell, or make him hold. Why, bless your innocence, what do you know of stocks, you "Outside Fools?" Do the directors give you information of their next half-year's campaign in Rails? What bills they may defer, and what crowd in to this account? Do we come out and let you know when everyone can see a certain stock is going to rise or fall? And that we can do, not so very seldom as you think. When suddenly four millions of fresh capital is

M*

wanted for a line, does that announcement come out vaguely and bang down the stock, or is a reassuring statement added to the declaration of the want? Does not, in nearly all these cases, first a fall occur, and then, when weak bulls have all sold, a rise ensue? Reflect, ye "Outside Fools," and catch the snarers thus. Buy when none else will buy, sell when none else will sell, see that ye operate in stocks that have backbone, no foreign I O U's will do.

Our system on the Stock Exchange is based upon this craving in the human breast for mystery which I alluded to above. Those strange philanthropists who oddly try to cope with over-population's growing ills trade on this craving for a mystery. The penny dreadfuls live upon this craving for a mystery. How grim the satire of the names quacks give their deadly opiates and filthy drugs. Oh, Science! oh, Philanthropy! are we to kill instead of hesitate to bring so many lives into the world?

Yes, it is mystery and misery combined these harpies trade upon. They puff their ghastly "*Infant Soothers and Preservers*" with impunity. The ghouls and slanderous scribblers who disgrace the pen by their attacks on persons in high places trade upon this craving for some mystery. A man who makes a fortune from his fellow-creatures' sufferings, well knowing how small aid his panaceas give, does nearly as much harm as does a great financing conjurer.

And gambling is the essence of all mystery.

Are we to blame the men? Not so, but legislate and educate. If one be tried without the other, it must fail. How puerile the Glasgow outbreak against gambling was. Those fond reformers seemed to think that simple legislation could put gambling down. Do those who howl so fiercely at our jobbing class think legislation can make us superfluous? And yet I do believe, though I'm not authorized to speak on this, that jobbers without brokers or brokers without jobbers would be quite enough. Again. The public ought to be allowed to see the purchases and sales, and not be often at the mercy of two gentlemen, who make the price between them and then share the difference.

Ye "Outside Fools," don't be deceived. My brothers of the "Inside House" would not have let me tell you this did they not now begin to see that these black sheep were killing by degrees the goose that lays the golden eggs.

The late revulsion in the public mind, through hearing strange dark hints of these tricks, and knowing not how far they may extend, together with the wholesale robbery of usurers, is making honest business less and less. The business now is most unsound. When I began, men used to deal in thousands, boys now deal in ten or twenty thousand at a time. We could then form some slight idea of value, and of when a rise should come and when a fall, and we could tell our clients something that was not all falsified within an hour. Now we are (that is the honest ones, not in the speculative swim) all at the mercy of the cliques, who spring their mines upon us with most startling suddenness, and when a stock should rise they make it fall, and when it ought to fall they make it rise. It is no pleasant business being dealer in the House if you are not dishonest now. If but the Glasgow brokers had empowered one of their own class to show where their own system was defective—to explain their intricate machinery, as I am authorized to try and do in London here, there would have been small need of legislation's aid. There are as many dirty tricks at Glasgow as there are with us. Yes, educate and legislate. The people's common sense, though greed of gain should try its best to deaden it, would show them that they must look out for other mysteries. Just so with nostrums and with quacks.

CHAPTER LXIII.

THE MAN TO BE DISTINGUISHED FROM THE GOOD HE DOES.—EGOTISM A FOE TO EDUCATION.—REMARKS ON SOCRATES.

WE have our Spelling Bees—why not establish Anti-Infant Soothing Bees, and Bees, where how the dice are cogged on 'Change is shown, and Bees where all the golden mystery of *MHΔEN AΓAN* is explained? And at these Bees blame not a single man. Attack the system and suggest reform, but don't try to persuade one class that it is so much better than another is, because it knows what others do not know. How fearfully has education suffered from this radical mistake! How much good is nipped in the bud because some attitudinizing fool will not dig out that *Ego* from his words and thoughts! The hearers often have a dim idea that what is said by him is true; but a resentful feeling rises in their breast to see his vanity, and so the man mars what he says, and they gain little truth instead of much. When will men learn that they are all but varieties of the unnumbered specimens that human nature has to show? Suppose his constitution, circumstances, or his style of mind induce and fit one of these specimens to teach his fellow-creatures something which 'twill do them good to learn—suppose no thought of money come into his mind—what then? It may be nothing but a hobby-horse—one of the many forms of necessary narcotism in this life. Society may well encourage such a specimen; but don't let prating fools talk loud about his moral excellence, and freely use superlative and vicious epithets which satire may sometimes employ for good, but never sober truth. Superlative in praise or blame does harm.

You've heard of Socrates? You might suppose a man possessed of all that wonderful philosophy could have been anything he liked. It was not so. He was unfit for any post in politics; he did not care for money, for he said, "Divinity requires nothing, and that wants least that comes the nearest to Divinity." But Socrates both liked a joke and glass, and would spend hours in arguing with anyone he met. And why? Because to teach was his, more than all other men's besides. He taught so well that it brought death to him. And what of that? it did good to unnumbered other men. Observe. God in this world, and doubtless in some other, has placed these rare specimens to keep the store of education growing gradually larger day by day, until each world is ready for its next great change, whenever God may will. "But," say you, "the same country that produced a Socrates is now more ignorant and false than then." And you may add that Socrates did no good to himself, and ask, "How, then, do these rare specimens of yours do good?" Ah! there is the mistake.

You think if one man has more knowledge than another, and because that knowledge is fresh power, he ought to use it so as to exalt himself. If he know anything worth much, he will do no such thing; why should he take to aping other specimens, instead of doing what he's fitted for himself? Why should he lose his happiness and rob the world of what small good he might have done to it? If taken on the lowest ground, this view of man is right. Who's so unhappy as the envious are? Who is more happy than a laborer who has his health and does a good day's work? Why do so many men get drunk when out on a day's pleasure, as 'tis falsely called? If they could analyze their secret motives they would find that often they're induced to take a gross narcotic to keep up the sham, and bring them down to the low level which the wretched votaries of so-called pleasure need. But to return. It matters not that countries once so highly civilized and so refined have sunk back into semi-barbarism. You must first prove that in the aggregate the world has not learnt more. And even the country that produced a Socrates, and was then in the zenith of its fame, was perhaps not *really educated* better than the other countries were, but only more *refined*. Though Socrates himself had found out what real education was, it does not follow that his countrymen had too. Indeed, their putting him to death is a good proof that they had not, for had they seen the truth they never would have done so foolishly. Refinement, the *belles lettres*, the study of abstruse and hidden subjects, the art and taste that form an appanage of luxury, are not the education that a nation wants. These studies should, undoubtedly, be ardently pursued by those few rarer specimens who are best fitted for the work, for they may find some germ of truth, although it's wonderful how little fresh truth we have learnt, that bears on life and death, on heaven and hell. A nation's education should be this—instruction in the relative value of all common things.

Mathematics, Greek, and Latin are all very well, especially the first; but when a man has learnt these thoroughly, he's only then just ready to supply a keener test to this comparative estimate of common things. A man is better able doubtless to explain and understand, and may discover something somewhat new after a training such as this, but is the game worth such expensive candles, and don't many turn out prigs? If the examiners for Indian appointments chose men who could do the papers fairly well, and ride, and shoot, and manage men with tact, in preference to those who only could do papers in a very clever way, our hold in India would perhaps be firmer than it is.

But to return. Though Greece has retrograded so, and though Jerusalem is now in Moslem hands, the truths which that strange Specimen, Socrates, taught Greece have been acquired by other countries in the world, and though the glory of Jerusalem be dimmed, no argument can prove the Christian teaching not to be the best as yet revealed to us. These views are not a broker's; they are those of my oft-quoted doctor, Sana Mens.

Return we to our Guinea Pig.

CHAPTER LXIV.

HOW TO ANGLE FOR AN AMATORY FOOL, AND MAKE A PRIGGISH RECTOR YOUR FAST FRIEND.

EMMA* was the subject of Josiah Fetchem's thoughts that evening at the rectory. Louisa Pantosniffle was disgusted and perplexed. All that elaborate silk sheath, so gay, so wonderfully planned and built by Messrs. Tricke and Trimme, the celebrated *artistes* to the Upper Ten, who can both fascinate and terrify all female snobs and make them spend as much as they can get, and often more, on dress, seemed likely to be wasted now. What could it mean? Josiah never was like this before. Had he some other flame? Vexed with these queries, which she could not answer, when the rector took up his work upon the—DE-SECRATED TITLE, "REVEREND"—and settled down to read it to his Guinea Pig, the plump and fair Louisa rose, and bade the gentlemen good-night.

Ye single ladies, take a hint. Louisa smiled a beamy smile upon Josiah as she said good-night—a smile full of intelligent appreciation, if not love—a sort of smile to make a man say as he was undressing, "A warm-hearted little thing is that Louisa, I believe she'd make a fellow a nice cheery wife."

Yes, marriageable spinsters, who would wed an Amatory Fool, don't be too chary of these beamy smiles. Indifference is love's worst enemy. Your

---

* The mine, not the lady, is of course meant.—*Erasmus Pinto.*

fish will think of that last smile at night, and very likely it will dream of you. And dreams awaken interest. And interest may soon turn into love. In angling for an Amatory Fool, the first great step is this, to stir him from his hole of calm indifference. When they were left alone, the rector droned along for a good hour, explained what was quite clear, and criticized imaginary difficulties, and, in short, so talked at Fetchem that at last he was obliged to stop through want of breath.

Ye Guinea Pigs, if you would make a priggish rector your fast friend, go listen to his muddled lucubrations cheerfully, and when you can, discreetly praise. Suppose your learned lecturer should flag, just differ on some trivial point, but differ only to give way with facile grace. A still tongue in a careful listener, combined with aptitude for clever flattery, and a creed that changes on the minor parts to suit the hearer and the place, has often changed a Guinea Pig into a Dean.

CHAPTER LXV.

THE REVEREND JOSIAH FETCHEM HAS A VERY CURIOUS DREAM.

JOSIAH FETCHEM went to bed. And still his Emma was the subject of his thoughts. After one half-hour's pleasant musing, during which, I grieve to say, Louisa Pantosniffle was not thought of once, he fell asleep. His dreams, like our "society," were just a little "mixed."

At first Josiah dreamt that he went down into a

yawning fissure in a foreign mountain capped with snow. The chasm was of awful depth. Within its caverns twenty-thousand men were piling silver ore in heaps and grinning horribly while at their work. A thousand trucks kept running past Josiah's gaze all filled with virgin silver ore. Why did they grin? he thought.

The scene now changed to a vast theatre. A play was being acted on a stage. This was the title on the bills, "HONESTY and HONOR are worth more than GOLD." The actors played their parts so well that the vast audience rose to a man, and clapped their hands with admiration and delight. Their playing struck a chord which was not dumb though dull through want of use. The curtain fell.

It rose once more. The world-famed Brothers Gotthemtite appeared with acrobatic feats and juggling tricks. At first the audience seemed listless and unmoved. But when the elder Gotthemtite made those Satanic dragon sovereigns, cheques and notes float through the air and almost touch the hands of those who sat in the front seats—when now the orchestra, as the baronial leader waved his magic wand, struck up that well known operatic air, "L'ARGENT REINE DU MONDE," up sprang with one accord the presidents and senators, ambassadors and members, and each one tried with frantic efforts to secure the dancing coins, the floating cheques and notes. More fast and furious played the orchestra, more wildly the conductor waved his wand, more frantically did those in the front seats grasp, and rush, and struggle, until many fell through sheer exhaustion, and a few were even crushed to death. Those in the gallery and pit howled like wild beasts with baffled rage, to think they were not near the coins, and cheques, and notes. They were railed off with iron rails from them.

Again the scene was changed. Madame Emma La Fargue appeared to Fetchem as he slept. The same Satanic sovereigns, each with a grinning evil face upon them stamped, danced all around her form. She, with alluring look and winning accent, seemed to say, "I give you these, Josiah, for your love."

Josiah Fetchem dreamt no more, but slept a heavy sleep.

CHAPTER LXVI.

TREATING OF THE THREE ODORS PECULIAR TO RELIGIOUS SECTS.

UPON the Sunday morning, about nine o'clock, Josiah woke. He felt like one who had drunk deeply of strong drink, or taken a large dose of opium. Had it not been for duty he would not have risen. He felt so enervated and so heavy in the head. No wonder, after what the man had seen. But he remembered nothing of his dream except that part relating to the twenty thousand men and thousand silver-laden trucks within the wondrous Emma mine. He positively gasped with his emotion when he thought of this stupendous wealth. With automatic habit, though he felt so dazed and tired with this cerebral excitement, he began to don his *reverend* clothes. Don't smile, dear Outside Fools, the epithet is right enough. But I will give you my authority. It is the Reverend Jedediah Tring's own latest work. "The DESECRATED TITLE REVEREND."

That work, alas! that did Josiah such small good

the night before his dream. This learned book thus lucidly explains my epithet.

"And further, let it be well known to all these godless desecrators of titles, tombstones, and graveyards, and to those impious heretics who would reduce those few elect apostles of the one true church, to wit :—Your Lordships and your humble servants, like myself, who are in name, and deed, and person truly *Reverend*, to the low level of an ordinary man, —that not only are the persons, acts, and thoughts of these holy apostles themselves *Reverend*, but that all their sacerdotal symbols, accessories, and vestments are *Reverend* in the same degree. And I would venture to assert, with all due submission to your Lordships, that the very coats, vests, breeches, head-gear, and other articles of dress belonging to these holy pillars of the Church, the true salt of the earth, without whom it would soon become corrupt, do contain within them that rare and peculiar odor by which, as though by a masonic sign, the elect alone are distinguished from all other men and known to one another. This odor of sanctity, your Lordships, I term ὀδμὴ θεόσυτος,' and this divine odor I should recognize myself, though it were dark. And I hold, on the contrary, that in or around all the coats, vests, breeches, head-gear and other articles of apparel with which those enemies of the true faith do clothe their godless bodies, there will ever be found a truly Satanic odor, differing completely from the *Reverend* and savory smell of the afore-mentioned holy apostles, and this I term ὀδμὴ βρότειος.

"There is yet another odor which I propose to apply to those men who are very near to us in creed and seem to wish.us well, and this I term the ὀδμὴ κεκραμένη, which, though very far removed from the θεόσυτος, is yet somewhat better than the βρότειος ὀδμή.

"The first named odor belongs exclusively to your Lordships, and such of your humble servants who, like myself, hold the one true orthodox and strict creed.

"The second applies to all those insidious enemies of the church who, to my thinking, are far more dangerous than the Mahometan infidel, who, has at all events, paid a liberal rate of interest to many good and holy apostles of the true faith, and does not profess to be more than an infidel. I mean the Broad Church and the High Church, the Recreative Religionists, the Peculiar People, the Independents, the Christadelphians, the Eclectics, the Progressionists, the Christian Eliasites, the Free Grace Christians, the Spiritualists, the Humanitarians, the Swedenborgians, the Free Christians, the Reform Glory Band, the Protestants who reject Ritual, the Free Grace Gospel Christians, the Independent Religious Reformers, the Separatists, the Unitarians, the Advents, the Apostolics, the Christian Israelites, the Glassites, the Inghamites, the Quakers, the Ranters, the Ritualists, the Reformers, the Calvinists, Arminians, and Moravians, and the Nonconformists too numerous to mention here.

"The third odor I have sometimes thought I have perceived in certain of the Wesleyans and Wesleyan Methodists, the Evangelical Dissenters, and here and there a Revivalist, who have all shown your humble servant great respect on all occasions that have offered; but I humbly ask your Lordship's advice as to this uncertain odor, seeing that I am but as a farthing rushlight to the sun compared with your Lordships."

There, my dear "Outside Fools," I think I have quoted sufficiently from the treatise of this prosy and long-winded ecclesiastical pundit, who goes on anathematizing all other *doxies* but his own, and kissing their Lordships' hands for 470 pages of close print. Faugh! the book itself has the odor of sanctity too strong for my nerves.

Now if any captious critic should venture to affirm that the true and *Reverend* apostle cannot scent the presence or approach of a brother-apostle, who is also worthy of the priceless title of *Reverend*, or if such critic or late learned sciolist should rashly declare that it is impossible to distinguish the two odors, to wit, the θεόσυτος ὀδμή and the κεκραμένη ὀδμή, by their different degrees of sanctity, or to recognise through the agency of this keen religious scent (which is in most cases further aided by the stimulating influence of the *Odium Theologicum*) the presence or approach of that grosser carnal odor of the heretic, the ὀδμή βρότειος, which is in unsanctified rankness as the pungent smell of the negro to the civilized perfume of the European, such critic or sciolist must be an unlettered, unimaginative dolt.

However dark the night may be, no less an authority than Humbolt assures us that the Indians of Peru can distinguish the approach of a stranger, even though he be far away, and can readily determine whether he be a European, Indian, or Blackamoor. If, then, the untutored savage can with such unerring perception distinguish, even from a distance and in the gloom of night, the odor of those different races, with no *Odium Theologicum* to assist his natural instinct, has civilisation, has the learning of the great divines not taught a holy man to know his brother by the odorous sign? can he not tell, though pricked by *Odium's* goad, the evil-smelling heretic, or diagnose that fainter odor which is "just a little mixed?" Go to, I will not waste my words upon such unbelieving critics. Why, such men would never know a nigger from a holy man by scent.

I suppose you will allow that I have now ample authority to apply the term *Reverend* to the breeches of the Rev. Josiah Fetchem. Let us see. We left him putting them on while musing still upon the wonders of his darling Emma's wealth. Said he, while bracing up the ὀδμὴ θεόυντος to its proper height,—

"I really think I shall turn optimist. It is the most astounding proof of human nature's goodness that I've ever seen, nor would I have believed, had not the dividends been paid, that keen Americans would have transferred to Britishers for such a sum an Eldorado like to this. Emma, Emma, there is something in the name; I always did think trochees very pleasing to the ear."

Has Josiah got his reverend breeches on? Madam, the odor of sanctity is now braced up. Indeed he has put all his reverend vestments on, and is now going down the stairs.

CHAPTER LXVII.

TREATING OF HABITS, SECONDARY AUTOMATISM AND THE ASSERTION OF PHILOSOPHERS THAT "WHEN THE SUM OF THE CONDITIONS OF A CASE ARE KNOWN THE RESULT CAN BE PREDICTED WITH CERTAINTY."

'Tis Aristotle, I believe, who says that a habit is only a series of acts. If this be true, which there cannot be the slightest reason to doubt, the Reverend Josiah Fetchem had acquired a fresh habit. By a rapid series of repeated blows of thought he had so hammered the word *Emma* upon the anvil of his brain that it was there stereotyped as firmly as a shoe is impressed upon a horse's hoof when affixed by a clever blacksmith. Observe, philosophers, how wonderful the power of money is. Josiah's new habit of thinking of Emma had disregarded the rules of science, which forbid any unseemly or abnormal celerity in the acquisition of habits, and, under the stimulating influence of the *Root of Evil*, had actually passed into the stage of *Secondary Automatism*, which in intensity and strength of influence upon the man was little short of *Congenital Automatism* itself.

Now I doubt not but that your Worships and your Reverences have frequently observed how, in the process of taking a constitutional, you will often walk over the ground you are used to, without either heeding your progress much or exercising any appreciable mental effort during your perambulations.

It is not unfrequently so with a parson in reading

the prayers. If his body or mind, or both, happen to be abnormally wearied, he becomes for the time being a devout automaton, and as the volition and the cerebral organs are, so to speak, in a state of *automatic narcotism*, the *afferent* nerves convey without mental aid the necessary stimulus through the spinal cord to the *referent* nerves, and the result is, your Worships, and your Reverences, that the prayers are read. You are doubtless aware that certain heretical philosophers have asserted that, "*When the sum of the conditions of any case be known, the result can be predicted with certainty.*" This inference is true enough, as your Worships will doubtless allow. But in *what* case is the "*sum of the conditions*" sufficiently known by a mortal man, so as to confidently predict the result? If there be any such cases it certainly is when a client begins to deal with a broker on 'Change. Arguing from Experience, which I suppose is Reason—seeing that if you showed a broker's infant child at the very instant when it began to notice anything for the first time, half-a-crown, it must inevitably expect to see, from its experience of what it had seen, nothing more or less than another half-crown—so arguing, I say, we might certainly, with as much justice assume that we knew the "*sum of the conditions*" in the client's case, and could therefore confidently predict the result, viz., ruin, as these heretical philosophers can assume that it is possible for a human being himself to know, or for other human beings to know with regard to him, that he is predestined or predetermined to be saved or lost. I can assure your Worships and your Reverences that we brokers and jobbers watch these important philosophical speculations with the deepest interest, for if we can once regard ourselves as simple machines, and accept the proposition that every client who deals with us is predestined and predetermined to lose his money, and that we are predestined and predetermined to be the instruments through which he loses it, a load will be removed from our consciences, seeing that all trifling distinctions between right and wrong will vanish as smoke, and we shall, with our hats stuck well at the back of our heads, continue to clean out our clients with automatic indifference and content, and shall be freed from that fear of the hostile designs of Sir Henry James which we, in common with the speculative members of parliament, have felt for some time past in no small degree.

One thing I am sure of. Aristotle's series of acts with all of us has long since become a habit. This habit, in the case of most of us, has been constitutionally transmitted from father to son until it has become no longer *secondary*, but *congenital* automatism.

We, therefore, in all justice, cannot be so much to blame as a man would be who began to clean out clients before he had passed from the stage of acquired or secondary into the stage of original or congenital automatism.

But, your Reverences, the thinking portion of our community declare that they are quite unable at present to get rid of this disagreeable moral responsibility, and they can see no convincing evidence yet adduced by these heretical philosophers, which proves that this "*sum of the conditions of any case*" is ever completely known by the finite creature called man, be he a broker or a philosopher.

CHAPTER LXVIII.

A PHILOSOPHICAL DISCUSSION BETWEEN NATHANIEL SEESAW, REGINALD MEEKIN, AND DR. SANA MENS.

I WILL just relate the conversation that passed between Dr. Sana Mens and Reginald Meekin, of our set, on this important point, which I myself took part in. Mens is a man of fair average health, and great logical power. Meekin has a wonderful physique, and both from constitution and profession is a man of action rather than thought.

"My dear Mens," said Meekin, "there can be no doubt at all, in the case of 'Outside Speculators,' that what your philosopher terms '*the sum of the conditions*' is completely known by us, and that being so, of course such speculators are predestined to lose their money. Our system never fails.

" Its machinery is mathematically adjusted, silent, and to a great extent, unseen in its working, for it is the elaborate and complete production of many brilliant and logical minds in many ages, minds stimulated to exertion by that greatest principle of action *desire to gain or keep*, and every individual speculator has to contend unaided against this magnificent and perfect system, besides being most materially and in many ways invisibly hindered and hampered by his dealing and broking agents, by the second-hand gabble of his fellow-speculators, the interested lies given to touts by financiers, and the planned and garbled statements of the money articles in the newspapers, and, lastly, by the fact that he pretends to be, say, for example, a shoemaker, and competes with skilled shoemakers, though he does not know the proper use of leather, knife, or last. And, more, he is not able to get the knowledge if he would, for we shoemakers on 'Change take care that none shall lift the curtain that conceals our cobbling tricks, the pall that hides our inside mysteries. On speculation's chess-board we know what the public's moves will be. They don't know ours. That makes all the difference. The moment that we find the public (not the strong financial clique) has done one thing much, we do the opposite. If they did right, we should do wrong. But our wrong would make money, and their right would not. Of course I'm talking of the majority, and not the few. The thing's as plain, old man," said Meekin, "as the nose upon your face, and goodness knows I might see that full half a mile away on a straight road and a fine day."

That Reggy Meekin could not do without his joke, and certainly he had a nose, a very large, sagacious, and assertive nose.

"Your inference is quite correct," said Sana Mens, "and so is the philosopher's; but how about the premises? I grant you that speculators are more likely to lose on 'Change than you or I to fail to get to heaven; but that is not enough. You must prove incontestably that '*the sum of conditions*' is completely known to you, or to your clients, or to both, before you can assert correctly that *you* know that *they* are predestined to be ruined, or that *they* know themselves to be predestined so."

"And have I not proved this?" said Meekin to his friend.

"Indeed you've not," said Sana Mens. "Will you

allow that, of one thousand clients, one may die before he is 'cleaned out,' as you would say?"

"Of course I will."

"Will you allow that one may, through a long experience, unusual opportunities to learn, or being by his constitution rogue and cheat, see through the plan sufficiently to keep away or imitate our way of dealing so as to make something, or, at all events, not lose."

"Why, yes, I must grant that."

"Then, my dear Meekin, though it may be true that scarcely one escapes, still you do *not* completely know this '*sum of the conditions*' in the case, and so you can *not* predicate of any single client that he is either predestined to be ruined or escape."

"Well, now, that's very odd," said Meekin. "What you say seems true, and yet it ought not to be true. Proceed, perhaps I shall see better soon." .

"We said above, that it was much more likely that a broker's client should lose all on 'Change than that either you or I should lose our chance of heaven, did we not?"

"We did."

"'*The sum of the conditions*,' then, is harder to discover in the latter case. Is that not so?"

"It is."

"Suppose you saw a man going quickly to the bad, through drink, or dice, or crime, could you assert that he would not reform?"

"I should not think he would."

"That's not enough. Could you declare that he would not."

"Well, no, I do not think I could."

"Suppose a man should say, 'I am an atheist,'

could you positively affirm with truth that he believes the words he speaks?"

"I do not think I could; for men who simply don't believe in one set creed, have said that they were atheists."

"I think this term is loosely used for *Deist*, or for *Pantheist*, and that these self-styled 'atheists' are but Dissenters in some other form, however odd that form may be, and however little recognized, because there are so few belonging to that form. At bottom, whether the first motive be a superstitious fear or a blind faith, each human being who is sane believes in something stronger than himself, and that is God in some one of the unnumbered forms and ideas of God there are to suit the different minds, just as the Evil One will take unnumbered shapes to suit each man's idea of what a Satan's personality should be. There is *some* good in all beliefs. By far the best is that of Christians who interpret what the Bible says with charity. But atheists cannot have a belief. I never will believe that there has lived an atheist who was both sane and honest when he styled himself an *atheist*. And even granting that a man's an atheist, can you affirm that he will die an atheist?"

"Oh! no."

"Have you not seen men in good health with strong convictions and strong prejudices, who when they have lost their health, or undergone a course of lowering medicine, have altered those convictions and got rid of their strong prejudices, even if they have adopted other ones?"

"I often have; but never thought about it much."

"Then any human being *may* so change in body,

thoughts, and acts that no one can affirm at any period of his life that he correctly knows '*the sum of the conditions*' with reference to that being?"

"This would seem to be the case."

"And can you tell when any human being is to die?"

"Why do you ask? Of course I cannot tell."

"Then, my dear Meekin, there is no philosopher alive, there never has lived one, who has the right to say that any human being is predestined to be saved or lost.

"As for the probability of this or that, it's nothing to the point. God never made one fool a judge of other fools' first motives and morality; that is between their conscience and their God. I challenge and defy philosophers to prove that in one single case they do completely know '*the sum of the conditions*,' as their language has the term, that's requisite to draw conclusions so untenable and dangerous. And if they cannot prove this thing, what right have they to trouble weaker minds with doubt? What right to try and pull an admirable fabric down, and build none other up? It is a burning shame that Science and so-called Philosophy should idly speculate and attitudinize to gain applause, instead of working honestly to illustrate what is. 'Whatever is, is right,' to-day. To-morrow the improved '*whatever is*, is right' and only needs explaining more, and this should be man's aim, to make it clear."

"But, Sana Mens," said Meekin, "though a broker cannot get '*the sum of the conditions*' requisite to predicate the certain ruin of a client, and although philosophers cannot affirm with certainty that one man is predestined to be saved, another to be lost, cannot a client tell himself that he is so predestined, and cannot man's inner consciousness enable man to say, ' I am predestined to be lost or saved ? ' "

"Well, let us see," said Sana Mens; "this must be sifted carefully. Books do not help us here. Why do your clients speculate, Nathaniel Seesaw ?" said he, turning towards me.

" Because they like it, I suppose," said I.

"That is too general; besides, it is no reason really."

"You give your reasons," I replied, to Sana Mens, "and I and Meekin will correct you when we think you're wrong."

" Well, I will try. Old Horace says philosophers are the best workmen at all trades, and so, by arguing on, they're kings. I wish that Horace was alive; I warrant if he tried that theory on ' Change he'd say it was a fallacy before a year was past. However, I will do my best.

" 1. Man is a gambling animal. Life has itself a gambling element, though slight to those who think and work ; but still it has the element, and rightly so, because this world is not the only world we have to live in, in a state of misery or happiness ; what seems incongruous in this world will seem all right in the world to come.

" 2. Man craves for mystery, or if he do not, then he dies, for all is clear to one who has no craving of that sort.

" 3. Man likes excitement. His physical condition often is the stronger cause of this, especially in nervo-bilious temperaments, and when there's fog and damp about.

" 4. Man is allured by greed of gain.

"5. And man is vain, and fain would seem more clever than his fellow-man.

"6. Man is gregarious and proud, and dearly loves to mix with bigger men."

"But will these reasons do? They are all true enough," we both replied.

"Well now, my friends, I hold that ignorance is vice, up to a great extent; and do you think, pray, that your clients would keep speculating on if they once know '*the sum of the conditions*' of which their speculation is but the result?"

"By heaven, I think they would be scared away as crows at sight of gun," said I.

"Most would give up, no doubt," said Meekin; "common sense would save their purse."

"Then no client can say, 'I am predestined to be ruined upon 'Change,'" said Sana Mens. "Just as in racing, one alone can win, but still all hope to win, and hug the narcotizing hope, so in the game of speculation, although scarcely one may win, unless he be a rogue behind the scenes, or have so much that he can influence markets by his capital, still each thinks he may be that one, and none can prove he may not be. All human weakness, ignorance, and vice, conspire to make him think he may prove the exception to the rule. And this is why, though legislation may reform and circumscribe the area of chicanery, it will be powerless to do much good. The cards will but be dealt and shuffled in another way. Nor are the men who deal and shuffle so much more to blame than those who play with them. There is no cure for speculation, never will be while the world is what it is. But much may still be done to stay the spread of speculation, and the fearful losses that are made, if the public will but learn and think, and not act blindly like insensate fools. But if they read no books but novels that contain adultery and bigamy, and mystery, and slander, all combined, there's nothing to be done but wait. God always cures ills in His own time. But to return. We've shown that broker's clients cannot truly say themselves that they are predetermined to be ruined on 'Change?'"

"We have," we both replied.

"And we have further shown that no philosopher can truly say of any man, 'I have "*the sum of the conditions*" requisite to tell that you are predetermined and predestined to be lost or saved.'"

"We have," said we.

"Now let us, lastly, see if man can ever get sufficient knowledge of '*the sum of the conditions*' to assert with truth, about himself, 'I shall be saved, or I shall not be saved.'"

"We both have heard men say so of themselves," said we to Sana Mens, "and men have their own conscience to assist them to obtain this knowledge of themselves, while the philosopher has no such aid to guide him in his efforts to obtain this knowledge of another man."

"They have a better chance than the philosopher," said Sana Mens; "but is it good enough? You know these words, 'Whom HE did foreknow, him he did predestinate.'"

"We do," we both replied.

"Does man foreknow what he shall do, or think, or say next month or year?"

"He does not," we replied.

"Does not his body change with exercise or rest,

with sickness and with health, and does not his mind alter much with all these agencies?"

"It does," we both rejoined.

"May not man's conscience tell a man at one time that one course is right, and at another that a different one is right?"

"We do not think it likely," we replied, "but still it *may*."

"The possibility is quite sufficient for my argument," said Sana Mens. "Then, though man's conscience said to man, 'You are predestined to be saved or lost,' he must not trust to it in *that* respect. His conscience, like his body and his mind, may change with further light."

"It seems so," we replied.

"Then, my dear friends," said Sana Mens, "if man does not and cannot *foreknow* what he is going to do, or think, or say next month or year, and if he cannot trust his conscience on this one point, because it, like his body and his mind, may change, *a fortiori* can man *not* foreknow that he is predetermined or predestined to be lost or saved."

"He cannot from our argument," said we.

"But, Sana Mens," said Meekin, "do not men more often say that GOD and not that they themselves foreknow that they are predetermined or predestinated to be lost or saved?"

"They do," said Sana Mens; "God has predestinated all to be condemned or saved. What then?"

"Why, this," said Meekin; "it takes away free agency if God has predetermined and predestinated what man's fate must be. And so it is, some men give up all thought about a future state, because, say they, it makes no difference what we may do to the result."

"Well, let us sift this argument," said Sana Mens. We have already proved that God foreknows, but that man does not foreknow."

"We have."

"We have already proved that man can never gain sufficient knowledge of '*the sum of the conditions*' requisite to say correctly, 'The result is that I shall be saved, not lost,' or, 'The result is that I shall be lost, not saved.'

"We have."

"Then all the knowledge man can hope to gain of this is this one fact, that God foreknows if man is to be saved or lost."

"It is."

"Then man has not the smallest right to say, 'It makes no difference how I may act.'

"God does not tell him which fate his must be. God does not give him any means of knowing which it is to be.

"And yet man dares to assume an attribute of God and say, 'I am *saved*, or I am *lost*,' just because God knows that he is one or the other.

"God's foreknowledge does not take away man's free agency.

"He voluntarily surrenders it himself when he asserts without a warrant that he is—not *either saved or lost*—for there would be no harm in that, but that he knows he will be *saved*, not lost, or that he knows that he will be *lost*, not saved.

"The moment he makes this unwarrantable choice, trying to draw a warrant from God's foreknowledge, man voluntarily surrenders his free agency, and God does not take it away.

"My friends, we may safely assert that no broker

can predict with truth, '*That client will be ruined;*' that no client can predict of himself with truth, '*I shall be ruined;*' that no philosopher can say, '" *I have the sum of the conditions*" requisite to correctly predict this man's future;' or that a man can correctly say of himself, '" *I have the sum of the conditions*" requisite to predict with truth whether I shall be saved, not lost, or lost, not saved.'

" Let a man have faith that he *may* be saved, and work hard to see that he *is* saved, for that is the only way to have any chance. These quibbles about phrases and words will never help him on the road to heaven."

" Well, I believe that's true," we both replied. And so our dialogue came to its end.

CHAPTER LXIX.

CONTAINING APOLOGIES TO THE READER AND A VERITABLE HISTORY OF THE STARTLING EFFECTS OF CONGENITAL AUTOMATISM UPON A DOGMATIC BRIDEGROOM AND A SCIENTIFIC BRIDE.

My dear " Outside Fools," and more particularly my fair readers, if I should have the luck to find any, accept my apologies for the sermonizing you have had to listen to ever since our Josiah had that curious dream. On my honor as a broker there was no help for it.

Both I and Reginald Meekin knew what we had to expect when we went to dinner with Sana Mens, at whose house all the sermonizing took place. He loves his fellow-creatures, I am sure, does Sana.

Mens, but I believe that he loves an argument better. Once get him started on a topic where there is room for original views, and he will go on without stopping for a week or more, just as an eight-day clock without winding up. Sana Mens always seems to me to be wound up. Yes, madam, and nearly always ready to strike. The "Madam" referred to here, my critical friends, is Mrs. Curiosa Sciolist, who, as well as Mrs. Sana Mens, was a listener to our discussion.

The only remark Mrs. Sana Mens, who is an admirable wife, and foolishly believes that women are more happy when the grey mare is *not* the better horse, was this. She said,—

"I am quite sure that reason has nothing to do with speculation, Mr. Seesaw, and I always told my husband so, when he would dabble a bit, fancying logic would help him, for, as you say, the pieces are often moved on the chess-board of speculation in an illogical way on purpose to catch the ' Outside Fools.' I could not express this in words, but I had an instinct that it was so."

"Yes, madam," said I "the instincts of your sex are often nearer to the point than the reason of ours."

Madam Curiosa Sciolist, who is a widow, and staying with Dr. Sana Mens for treatment is an advanced believer in "*Woman's Rights*," longs for a vote, has already discarded the petticoat, and will often sorely puzzle Dr. Sana Mens himself in argument. It is on record that on the day when she was married to Septimus Sciolist, Esq., M.A., A.S.S. whose name often appeared on the prospectuses of some of the minor joint stock companies of the day for a consideration, when they had dined at their hotel at

Dover, which place the god Hymen had selected for the consummation of his rites, after an excellent dinner, and when now it was time that they should retire, and bethink them of the main business for which the holy rite of matrimony was chiefly ordained, Sciolist, with the best possible intentions, thinking it to be, as he afterwards told me, over a glass of wine, a graceful piece of strategy, made this remark,—

"My darling Curiosa, you must be tired to death. Go to bed, there's a love."

I give you my honor, ladies, it was nothing but one of society's little subterfuges, a sheltering phrase to cover a virgin modesty and give the bride the opportunity to avoid saying, "I want to go to bed."

Of course, if Jane Smith should marry Richard Hodge, there is no need of any subterfuge or finesse, for nature is not trammelled by art or fashion, and so the business is easily concluded.

But it was very different in the case of the Sciolists. They moved in very good society. The fashionable world had its eye upon their movements, and before Curiosa Hairsplitte, to the wonder of her female friends and admirers, had deigned to wed her Septimus, she had been looked upon as the coming champion of the rights of her sex.

Indeed she had a sense of degradation upon her even on the wedding-day, a feeling that she was a renegade to her supporters for having so tamely made this very important concession to man's supremacy.

No doubt, my fair readers, it was not this simple remark alone, nor even its slightly dictatorial character, that roused the argumentative and combative qualities of Curiosa's mind; but, as philosophers would say, her mental *passivity*, of which she was unconscious, manifested itself by effects of which she was conscious. And so was Septimus ere long. So instead of retiring, as you and I, madam, would have supposed she would readily have done, her mental passivity, having suddenly become active, made her say, " I am not the least tired, Septimus, thank you."

Now Septimus Sciolist was an M.A. and A.S.S., besides being possessed of other honorable titles of distinction too numerous to mention, and, alas, like many others who may append an M.A. and A.S.S. to their names with perfect justice, he was dogmatic.

Instead, therefore, of discreetly waiting for events to unfold themselves easily, as no doubt they would have done—instead of giving his bride a loving embrace, as a newly-wed M.A. ought to have done, and holding his tongue, our bridegroom must needs rejoin, with that dogmatic tone with which I do believe that each corporeal particle of his whole frame was tainted, " Curiosa, you *must* be tired, your eyes are half shut now."

Now, observe, my dear readers, this was the second time that Septimus Sciolist, Esq., M.A., A.S.S., had made use of the word *must* to his scientific bride. The repetition of that word *must* would have been trying to any unscientific lady who was not a champion of her sex's rights, but it instantly and completely banished any lurking *passivity* of which the fair Curiosa might have been still unconscious.

With eyes by no means *half-shut*, but wider open than was good for their beauty of expression, and in the lively tones that are appropriate to positive *Mental Activity*, she exclaimed,—

"I tell you, Septimus, I am *not* tired in the least, nor did I deign to marry to be dictated to."

"My dear Curiosa," replied the bridegroom, "I did not mean to dictate (and here the devil or the dogmatic corporeal particles tempted him to add), although, if you come to argue the matter, the wife is bound to obey her husband, in all reasonable matters such as these."

"Such as what?"

"Madam! I beg you will not interrupt me. Have patience."

The only chance of peace was destroyed by this last unfortunate remark. Curiosa Sciolist was again in imagination Curiosa Hairsplitte, and she at once brought to bear all the logic, rhetoric, syllogisms, enthymemes, similes, metaphors, tropes, arguments, and all other weapons which the now-awakened *Mental Activity* had at its command to demolish that heretical notion of feminine submission to which our sex so fondly clings. Septimus, on the other hand, called forth all the *Latency* of his mental and corporeal dogmatic particles, and as the belligerents were worthy of each other's steel, the battle raged with alternating fortune, and with not a sign of either champion giving in. They kept it up with most unflagging spirit till the clock struck three. The waiter, thinking something must be wrong, tapped at the door, and from the excited looks of both belligerents, he thought the row was serious, or else they were both lunatics. They neither of them knew how loud their voices were. This calmed the bridegroom, who began to feel ashamed. Dismissing the waiter with some lame excuse, he went to bed without another word. His bride in dudgeon sate there still, dissatisfied, and feeling that, at all events, she had not gained more than she had already lost. And still her pride kept her upon her lonely chair, until the gas went out, and till the chambermaid, with candle in hand, said, "Would not madam like to go to bed?"

She went; there was no help for it, or else she would have stayed up all the night. She found that her dogmatic lord had gone to sleep.

Still vowing, "I will not *submit* unless he owns he was wrong," the beauteous Curiosa laid aside her robes.

Don't start, ye prudish, canting, hypocritical, immodest, and immoral "Outside Fools." It is not I, but ye, who are indelicate, and as for Mrs. Grundy let her get to heaven if she can. There's nothing to conceal. The beauteous Curiosa laid aside her robes. Had her dogmatic lord not been asleep he might have seen—a woman, that is all. And what are you, pray, Miss Demure? It's not my fault if you are not a woman too. A woman now-a-days looks sometimes more indecent when she's dressed. Ah! don't you know that woman is the sweetest mystery of all the many mysteries in life? But if you ladies will dress so, she'll soon not be a mystery at all.

The beauteous Curiosa laid her down to rest. Her Septimus awoke. She vowed, "I never will submit," and while she still was vowing, had submitted to her Septimus. Philosophers, ye are right here. *Congenital Automatism* conquered both the champion of Dogma and of Woman's Rights, and, I rejoice to say, proved this, that nature still can hold her own against the philosophic mists and barren theories that now perplex men's brains. Ye scientific maidens, do not trifle with these mysteries. Submission in this case, observe, came rather late. And the insulted god of marriage vowed he'd be revenged. The Sciolists were bound to Paris the next day. What with Science, and the Dogma, and the late submission, both the combatants were very weary when the time to cross the channel came, although they both were quite at home now with each other, and each tried to gratify the other's slightest wish.

But Hymen vowed he'd be revenged, and Æolus conspired. It was a breeze when they first started, but it soon became a gale. Our Master of Arts was standing upon deck, not feeling quite himself, nad holding in his hand a glass containing S. and B. Behind him stood a short and puffy gentleman. Both gentlemen were back to back, and Septimus was tall—the puffy, as I said, was short. The vessel gave a heavy luch, just as our friend was going to drink. Backwards he fell, and raising up the still full glass in vain attempt to save himself, the contents were shot down the neck of the short puffy gentleman, who stood behind, and passed out at his shirt cuffs in abundant streams, and down into his boots. He swore, not mildly, by his gods. But Septimus was far too ill to quarrel or apologize. So was his wife. Drenched, wearied out, and wellnigh tired of life, the married pair reached Paris safe at last. They did not sit up long. Philosophers, ye score again. Congenital Automatism surely made them sick. How so? Why, both the father and the mother of the bride and groom were always sick at sea. Or was it outraged Hymen? I can't tell. They got on pretty well as married folk, with now and then a little breeze of science, or a gale of dogmatism, until the *missing link* arrived. The what? The missing link, madam, to wit, a fine dogmatic scientific boy. It spoke six months before all other children do. Its first articulate sound was "won't." Its next was "will." The parents were amazed. They gave up science after this, and dogmatism too, the wife submitted to her husband's will, and both were happy then. A fine old mystery this, ye sage philosophers. But ye are right again. Congenital Automatism made the child say *won't* and *will*. The parents were so much alike. Each gave an equal share of wilful and of won'tful particles unto their child.

It's wonderful how much that *missing link* changed Curiosa and her spouse. They both have often laughed since then to think that they could be such fools.

But, perhaps you don't believe that this brat of the Sciolists possessed the parents' tendencies so strongly marked?

Lend me your ears, ye "Outside Fools."

I had a little Guinea Pig. It was not *Clerical*, but it was *Lay*. I made a lesion, by unlucky chance, in Guinea Piggy's spinal cord; and then I slightly pinched its face to see if it was dead. My Guinea Pig had straightway epileptic fits.

My epileptic Guinea Pig took to itself a wife. In course of time the married pair had little Guinea Pigs. These little Guinea Pigs had epileptic fits, without a lesion of the spinal cord.

Observe, ye careless parents, what ye may and can do for your little ones that are to be.

Be very careful of your *wills* and *won'ts*, for they are fraught with consequence.

Such was my Guinea Pig, but it was Lay.

Now was it not transmitted automatic power that made this brat of Sciolist's say *won't* and then say *will?*

"But, madam, pray where did we leave our Clerical Guinea Pig?"

"He was just bracing up the odor of sanctity, sir, if I remember right."

"Nay, madam, had he not already braced it up, and was he not just going down the stairs?"

"But surely, sir, the going down the stairs is nothing to the point, whereas the bracing of the odor of sanctity has everything to do with it."

"Madam, you are right; I stand corrected.

How a woman jumps straight to the point, as though it were with one instinctive leap; while men keep fumbling with their "Shall I?" and their "Shalln't I?" then, "Does it?" and then, "Don't it?" and their *pros* and *cons*, until the whole pith of the matter has escaped unknown to them!

CHAPTER LXX.

TREATING OF THE STARTLING AND NEVER-BEFORE-IMAGINED EFFECTS OF UNCONSCIOUS CEREBRATION ON A CLERICAL GUINEA PIG.

JOSIAH, as I said, went down the stairs, and took his odor of sanctity along with him. The rector and the fair Louisa were already breakfasting. It was now nearly ten o'clock, and service should begin at half-past ten. Our Guinea Pig made efforts to collect his wandering thoughts at breakfast-time, and raised Miss Pantosniffle's spirits to not a little above par by the attentive way in which he seemed to listen when she spoke.

Between ourselves, dear "Outside Fools," Josiah, with a *Secondary* Automatic Thought, was dreaming still of his dear Emma, while his body, in response to that so natural prompting which most men feel towards the other sex, and in obedience to a *Primary* Automatism, was paying heed to what the lady said. Had there but been a short brisk walk to church, Josiah's brain would very likely have regained its normal state, and no result so startling and important would have happened to our Guinea Pig. But, doubtless for the good of all philosophers, the rectory was close to the churchyard, the church not fifty yards away. It now was half-past ten. The congregation were assembled, and the members of the orchestra were seated in the long low gallery that ran across the west end of the church, and sundry scrapings upon Captain Dudman's violin, with one or two premonitory grunts from Barloe Healey on the reedy-toned bassoon, struck on our ears. Louisa Pantosniffle and some village nightingales sat in the gallery to aid with vocal melody the instrumental efforts of the gentlemen I have already named in chapter sixty of this Book.

Madame La Fargue was in her pew close by the reading-desk, and had her ocular artillery directed to the spot where our Josiah's face was soon to be. A very striking-looking woman was Madame La Fargue. The Great Whoppliddians looked on her with wonder and respect, as one who knew so much more than they did. Her golden hair was envied by the simple village girls. Her nose was a straight beautifully chiselled Grecian nose, the nostrils well distended, showing sensibility and taste, and Byron's "*beautiful disdain.*" Her eyes were very bright, the pupils large and full, her lips like coral, her complexion fresh and blooming as a rose, her teeth were regular and white as pearls. Her forehead's veins, so well defined, bespoke the aristocrat, her ample bust the matron rather than the maid. And yet, though she had all these charms, Miss Pantosniffle was the favorite at Whopplidde-in-the-Fen. There was more nature there, the other was all art.

Dear "Outside Fools," the service has begun. The singing of the village girls, led by the fair Louisa, really was not bad. Bocuda Sinales broke in with fitful and discordant roar that rather marred the melody; but that was only now and then. Gad Vossey was all there, his sanctimonious whine was at its best.

He rapped the irreligious village boys' heads till they rang again, and smiled upon them with a saintly smile as whimpering they rubbed their aching pates.

Yet even while Josiah read, *Unconscious Cerebration* did its silent work.

I grieve to say, your Lordships, Worships, and your Reverences, that if you come to a philosophical analysis, it was but an *Automaton* who read the prayers. The *EGO* was with Emma still.

Observe, philosophers. This Guinea Pig had dreamt no ordinary dream. And though there was no lesion of the spinal cord, think how the man's *Sensori-Motor Apparatus* had been taxed. How the *Sensorium* had been diverted from its intellectual or Cerebral to its Sensational side. Josiah never had much *will* when in his normal state of mind. But now he was a bull of Emmas, which had risen more than two per cent. Satanic dragon sovereigns danced around his wearied brain.

And well you know, philosophers, that if you wish to fix your close attention on some object, the effort will be greater in proportion to the charms of any other object that may synchronously magnetize your sensory.

A college-friend of Turnabout's young brother's married a girl-graduate, with golden-hair. And he was very fond of problems, and was just about to solve a problem worthy of his wrangler's steel. His sweet wife-graduate, with golden hair, came dancing gaily to her wrangler's side, and simply said, "Dear Charley, do this little sum for me." *Congenital Automatism* drove all secondary problems far away. Of course he did her little sum. And so would you, philosopher, unless your telegraphic cable offices were bare of furniture. And such philosophers are worse than any fools. What? Did not Aristotle go down on all fours and take a beauty on his back, while Alexander's court looked on? He did, and it was doubtless done to show how strong is this *Congenital Automatism.*

Well, sages, fight it out among yourselves. It is not mine to analyze, but chronicle. I know saliva flows with readiness when hungry men but think of savory food. And Aristotle's burden was most savory, and Emma was a dainty morsel to our Guinea Pig. The prayers were ended now, and he was just going to give out the hymn, when his unlucky eye caught that of Madame Emma La Fargue, and ere he knew what he was saying, *Emma* had slipped out instead of what it should have been. The magic word was telegraphed by female agency to our Josiah's *cerebellum*, and at once *passivity* of mind became *activity*, most novel and distressing in this case. For Emma was the lady's name, and Emma was the mine's. He meant the mine; she and all those who heard supposed he was in love with Madame Emma La Fargue, whose rapt devoted look deserved the love of any Guinea Pig. And all the parish knew that either she or else Louisa Pantosniffle was to be the bride. The great Whoppliddians, like other human beings, craved for mystery, and gambling is a mystery.

So though no brokers' telegrams had reached the simple village yet, the devil took good care that there should be a something there to bet about, and, as I have already told you, all had something on. Those in the gallery were all too far away to hear that one dissyllable that sent a thrill of joy, though blent with great surprise, through Madame Emma's heart. The fair Louisa heard it not, but sang on in her happy ignorance. The instrumental operators heard it not, but went on with their violins, their ophicleides, their clarionets, and their reedy-toned bassoons. 'Twas lucky that they did not hear, for they were all most interested in the issue of their bets. It might have interfered with the religious sensory.

But there were plenty who did hear this fatal word, and who decided in their minds that they had lost or won, and that Josiah must be very bad with Emma on the brain to make so awkward a mistake. They stared and tittered, but they did not think it wonderful. The great Whoppliddians believed in nature and in love. Indeed, their life was automatic and emotional. Sublime volition such as Madame Emma shortly showed was quite beyond their ken. And as for Emma mines, they knew not of such things. Madame La Fargue, to speak unphilosophically, was a woman of the world, of ready wit, and not much hampered by fastidious moral sense. So, while the Reverend Josiah did just what he never should have done, to wit, blushed, looked confused, and altogether foolish at his odd mistake, the quick-witted Emma, taking in the situation with a glance of genius, sent all her previous automatic tendencies about their business, and determined, though she was in church, that she would never throw away so good a chance. So after darting from those full expressive eyes one tender arrowy look upon her Guinea Pig, she fainted right away. Yet, singular to say, the ganglionic matter of her spinal cord was in a state of normal calm. The volitional control antagonized hysterical impulse with a complete success. Recovering decorously just at the proper time, though looking ghastly pale, she was conducted by her maid, both walking slowly, from the church. The rectory was close at hand, much nearer than her house. So to the rectory she went, with busy brain and *will*, enough to win a score of Guinea Pig-Affinities. The air and rest restored her outwardly. Her inner consciousness had never been disturbed. Philosophers, attentively observe this curious female specimen. How those emotional impulses which a woman mostly has more strongly marked than man were in complete subordination to her Will. And how abnormally her *Ego* knew all changes taking place in the external world. All her congenital and constitutional automatic tendencies, all that surprise, all the education she had received from others' will or from the discipline of circumstance, was powerless to trammel the sublime volition that enabled her, in spite of all the hindrances of time and place, to form a grand strategic plan to catch a Guinea Pig.

To think, said she, to her maid Fanny, that he should have chosen such a place to make it known. This hint was quite enough for Fanny, who replied,—

"Why, madam, I consider it was beautiful. They say, as love is heavin, and heavin is love; and sure, to see the parson blush as he forgot hisself and spoke your name, was quite a pretty picter like. You know he has been called a cherubin, although he's rather too deep-colored to my fancy for a cherubin; but love improves the looks most wonderful. I only hopes the rector will not blow poor Mr. Fetchem up."

"He can't do so," said Madame Emma, "without being rude to me. Just see if you can get a glass of wine, I feel so overset."

Away went Fanny to the kitchen, and with gleeful pride detailed the news, and added that it was a very strange affair, and licked her quite, it did; and what would poor Miss Pantosniffle say? "I warrant me she'll vow there is some gillery in this. And so I think, for Mr. Fetchem never was so sweet on madam as all that. But as I said before, it licks me quite."

Meantime Josiah went on with the service, but it was very clear to all that he had something on his mind, or else was very ill. His manner was unwontedly confused. He lost his place, repeated what he had said, and went from bad to worse. Of course to those who heard what he had said before the lady left the church each fresh mistake was but a further proof how deeply smitten he must be. Had but Volition checked Emotion just a little, he might have saved himself; but as it was, he played into the lady's hands as well as it was possible to do. However, all things have an end, and so this memorable service had at last, and dazed, and angry with himself and everything, Josiah, waiting in the vestry till the congregation had all gone, went over to the rectory. Madame La Fargue had, like a skilful general, retired. It would never do to face her swain before he knew what wonderful effect that little slip of his had brought about. Before another day or two was past he would be sure to know. You see, just as your Worships and your Reverences affect disdain for money's sordid influence, so he was forced to ape the same disdain, and dare not say, "It was a mine I thought about, with shame I own it was; and yet, to tell the truth is always best, however hard it seems to be." All he could say to kind inquiries was, "I was not well;" but people don't say *Emma* in a church when they're unwell. The Great Whoppliddians pitied him, and Barloe Healey said to Mr. Smales, who stood to win a monkey on the event,—"

"Becuda, you were right; that foreign madam has such ways o' lookin at a man as makes him think o' things."

Ye pundits and philosophers, can ye surpass the wisdom of Becuda Smales? He recognized intuitively that a woman's will is the great wonder of the philosophic world.

Josiah found out but too well before next day was over the true state of things. The maid had been so active in her mistress' interest that all the village knew, or thought they knew, which was the same thing in effect, that parson was over head and ears in love with Madame Emma La Fargue. The rector was the worst to pacify. He talked of "desecration," "prostitution of the dignity of holy men to carnal sense," and got so hot that, had not our Guinea Pig discreetly begged him to consult his great work upon "Desecration of the Title, *Reverend*," I really think he would not have forgiven him.

Just like the captive with neck-stretched out for the sacrificing knife, Josiah listened for two hours to the rector's lecture from this priceless book, and as no passage could be found that could be made to suit the case, he got off with a reprimand.

"Of evils choose the least," say the philosophers.

Josiah chose the least. He had a wholesome fear of British juries when appealed to by a Buncombe's rhetoric on the behalf of spinsters' harrowed feelings —widows' broken hearts; and well he knew that if his Emma fainted at another Emma's name, she could get up an admirable scene to aid her counsel's powerful appeal. Josiah, madam, was afraid of damages, and so he chose the smallest ill, to wit, Madame La Fargue. As there was so much art and plan, so little natural telegraphy about the case, I'd rather let the wooing pass. They were engaged. And as the "objects" had not been selected by the odic theory, or in our halls, it was more a mercantile than love affair. The wedding-day was fixed for Thursday, six weeks from that date. Josiah left for town, to court his other love.

CHAPTER LXXI.

THE REV. JOSIAH FETCHEM RETURNS TO THE CITY AND FINDS HIS EMMA SHARES DECLINING.—MADAME EMMA LA FARGUE PREPARES FOR HER WEDDING.

Josiah left Great Whopplidde-in-the-Fen as the affianced husband of Madame La Fargue. When he came to my office his first Emma seemed to have pined through his neglect. At all events the shares were down to 29. Poor fellow! it was rather hard that Emma, the American, should first have worked on his emotions by the expectation of success so strongly that the Gallic Emma's wonderful volition should have made him ask her to be his for life, although she was not his "affinity," and then as soon as all this mischief had been done, that his American first love should harrow his emotions by the fear that she would prove a faithless jilt. But so it was, and from that date the shares began to steadily decline. Now, as you know, dear "Outside Fools," a dwindle is a nasty thing for any bull to face; but when he feels that he has been trapped by a fair one that he does not love, and may be jilted by another fair one whom he passionately loves, the prospect is enough to drive a bull with weak volition and abnormally excitable Sensori-Motor Apparatus into the condition of hysterical automata.

There seldom is a middle course with mines; eighteen per cent. or nothing is the usual thing.

I recommended Fetchem to return to court his other Emma, if but to distract his thoughts.

This other Emma was preparing for her wedding

with industrious alacrity. Another batch of parcels came from Paris, and she was locked in her room most days for two or three hours at a time. Now Fanny Pratt, her maid, resented this, and tried her best to worm out madame's secret, but in vain. The door was always locked when she was in the room, and when it was unlocked there was not anything to see but Madame Emma looking very nice and fresh and trim. By dexterously laying the letters on the top of the hot-water jug Miss Fanny Pratt had opened all but sealed ones easily; but as the writing was in French, it did not tell her anything.

CHAPTER LXXII.

THE BRIDE ELECT MEETS WITH A TERRIBLE ACCIDENT, AND A VERY SINGULAR DISCOVERY IS MADE.

JOSIAH had taken my advice, and was expected to arrive at Great Whopplidde-in-the-Fen on the next Wednesday at eleven o'clock. Madame La Fargue complained of headache on the Tuesday evening, and retired to her room at half-past eight o'clock to have a good night's rest, as she remarked to Fanny Pratt.

It was just ten o'clock. The maid had done her supper, raised her spirits, which were rather low, with just a wine glass full of madame's *eau de vie*, had fastened all the doors and windows, and was going up to bed, when she was startled by a piercing shriek. She knew her mistress' voice, and rushed upstairs. The door was locked. But Fanny was a strong and heavy girl, and, stimulated by a second scream for help, she burst open the door with a tremendous lurch. She was only just in time. Her mistress was in flames up to her waist. She had passed too near the fire-place, which had no guard, and the flames had caught the bottom of her dress. She rushed towards her maid, who with great presence of mind seized two thick blankets from the bed and met the burning lady with them spread out wide. She flung them round her and then threw her on the ground. Nor did she stop at that, but emptied both the water-jugs upon the lady's prostrate form. It was enough. The energy and promptitude of Fanny Pratt had put the fire out, but it had sadly burnt poor madame's lower half. The maid, without assistance, got her mistress into bed, and sent off for a doctor's aid. But what a mistress met the astonished Fanny's gaze, now that the excitement was somewhat subdued!

Where now was all that golden hair, the admiration and the envy of the village girls?

Where now the nostrils, beautiful disdain, the coral lips, the teeth as white as pearls?

Where was the fresh complexion and, alas! where was that bust, so ample and so matronly?

Ladies, turn we to the dressing-table, there to see the triumphs of high art.

There lay the skilfully constructed wig, tinged with Sol Aurine's lovely hue.

There lay that miracle of modern days, the Nose Machine.

The silver nostrils' beautiful disdain was still upon the injured lady's face, but coyly peeping through the forehead's skin, which had been peeled down and then drawn over it by artistes's hands. Poor thing! when set alight she fell upon the floor and struck her chiselled Grecian nose as reckless rinkualistic maidens fall while skating with their hands entangled in a muff and break the Grecian or it may be, the "tip-tilted" nasal bones.

The lips, alas, were white and rough, through want of the Lip-Tingeing Pencil which lay upon the dressing-case.

The teeth lay by an Eyebrow Pencil's side; they looked as white and regular as heretofore, but they were not in poor burnt madame's mouth.

That former fresh complexion was now changed for yellow wrinkled pock-marked skin. Oh, fire! ruthless element! what ruin hast thou wrought!

Close by the mysterious dressing-case were boxes of Complexion Pills, and packages of Ninon's Liquid Bloom. Not far away there was the wonderful Small Pox Eradicating Pigment, with two packets of Skin Tightner, and three of Nile Deposit, to close up the pores, and scare loose flesh away, a Pimple Startler, with a pot of Rose Emulsion and of Nymphéine.

Next to these wonders of the woman-building art were Nail Enamellers, Throat Garglers, to improve the tone, and the far-famed AZURINE that can produce aristocratic veins of blue on temples of an Indian squaw—how much more easily on those of a La Fargue!

And there, on each side of the mirror, rested gracefully, though false, alas! and cold, that noblest triumph of American philanthropy, Achilles Gilead's Saratoga Palpitators, for the flat-breasted fair. These bosoms were so natural, that they would have taken in the keenest baby out; they all were magnetized and, warranted to rise and fall at wearer's will, and could be worn by day and night alike.

The mystery was solved, and Fanny Pratt was satisfied. She turned, but Madame Emma was in a deep swoon.

CHAPTER LXXIII.

DEATH OF MADAME EMMA FARGUE, AND DECLINE OF THE EMMA MINE.

THE doctor came, and after a brief examination was quite satisfied that there was not the slightest hope.

"The shock," said he, "has thrown the *Cerebro-Spinal* system altogether out of gear, disorganized the *Semilunar Ganglia*, and superinduced incurable derangement of the *Hypogastric Plexus*.

"It might be some satisfaction to the friends," said the learned Galen, "to have another opinion," for he was aware that the mimetic power of the sex, combined with an abnormal will, had occasionally produced astonishing phenomena, having all the appearance of disease, from which, however, the patient subsequently recovered, although, for his part, he was quite sure "that all that the most captious of his class could do was to fix on the *Cardiac Plexus*, instead of the Hypogastric, for, as for the great *Solar Plexus* being affected, the thing was simply ridiculous."

Whichever Plexus it was, poor Emma La Fargue went to her rest. The fame of her silver nostrils, with their beautiful disdain, still lives in the memory of the Great Whoppliddians. She was no more before Josiah had arrived. I wonder if her *will* would have been quite so strong if she had not required Achilles

Gilead's philanthropic aid. Just crack that nut for me, philosophers; my teeth are not quite good enough.

Josiah arrived with heavy heart, for American Emma tended downwards still. It very much depressed his weak emotional mind did this catastrophe. Although he never wished to marry, and was staggered at the story of the silver nostrils and the palpitators, yet Josiah's agitated cerebrum responded automatically to the sad impression of poor Madame Emma's death, and he was very much afraid that it portended death to American Emma too. Alas, the omen was too true.

Remittances began to cease; not even dare they borrow more to send, as though it were great Emma's virgin ore. Some ugly rumors were afloat, yet some directors pledged their faith anew that all was right. As none could find out what was true and what was false, the old directors all resigned, and a new board was formed. Among the shareholders who still were left was our Guinea Pig, and though his spirits now were low as were the shares, the pleasant theory of a *Fissure Vein* was started by some philanthropic and imaginative wag, and Phœnix-like, our American Emma was to rise triumphant from her ashes through this " Fissure Vein." But truth is stranger yet than fiction, and the damning proofs were soon to hand that Emma was a "pocket," a miserable flirt, a lying jade, and not a matron with those solid stores of wealth that now-a-days add so much to a lady's charms. The American Emma was played out. She once was worth £100,000, or, some say, half as much again. Co-operation here was gained for not much more than that; and what co-operation!

Should you have thought, dear "Outside Fools," that such co-operation could have been so cheaply bought? I never should, and I know something of the City's ways. But wasn't that a funny dream Josiah had?

Poor man, he was a spectacle to see. The ganglionic centres were all frightfully disturbed in this sad case, most interesting to philosophers.

CHAPTER LXXIV.

A BROKER'S CLASSIFICATION OF OUTSIDE FOOLS, AND A DOCTOR'S OPINION OF JOSIAH FETCHEM'S MENTAL STATE.

THERE was a *Mental Latency* about the man most puzzling to a non-professional. I had heard that one class of feelings will intensify, and another nearly paralyze the *will;* but I never saw a case like this. Josiah's whole volitional control seemed gone, and he was simply an hysterico-emotional automaton. Now, my dear "Outside Fools," we brokers don't feel comfortable when we cannot make our subjects out. It's next to never that we can't, for about three classes will include you all. I have in what I term my broker's cerebrum three ideal shelves, on which are ranged unnumbered "Outside Fools." The shelves are not alike in size. Upon the bottom, and by far the largest shelf, are ranged the "*Ignorant Outside Fools.*" Upon the middle shelf, that's not so large, are ranged the "*Greedy Outside Fools.*" Upon the top, and smallest shelf, are ranged the "*Vain and Imitative Outside Fools.*" Josiah had been on the greedy shelf, but now his manner was so strange that not one of the three would suit his case, and so I got him to see Dr. Sana Mens.

Next day I called to hear what Mens thought of his state.

"This interesting case of Fetchem's, Seesaw," said he, "is an admirable illustration of the power that *Money* can exercise upon the structure of the human brain. The chief *Dynamical Causation* was an exaggeration of Rectorial and Vicarial Deference. This placed your Guinea Pig at once upon the *greedy shelf* of 'Outside Fools.' Then came that curious dream that made the mischief spread so far.

"*Unconscious Cerebration* since that time has been at work at intervals both day and night, but more especially at night. Thus a distinct organic impression was produced upon the *cerebrum*, which, just like any other organism, ever tends to *form itself* in accordance with the mode in which it is habitually exercised. The brain, then, of your Guinea Pig had, as it were, unconsciously been *Emmafied*, to make my meaning clear to non-medical 'Outside Fools.'

"As time went on, the *Ideational Activity* of his mind completely *objectified* the *Emma*, so that the least circumstantive agency could bring the mind back from the will's control, into the *Emmafied condition*. Now, Seesaw," continued Mens, "there's a mental *Law of Contiguity*. Two states of consciousness will often co-exist, or follow in immediate sequence. Such states tend to cohere, so that the subsequent occurrence of one revives the other too.

"Now the American *Emma* and the Gallic *Emma* had become compacted into a *Composite Notion* that was the resultant of two distinct states of Ideation.

"At the moment, therefore, that the Gallic Emma's face, surrounded with that profusion of *golden* tresses, struck the eye of your Guinea Pig, while the Satanic dragon sovereigns of his dream and the rich stores of his American Emma were secretly acting upon his *Mental Latency* by the *Law of Contiguity*, a vivid Ideal reproduction took place of the theatrical scene, the golden tresses of Madame La Fargue suggesting the golden and Satanic dragon sovereigns of the theatre, and the startling resultant was that unseasonable ejaculation, the remoter consequences of which were the *desecration* of the θεόυντος 'οδμὴ as well as of the sacred building itself."

"In plain English," said I to Sana Mens, "you mean that his brain was unconsciously *Emmafied* by the mine, and that Madame Emma La Fargue's golden hair made the brain become conscious of its *Emmafication* and automatically ejaculate, in spite of the man's *will*."

"I do," said Sana Mens, "and I should recommend your Guinea Pig to keep away from the scene of his emotional suffering both in the City and at Great Whopplidde-in-the-Fen, and to try some other pulpit. I am certain that it is the best and only rational course to pursue."

"What a splendid broker you would have made, Sana Mens," said I.

"Why so," asked he.

"Because you have such wonderful power of analyzing motives and tracing the causes of human action, and that faculty is the groundwork of our successful operation. Once give me the knowledge of the client's mental proclivities, and I can select the exact kind of speculative matter to suit him. We have all sorts of pleasant narcotizing stocks in hand for every class of brain. Yes, Sana Mens, you would have made a first-rate broker."

"Thank you for the compliment, Seesaw, but I have no wish to become a broker. You are one, and it is not your fault; but I am lucky enough to be a doctor instead of a broker, although, for the matter of that, but for dunces, most were doctors. Surgery, I grant you, is a respectable and honest trade, but as for medicine, it is mostly empirical. I have sometimes thought, Seesaw, that God never meant one man to save the soul, to cure the body, or to make money for any other man. In these three cases man must do the work himself, or fail, and the more he leans on others' aid the more unhappy he will be. You'll let me know how your client goes on; I should like to hear the result of the change."

I promised that I would, and left the house. I like that Sana Mens; but he don't seem to know what protection means; and he is all for the majority.

That's not my creed. Long live the "Outside Fools!" say I.

Now, my poor Guinea Pig had lost much of the power to produce Rectorial and Vicarial Deference; but neither rectors nor vicars *knew* he had, and so he could still go to some other pulpit without a shock to his personal vanity, which in his then hysterico-emotional condition would have been in the highest degree dangerous, if not fatal.

It happened that the vicar of Littleprice-cum-Kiddleton, in Clayshire, was in want of temporary assistance, and engaged our Josiah's services through the medium of the *Clerical Advertiser*. He was to take part of the duty for a month and reside with the vicar.

CHAPTER LXXV.

THE REV. JOSIAH FETCHEM TRIES A CHANGE OF PULPIT, AND MEETS WITH A MOST CURIOUS AND DISTRESSING ACCIDENT.

HE went to Littleprice-cum-Kiddleton, and arrived in the middle of the week. The change of air and the kind attention and jovial disposition of the vicar had a good effect upon our Guinea Pig, and on the Sunday following he got through the prayers and passed the critical place at which he had so sadly failed before without mishap. But wonderful and various are the devices of the Evil One to desecrate the sacred odor of a saint.

The church was very old at Littleprice-cum-Kiddleton. 'Twas in the Gothic style, and many were the quaint gurgoyles that both inside and out looked down upon you from above. The fancy of emotional automata might have perceived a Satan's personality in every gurgoyle's grinning face. But from what happened I believe the Evil One's abode was then a wooden pulpit's floor.

I'll just describe the mechanism of this trap for holy men.

The floor of the pulpit at Littleprice-cum-Kiddleton was a moveable one, raised or lowered by means of a perpendicular screw about three quarters of an inch in diameter and three feet in length. The screw was acted upon by another of similar thread or diameter, but quite short. This short screw was inserted in the end of a long bar, which reached into the clerk's pew under the floor of the church in a horizontal direction. The longer screw of course acted vertically. By means of a crank also in the clerk's pew, and by the aid of two cogged wheels, the pulpit floor could be raised or depressed at clerkly will, although the odor of sanctity should be there at the time and weigh from ten to twenty stones. The custom was to adjust this pulpit while the hymn was being sung and just before the sermon had commenced. Now although Josiah Fetchem was a stranger Guinea Pig, and in weak health, he was left quite in the dark as to this customary mechanical arrangement. So while the hymn was being sung, he entered the pulpit in blissful ignorance, and as he was a-weary he sat down, which it appears he never should have done. The clerk, according to his function, looked around to see if the floor was the right height to give effect to his appearance and delivery. Josiah, as I have already said, was like a turtle raised on its hind legs, and short, and as he had sat down, he was not visible above the pulpit's edge. And so the clerk began to wind him up. Josiah, being weak and nervous, thought the pulpit was going to give way, and started from his seat. This brought his body quite three feet above the pulpit's edge. Again the clerk looked critically up, and saw that parson was too high. Round went the crank the other way, and down again went our Guinea Pig, supposing it must be a miracle, and thinking it was surely safer to sit down until the funny pulpit quake was over, he sat down. Again the clerk began to wind him up, till in an agony of fright Josiah cried,—

"Oh, Lord, forgive and steady me, and I will never touch another Emma in my life!"

The clerk ceased winding when he heard so strange a text, and Fetchem, thinking that his prayer and promise had made the trouble cease, began to preach. But soon emotion scared volition quite away; the shock was too much for his nerves, the blood rushed to his brain, and he was forced to bring the service to a sudden end. Now I can understand Josiah's fear at being wound first up, then down. But how was this, psychologists? Why did he ask forgiveness for imaginary crime? It seemed, and surely in this cranky case he spoke the truth, as if he were afraid of punishment. But though he had less will than the rectorial and vicarial pillars of the church, his odor still was the apostle's sanctified perfume. Had but this odor been *a little mixed,* or had it been the *heretic's* rank smell, I could have understood this fear of punishment to come. But as it was I could not make it out. Nor more could Sana Mens.

Josiah had brain fever, and was ill for several months before he was restored. To my surprise he came again to me. Sana Mens declared that he was now a *Secondary Automaton,* and would continue so. It appears that several rectors and vicars had taken some shares in Emma, upon hints that Fetchem had let fall, and as their speculation had turned out a failure, they looked coldly on their Guinea Pig. Take old Nathaniel Seesaw's tip, ye "Outside Fools" —don't recommend a speculation or investment to a brother fool. If it go right, he'll think it was his cleverness; but if it should go wrong, as it is ten to one it will, you'll get the blame. Their reverences' change of manner made Josiah wild; he could not bear it, with his weakened will, and so he came to dabble in the mud again. A friend of his read Broker Gabbit's famous circulars, and having acted on the wisdom there contained, was, as he said himself, in a most splendid thing, quite safe, no speculative venture, but a *bonâ fide* Industrial Joint Stock Company. Shudder when you hear that term, ye "Outside Fools," and stop your ears with wax, lest ye should listen to the deadly sirens' voice.

This noble enterprise was the great Neuchatel's Rock Asphalte Paving Company. An asphalte had been tried in Paris, and had been successful for some years. These Neuchatel Rock ten-pound shares were over £60 a share. Just as we now are narcotized with "rinkualism," so then the "Outside Fools" went paving mad. Wherever there is a demand, there always is a supply in the speculative world; it's different with butcher's meat. Just in the nick of time, the true bituminous rock was found in most abundant stores. Promoters had all got their oyster, and they lost no time in opening it. The *Weekly Locomotives* and *Hebdomadal Reviews*, who let out spaces for a price for speculative bulls or bears to write things up or down, were full of letters from so-called investors, calculators, addlepates, and interested rogues, imploring "Outside Fools" not to neglect so grand a chance. Ye "Outside Fools," just take a hint. Don't follow friends' advice. You think, perhaps, you are not listening to a broker then. Where does your friend get his advice from, eh? You buy for sixpence, do you, papers full of splendid tips? Don't be an arrant ass. Don't deal in anything you do not understand; don't deal in any new securities unless you're rich and can afford to lose. But if you should be stuck with rubbish through some other fool's or rogue's advice, or your own folly, don't add to that folly by a vain attempt to *catch at a falling market.* Don't average. This averaging in rotten stocks has ruined countless "Outside Fools." Buy something that, as Americans say, has *a rock bottom,* and when it drops, buy twice as much if you can spare the cash. What is there sound? Some English Rails.

Well, as I said, these Neuchatel shares had been over sixty pounds a share. Indeed, they had been in a soda water rise close upon seventy; but when Josiah's friend went in they were much less than that. The sapient friend remarked,—

"You see I am not taking brokers' tips, I'm buying when they're low, just when outsiders never buy. My broker says if all his clients were like me they'd never lose."

Our Guinea Pig, with weak volition, took his friend's advice, and bought just twenty Neuchatels. The price grew beautifully less each day that came.

His friend did average. Josiah, having weak volition, did the same. They kept them till they had dropped only £30 a share. The Neuchatels sell now with difficulty at three half-crowns a share. 'Tis true the shares have been reduced and preference stock been raised, but there's not much difference in the result.

Our Guinea Pig is in a private madhouse now. He thinks that Emma is the queen of a large island full of silver and of gold. That the air is poisoned with

the evil-smelling odor of the heretic, but that the
sacred odor can be found within the madhouse walls.
He thinks that bishops, rectors, vicars, and their
Guinea Pigs fall down before a golden calf that's set
up in all larger towns, and worship every day, and
that the each *'Doxy* hates each other *'Doxy* with a
deadly hate. That members of the island's government think but of place and opposition, while all
emotion is subdued by a *Satanic will*. He dreams
that other countries smack their greedy lips, and tuck
their tongues inside their grinning cheeks as they
behold this island's unprotected state, and say to one
another,—

"Let us wait till all our loans are floated and our
strategic railroads are complete. We must keep
friends with the Financial Acrobats and 'Outside
Fools' till then. But when that game is up, then
our time will come. Fling the sucked orange
roughly to the ground, and rush to arms. We
must let blood or else be ruined by our armies' cost.
See how that island's lion has become a lamb!
Alliance be our watchword, plunder is our aim!
Come on, my brother military tinkers, come; let's
shake the tree, the pear is ripe. See what free
trade and peace at any price has done for us! See
how the haughty military snob, who often does not
know one-tenth as much as many a common soldier of
the Fatherland, laughs down the volunteers, cares
more for his own small exclusive set than for his
country's good! See how place-hunting, jobbing fac-
tions strive to oust each other from their seats! See
how the very manners of the Stock Exchange have
crept into the Parliament! How there a battle-
royal oft is fought! How premiers are not allowed

to see their Queen, nor yet to look down at their boot, while noting silently each "Inside Ass!" A little of our autocratic rule would teach these jostlers, ugly rushers, and bear-garden members to behave themselves.

"See how their noisy EGOS struggle to assert themselves, although meantime their island home lacks army, fleets of active gunboats for the coast defence, and everything but gold and luxury, the sure precursors of a fall!"

You must excuse my Guinea Pig, your Worships and your Reverences, his emotions sway him so. I wonder if these madmen are not sometimes happier and wiser, too, than we?

My doctor, Sana Mens, declares that all are mad, but says that only those who are the enemies of ignorance and vice, and greed of gain, who will not kiss hands freely for preferment, or bow down to golden calves, need fear the Lunacy Commissioners. That Sana Mens quite frightens me. I wonder he is not afraid lest he himself should be shot down or stabbed. He has such little sympathy with roguery.

CHAPTER LXXVI.

CONTAINING A BROKER'S APOLOGIES TO A LEARNED CRITIC.

My learned friend Opsimathes observes that all this story of the Guinea Pig is well enough, but that I violate the "*id quod decet*," as 'tis called in Kikero, and that I desecrate what's termed "τὸ πρέπον" by the Greeks. In other words, dear "Outside Fools," our

YE OUTSIDE FOOLS. 335

learned friend implies that I offend propriety by calling true apostles Guinea Pigs, and by allowing such profanities as "Emmas" to distract the thoughts of odorous sanctity, or to be mentioned in a church. My good Opsimathes, let me be plain with you. These little tales, so easy as they seem to read, have yet an allegory which you might perceive, did not vast learning dim your mental sight.

This is the meaning of the book. That money, though the "Root of Evil," is a source of good as well. It is a mute epitome of truth more than all else but *MHΔEN AΓAN* in the world.

That seeing this is so, philosophers and learned critics and ecclesiastic lights would all do well to study money more, to bring their very hardest words, their terms so difficult and so abstruse to "Outside Fools," to bear upon this theme of universal interest, instead of fighting shadows so and making mountains labor to bring forth those funny philosophic mice.

My book would also teach that every man craves for a mystery, a narcotism, in some one of the many forms there are. It fain would show that EGO is the strongest foe that education has. Surely the EGO of these learned men is not afraid lest, if plain ordinary terms be used to illustrate the grains of wheat there may be in the chaff, *non-philosophic* EGOS should so quickly learn that philosophic EGOS should fall from their pedestals.

Real merit and true genius should have no EGO and no pedestals, but know how little worth is human praise, and how unmerited, although less frequently, is human blame.

I asked my doctor, Sana Mens, the other day how he explained this paradox. I mean that, learned critics, those who lived at the same time and occupied the leading critics' chairs, could scarcely find words coarse and scurrilous enough to lash the works of Byron, Shelley, Keats, Leigh Hunt, and countless other men of genius, which works both "Outside Fools" and critics now combine to praise and read.

"A critic on his deathbed told me this," said Sana Mens, and as a man don't often tell lies then, I think it is quite true.

This dying critic said with faint and feeble voice,—

"In theory a critic is the quintessence of the EGO placed upon the very tallest pedestal. His EGO looks down with sublime contempt upon all 'Outside Fools' and also upon men of genius, for they, it says, are bold invaders of the critic's realm, who should be thought odd specimens of 'Outside Fools,' and nothing more.

"We often praise the mediocre man of letters," said this dying critic, "because we're not afraid lest he should tell the 'Outside Fools' more than they ought to know, and he does not assail our EGO as the others do; but never yet have we, unless compelled by want of money or through fear of loss of critic's chair, praised genius at first.

"When we turn round and praise the very authors that we blamed before, it is not that our EGO holds a different view, but as some millions of besotted 'Outside Fools' have chosen to both praise and read the works, the critic's powerful *volition* brings his EGO well down to the level of the degenerate times, and his *volition* is oft stimulated by the price he gets for what he writes, and so he writes for money, peace, and publishers, and lets his EGO take it out in sneers at home. A critic is by far the greatest of all living men, for though one be a Byron, Shelley, or a Keats, one cannot, as a critic can, explain the meaning of one's works. Indeed, a critic has been known to find out *beauties* in a mediocre poet that the poet never thought about himself."

The dying critic died, or he would probably have told us more, dear "Outside Fools."

And now, Opsimathes, I'll tell you what I think a critic's duty is.

To drag this EGO from its pedestal, to tear it from its hidden lurking-place, and show how it is narcotized with human vanity, and not, as it supposes, with the will to do its duty as a simple specimen of the unnumbered variations of that interesting curious creature, MAN. Dear ladies, don't look cross, the term includes you too. Do this, Opsimathes, and you will do a public good. But do not let your EGO tickle the ears of "Outside Fools" with your "τὸ πρέπον" and your "*id quod decet;*" do not hurl big learned words at simple brokers' heads, who think that they have something to tell others which will do some good, and who are forced, through lack of other means, to tell it in a book. If we be wrong in thinking that a single dragon sovereign is a better study for a critic, sage, or "Outside Fool," why, show that we are wrong. But do not mystify us and our readers with the egotistic posings of an old-world barrister, who used his rhetoric to prove black sometimes to be black, and to be white at other times, according to his subject or his fee, and who cribbed his philosophy from Greece.

The rank smell of the EGO overpowers my comprehensive sense in Kikero.

P

And what have I to do with rules of art?

There are abundant "Outside Fools" to learn. Here is the "Inside Ass" selected by his brethren to teach. Each to his trade. My EGO does not want to learn a little art, and say to "Outside Fools," "Come, look at me, see what a clever and artistic EGO you have here." No, be it right or be it wrong, my EGO's narcotized with this idea, that some good may be done by drawing wiser men's attention to the power and working of this very common thing, this money, which so many in their words seem to despise and in their acts to value more than anything. To solve that paradox, Opsimathes, would seem an aim well worthy of the greatest sage's wisdom and ability.

Tear off my EGO's mask, Opsimathes; God knows we know the least about ourselves.

But just a word about your charge of desecration of apostles and the church.

The church is full of honest and good men, but, alas, the church's teaching now-a-days is often fatal in effect.

I don't believe that any title in the world can ever make men bad or good, condemned or saved, to be revered or be despised.

A man is *Reverend* according to his acts and not according to his name. The term itself is but a laudatory compliment. A Guinea Pig like Fetchem, may be a Reverend in deed. A Reverend in word may be a Guinea Pig in deed.

Both Emmas in my tale portray the "Root of Evil." If that root be not found within the precincts of a church, why, then I'm wrong. But if the "Root of Evil" made the rector and the vicar change their manner to their Guinea Pig, and if that change of manner urged him on to speculate, I do not think I'm wrong.

But when our common sense is scandalized by elephantine efforts to pick up religious pins, when holy men can quarrel bitterly about the writing on a dead man's tomb, when they can shock the feelings of a train of mourners as they bear their dead ones to the grave, when Ritualistic Mountebanks, who break the law, excite the sorrow of the Mother Church and ridicule of Rome, when men refuse to be addressed as Reverend because the members of another sect may be so termed, when they refuse to give the sacrament to those who cannot see a Satan's shape and form just as they think they see what never has been seen by man, and, when the legal right to have that sacrament has been distinctly proved, resign their livings, while six hundred of their congregation ask what they call "evil livers" to give up attendance at their church—talk not of "*id quod decet*" and "τὸ πρέπον," or of desecration of the church, but weep and grieve to see that Love and Charity are dead, that Holy Hate and EGO have so wide a sway.

But God forbid that I should cast a slur upon a single honest man; there is no EGO I respect so much as his.

Good-bye, ye "Outside Fools." I'd rather be an "Inside Ass," such as I am, than torn by this religious hate or worried by an EGO so.

CHAPTER LXXVII.

ERASMUS PINTO'S ADVICE TO INVESTORS AND SPECULATORS.

My Dear "Outside Fools," allow an "Inside Roguish Ass" to address a few more words to you.

Had my worthy father-in-law not quarrelled with his cook, no doubt he would have given you more veritable histories of his clients and their dealings, but his unlucky bath prevented that.

Whether I shall address you again on a future occasion will depend much upon the celerity with which you learn, and the permission of my brothers of the Stock Exchange. Perhaps you feel inclined to say, after reading these pages, with the inveterate playgoer at Argos, "*I swear, my friends, that you have brought me to my grave, not cured me, by wresting from me such a joy, and forcibly depriving me of a delusion so delightful to the mind.*"

There was much truth in what this old man said. Man will have his gamble in some form or other, and there is not much harm in it if he will play moderately and within his means. As when we try to follow virtue in excess, we often sooner fall back into vice, so you must rid yourselves of speculation's folly by degrees.

So, then, until you've learnt to keep away, observe these rules.

First, do your business upon paper, charge commission and allow for jobber's turns, keep strict account of the results, read all the daily papers carefully, meantime, and follow their suggestions carefully, whenever you feel naturally inclined. Do this for half a year, and give your profits to some charity You safely may. But gratefully rejoice that all your losses only need be paid unto yourself.

"Oh! hang that paper-plan! I want the real thing!" I think you said, dear sir.

Very well, do this. Go to two brokers, lively sinners, like myself, who know a thing or two. You'll have to pay, I grant, but then you'll learn so much more quickly from the sinners than the saints. Keep a still tongue in your head. Shun gush and gabble as you would the Evil One. Act the *rôle* of learner thoroughly and quietly. Take notes, remember what you hear, and check off the result. Don't tell your sinners what you want to do before you get a dealing-price. Mark well how often this price varies when they know what you intend to do, and how very seldom that variation suits your book. Compare the prices that each sinner brings you out. If ever they forget their duty and advise you in a casual sort of way, by word of mouth, by winks, by laying fingers upon noses, shoulder-shrugs, or knowing looks, just jot them all down upon paper (you can surely draw signs), then add the dates and watch for the result. Do just the same with "tips" and gabble that you hear outside, and money articles. Or if you act before, do just the opposite to what you feel inclined. You'll make some money so, but you won't like it much. It's very odd, but money made according to the views we hold is so much sweeter than what's made in any other way.

And just look here. If I had such an "Outside Fool" to do with as I've just supposed you are, I should establish "Amicable Relations" with your other sinner, and so deftly blend the false with what was true that were you not in league with the Old Gentleman, you'd never know which way to act with me. I tell you candidly you'd find your match with all the judgment, money, nerve, and mathematics in the world at your command.

Explanation of Terms.

Speculation.—Time-bargains, or bets for time on between bulls and bears, as to whether a stock will rise or fall.

A Bull.—A speculator who buys stock without paying for it, expecting to sell again at a profit at some future date.

A Bear.—A speculator who sells other people's property, or bets that other people's property will fall, and expects to buy back at a profit at some future date.

Account.—There are two account days every month in ordinary stocks and shares, one at the beginning, and the other at the end of the month, and one in Consols at the beginning of the month. Each account consists of three days, called respectively Carrying-over Day, Name Day, and Settling Day.

Carrying-over Day.—All stocks not closed before the first day of the next account are *carried* over, or *continued* to the next account at a fixed price, and at a charge varying according to the abundance or scarcity of the stock.

Name Day.—The second day of the account is so-called because upon it speculators who elect to take up, *i e.*, pay for any of their stocks, then pass their names or their bankers for the transfer of such stocks.

Settling Day.—Is so-called because on that day

speculative differences are paid and received, and money is also paid or received for stock taken up or sold and delivered.

A Jobber.—One who deals in the markets either as a buyer or seller, with a turn or margin in the price, varying from a shilling to £5 per cent. (or even more in panic times), according to the quantity of dealing and the price of the security.

Suppose A, an outsider, tries to buy through his broker of B, a jobber, 1000 Midland Railway stock. If the bargain be done without collusion between the broker and jobber, the broker would bring out the price, say $132\frac{3}{4}$-133, at which the jobber would profess to be prepared to do either, and the broker would buy the stock for his client at 133. I am supposing the most favorable case possible for the client in which a fair quarter price has been made by the jobber, and only $\frac{1}{8}$ per cent. commission charged by the broker.

A, then, has bought 1000 Midland stock at $133\frac{1}{8}$ net, if we add the commission to the jobber's turn. Now supposing A wished to sell the 1000 Midland again, and the market had neither risen nor fallen, he would be able, if there were no collusion, to sell at $132\frac{3}{4}$, so that no outsider can possibly buy a thousand stock for speculation under the most favorable circumstances without at once losing £3 15s. on the purchase. But suppose A went to a highly respectable broker, he would be charged $\frac{1}{4}$ commission and sometimes $\frac{1}{2}$; there would be no collusion, but there would be this, that the jobber would most likely guess the business of the highly respectable broker, simply because such men do seldom condescend to bear anything for their clients, so that unless he were selling stock to deliver, which would be against probability the jobber would read him a buyer, and instead of making the price $132\frac{3}{4}$-133, he would make 133-$133\frac{1}{4}$, and most likely 133-$133\frac{1}{2}$, in which case A would have bought 1000 Midland at $133\frac{1}{4}$ or $133\frac{1}{2}$, according to the attention and energy displayed by the highly respectable broker, and been charged either $\frac{1}{4}$ or $\frac{1}{2}$ commission, according to the degree of horror with which this respectable saint regarded speculation.

So that if A wished to sell his 1000 Midland before the market had changed, he would have lost the difference between 133, which was the price he could have bought at, and $133\frac{1}{2}$, and also the $\frac{1}{4}$ or $\frac{1}{2}$ per cent. commission, in other words, £5 in jobber's turn, and either £2 10s. or £5 in broker's commission. So that if you employ a saint, you will know the saint will not try to cheat you; but on each thousand you will probably lose £7 10s., without any change in the market price; while, if you employ a sinner, you will only lose £3 15s. This will make an enormous difference in three months' speculation. And observe, the saint is really an honorable man, but he unwittingly neglects his client's interest by haughty carelessness.

Perhaps you think this is done to discourage speculation. If so, it is very odd that when a man is known to be an investor, he has a wider price made to him and more commission charged than if he be a speculator. When you hear a broker say to you, "I am going to give up speculative business and take to investments," you may be sure of one of three things. Either he is a hypocritical would-be-saint, a straightforward liar, or wishes to get rid of you.

Investors' business, with the bother of transfers and stamps, would not enable the average broker to live.

No, my dear "Outside Fools," if you speculate, don't go to one of these highly respectable saintly persons who cannot endure speculation, and, to show their abhorrence of it, play, unwittingly of course, into the hands of the jobber, and wittingly charge you twice as much commission. Go to a man like Erasmus Pinto, and keep a sharp look out, and you will lose less and learn far more.

A Broker.—A middleman, who acts between the client and the jobber for a commission, varying with the price of the security and his own conscience. The client's agent and protector, or the jobber's friend and ally, as the case may require.

Contango or Continuation.—An indefinite and variable, but highly profitable source of gain to both jobbers and brokers, generally paid by the bull for the privilege of keeping his bargains open until the settling day of the next account. In theory, it is heavy or light, strictly according to the *bonâ fide* supply and demand of a stock, and when that supply and demand is exactly balanced, there should be no contango; but the bull should be enabled to continue his bargain for nothing, or, as we say, the stock should be carried over *even*. Should the demand for the stock be greater than the supply, *i.e.*, should the stock be very scarce, and the jobber find himself unable to deliver to buyers, who perhaps combine to take the stock off the market in order to create an artificial scarcity, he will in theory give the bull speculator something to carry over instead of making him pay.

There is no rule in the price of contango. Perhaps

we may say that from ¼ to ⅜ is the most common price for a bull to pay on Railway Stocks that are below £100 in value, and from ⅜ to ⅝ on those above £100. Just now the heavy lines are carried over at a cheaper rate, because they are beared, and well held. Practically the bull will find that when he carries over his stock the charge is heavy, and the bear will find that when he carries over his, the sum he receives is very light. You see there is a whole day for this mercurial contango to keep playing at hide and seek with both bulls and bears, and it never seems to get tired of the game. A novice had better carry over as soon as the price is declared, for this reason, that the jobber does not then know so well how to charge to suit his books. It is usual for a broker to charge the client half commission every time stock is carried over and not to charge for selling the same. Some brokers charge nothing for carrying over, but a fresh commission for selling. Erasmus Pinto prefers the latter arrangement, as, with "Amicable Relations," he would back himself to get his percentage every time the stock was carried over as well as the commission for selling. He would make things pleasant, dear "Outside Fools," for the jobber. Young brokers, if you have a fit of the blues, make things pleasant on continuation day with the jobber, the laughing and the profit will set your slow secretions right again. Make your bulls pay stiff contangoes, and see that your bears get little, and just take this hint. I find it work admirably. Manage to have clients who are bulls, and other clients who are bears of the same stocks. You can then in theory give the charge the bull has to pay to the bear; in practice you can divert half of the charge into your own pocket, and do without the jobber at all. This is a beautiful arrangement, so safe and simple. The only danger is that a young broker should not be able to keep his countenance while playing the game. I took to it very kindly, and now can even indirectly advise my clients so that I always have a good lot of bears and bulls of the same stock by carrying over day. And they used to say, " Now, Pinto, mind you don't let the jobber cheat us; " and I used to say, truly, " I will take care of that," and I never laughed. No, on my honor, never once.

Backwardation.—A charge paid by the bear for deferring delivery of the stock he has sold without possessing. This is the opposite of *contango*. It occurs much more seldom than *contango*. The causes of backwardation are these. A scarcity of the stock sold by the bear, produced either by a sudden influx of investors, who call upon the jobber to deliver the stock. Many jobbers, just like retail traders, always keep a certain quantity of the sound and fluctuating stocks on hand, enough to supply the average demand. But the presence of *backwardation* implies more than the average demand. If investors suddenly require the jobber to deliver what he has not got, he must offer the bulls something to continue their transactions, and charge the bears heavily for helping to produce the scarcity by selling what they cannot deliver. Wealthy speculators often combine to take off large quantities of a stock that is small in amount, and thus produce an artificial scarcity. The public have perhaps become bears of the stock. Officials behind the scenes have perhaps sold heavily, knowing that a bad dividend is to be declared, or that some other adverse event is to come off, which the general market is unaware of. In all these cases a backwardation has to be paid by the bear to the bull. In theory, the bull gets it all, allowing for the jobber's turn. In practice, the bear pays it to his agents, except the fragment that finds its way with difficulty to the credit side of the bull's account, When the supply of stock is large, the bear has no backwardation to pay, but receives a contango, varying according to the honesty and industry of his agents.

As mentioned above, when the stock is scarce he has to pay. No rule can be given as to the amount of this charge. It may be $\frac{1}{16}$ and it may be 2 per cent. Perhaps from $\frac{1}{4}$ to $\frac{1}{2}$ is the average amount paid by bears under such circumstances. Just like contango, backwardation loves to play at hide and seek with the bear-speculators, and when a good many frightened bears have paid a heavy charge early in the morning on carrying over day, backwardation will often disappear altogether.

Perhaps backwardation is afraid of getting a good hiding from the bears, whom it has humbugged by its antics, and frightened into paying so heavily for the privilege of deferring their transactions until the next account. However that may be, on its disappearance, the bear can "carry back" his transaction or keep it open to next account for nothing, or, as we say, "even."

Cover or Margin.—These terms are applied to money deposited with brokers by clients as security for the payment of differences. There is no rule as to the amount, nor is it customary between gentlemen, unless the client be a new one and the transaction large.

Making-up.—This means the arrangement between jobber and broker as to what securities are to be taken up, what delivered, and what carried over to next account. If no notice be given by the client to his broker, the securities "open" must be bought or sold on that or the next day, or a name passed to take up or deliver the same. If there be a special reason, brokers will, if requested, defer carrying over until the afternoon of the first day, and rarely till the morning of the next day.

The Delivery of Stock Transferred.—Sellers of stock that requires a transfer stamp, unless by agreement the transaction be done for cash, are allowed ten clear days to deliver the stock. If not delivered on the eleventh day, the broker should be instructed by the client to "*buy the stock in*" against the seller which must be done by twelve o'clock, after one hour's notice has been given. If not bought in by half-past twelve, the notice to be cancelled, but if bought in, the stock must be delivered by one o'clock on the twelfth or next day.

Receiving and Paying Money for Stock Bought or Sold.—Those who have paid the broker for stock taken up naturally feel that they ought to receive what they have paid for; but as the seller is allowed ten days to deliver, they do not receive it; indeed often, where no instructions to "buy in" have been given to the broker, it is a month before the stock is obtained by the purchaser. This is a disadvantage, as he might wish to borrow money upon it, besides the disagreeable feeling of having paid the money and received nothing for it. I am instructed to say that the honorable members of the Stock Exchange feel that some alteration of this law is required; but, meantime, I can assure investors and speculators that where they have signed the transfer, which is generally certified by the company, there is no danger. The danger lies here. Suppose you have an account with Erasmus Pinto, in which you have to pay £1000 for stock you have bought and intend to keep. It is customary to pay Erasmus Pinto on the settling day, although the transfer may not, and usually does not, come in until from three or four to ten days after that period. Now of course there is nothing on earth to prevent Erasmus Pinto, after cashing your cheque, from levanting with your money, and leaving you to pay again or go without the stock. It is all gammon, my dear "Outside Fools," to talk about not dealing with a broker unless you trust him. You have no right to be obliged so to trust him. We trusted Overend and Gurney pretty well. Collie had his share of credit. My brothers know what nonsense that is, and they want this rule altered. Indeed, some respectable brokers won't take the money until the stock does come in. Snobs, who know they are thieves, and think refusing to pay is as good as telling them that they are, would send you away if you refused to pay for stock on settling day.

Until the law is altered, dear "Outside Fools," keep a sharp look out upon your broker, and if he does not like it, you may take your oath he is a snob or thief.

In delivering stock, you must not expect the money from your broker until you have signed the transfer and given him the certificate; all you have to mind is that he does not give you a cheque that comes back with N.E. or N.S. on its face, and that he does not sell your stock for cash and retire from the scene altogether. Such cases have been known, and you need not be surprised that Erasmus Pinto's brothers feel rather sore that their good name should be dragged through the dirt by the malpractices of these black sheep.

Scrip or Securities to Bearer.—With few exceptions, this term is a synonym for rubbish, or, at best, the so-called securities are equivalent in value to a mine. One year they are worth 70, another 40, and at some time they die out altogether. Besides this, they depend entirely upon the great *financier's* name at the back of them. He will endorse them as long as he sees his way to get enormous pickings out of repeated loans for the same improving countries, as they are always termed until the public refuse more subscriptions. Then the great magnate of finance suddenly discovers that this improving country is not good enough for him, and passes the half or three parts sucked orange on to a brother financier whose tarnished name will let him deal in damaged oranges.

The former great supporter does not object to sell a huge bear of damaged oranges before he withdraws his valuable concern from the Jew's fruit shop. Not by any means. He rather likes it. Besides the other disadvantages of these I O U's, some of which are worth nothing, and others are on the eve of a heavy fall, there is this ugly fact, that they may be lost, like five-pound notes, and if you think the countries who issued them will give you fresh ones, I pity your innocence. Their principle is repudiation, and this is legal repudiation. The advocates of this sort of security say, "It is so negociable and so free from expense of transfer and fee." More shame to our government that it is so.

More than One Broker Desirable.—The advantage of having two or more brokers is considerable. You can check the prices, and see by the comparison whether there be collusion. If you have bought from one and want to act again in the same stock, his instincts would tell him that you would be likely to sell; whereas, if you go to the other, he would not know that. But, my dear "Outside Fools," if you played that little game with Erasmus Pinto, he would soon find out your other broker and make it all right.

Ex-Div., or Ex-Int., Ex-New, Cum-Div.— These abbreviations, so often seen in the daily share list, mean this. That a stock is, from the present date, to be considered in all dealing as ex the dividend or interest due upon it, or ex the proportion of new share that may be due to a bull. The rule is this. All purchases made before the stock is quoted ex-div., or ex-int., or ex-new, are entitled to the dividend, interest, or proportion of new shares, and all sales made previously to that quotation lose the same advantages. A bear of stock has to pay the dividends, interest, and proportion of new shares, and that is not to be despised in railway securities, Don't draw a wrong deduction from the recent drop in Rails, dear "Outside Fools;" see how large the rise was from the commencement before you form a hasty judgment.

Consols.—This word is an abbreviation for consolidated stocks. Nearly ten million of the national debt was consolidated in 1751, and the interest fixed at 3 per cent. The debt was three hundred and seventy millions in 1852, the increase being caused by war.

A Stag.—One who applies for shares in a new company or stock in a Foreign Loan, with the intention of selling the allotment-letter.

An Outsider.—This term applies to a dealer in stocks and shares who is not a member of the House; but as used in an article of the *Times* some few months ago, in the expression, "*the foolish outsider*," we presume it only refers, dear "Outside Fools," to your worthy selves. Never mind, it is much better to be a "foolish outsider" than a rogue who makes use of his position to plunder poor dupes, as, alas, Erasmus Pinto and others have too often done.

Pm., or *Prem.,* stands for the *premium* or price above its par value at which any stock or share is.

Dis.—Stands for the discount or price below the par value of stock and shares.

A Defaulter or Lame Duck.—One who absconds, levants, or cannot pay his differences.

What governs the daily price of stocks and shares? The two powers that regulate the price of all shares are,—

Supply and Demand.—If a corn-merchant finds the prospect of the harvest bad, he immediately bids for corn to secure a stock that he knows will be wanted, and his bidding or endeavor to get the stock puts up the price. On the other hand, if the harvest prospects are good, he tries to sell his stock, or most of it, for fear he should have it on his hands in a declining market. Too many corn-merchants for the last two or three years have been *stuck* with corn. Just so when the warm winds of April and May (when there are any) induce the speculative fish to nibble or bite freely, there is a run on worms and gentles, and some broker-anglers, who have not sniffed the coming feeding inclination, are short of worms and gentles, and have to bid for them and put up the price. Then has the "catcher of the early worm" his golden harvest. Your speculative fish are always found in shoals. The silent solitary pike is represented by the great Loan Monger, aided sometimes, we fear, by the City editor.

I and plenty of my brother brokers have seen the public rush at the markets so eagerly that the dealers were obliged to put up the price from one to two per cent. for several mornings to protect themselves, so universal was the inclination to buy. That was the time for an outside bull. But, hark ye "outsiders," don't buy on a jump at the opening. The jobber is a much more accurate gauger of the public requirements than you think; and nine times out of ten, if you buy on such a rise at the opening, you will find a lull ensue, when you will not buy again. But that is when you ought to buy.

The Best Time of the Year to Speculate.—At that time when the first chance occurs. Erasmus Pinto is not such a charlatan, dear "Outside Fools," as to try and pick your pockets by giving advice on what none but those gifted with second sight or some supernatural power can offer an opinion worth the words the opinion is couched in.

Riggers and Members of a Syndicate.—These are wealthy speculators who band together generally under the leadership of one or more leading spirits connected with the Rig or Operations of the Syndicate. Their *laches* are very simple, and much more dishonest than your speculation, dear "Outside Fools." They create an artificial scarcity of stock, generally a small one, because it is so much more easily handled, and often a bad one, because the public will probably be bears of it, by buying suddenly through their instructed agents large quantities of it, often offering to give money for the call of more at a price higher then the current one, so as to give the impression that something good is going to come off. They hire, when they are strong enough, columns in the papers and write up their selection. They establish "Amicable Relations" with brokers and jobbers whom they can tempt by a hope of some small share of the plunder. And so they force up the price of stocks which are by no means always fit for investment or sound speculation to a price far above their value. Well, they know that on a sudden rise the public bears will close, and bulls rush in to aid their philanthropic game of *Unloading*, as we term it, their expensive wares.

Wreckers.—This elegant appellation is bestowed upon those who make a similarly-organized attack as bears upon some stock, rotten or good, according to their power, and force down the price by large and successive sudden sales. They trust to the well-known fact that the ignorance of investors about the merit of the stocks they hold is so great and their fears so readily excited that they are sure to come to the help of the *Wreckers*, and enable them to close their transactions at a handsome profit.

A *Corner, Pool, Clique, Ring* are all terms equivalent to a *Rig* or *Wreck*.

Banging the Market only means producing a temporary fall by sheer audacity and impudent offering of stock in large quantities, or by the circulation of false telegrams and mendacious statements.

The American terms for "bulling" and "bearing" are "selling *long*" and "selling *short*," or, as they sometimes say, "To *go long*," or "*go short*."

CHAPTER LXXVIII.

ON THE WORKING OF OPTIONS.

OF all kinds of speculation none are more interesting than speculating by "Options." If speculation could be conducted by the public in this way, I do not think it would do much harm. And the exercise of the mind requisite to work them properly is beneficial rather than not. Certainly if a man be fond of theory, a good calculator, and desire to conduct his speculation upon sound principles, without incurring the practically indefinite risk attaching to most other kinds of speculation, he should speculate by options.

As I observe that writers on Stock Exchange speculation give no explanation of the working of these options, I will illustrate them briefly for the benefit of those cautious and mathematically-minded "outsiders" who may have thought that here, at least, they have found out how a clever "Outside Fool" may win money if he likes.

There are several kinds of Options. The most common are the *Put Option*, the *Call Option* or the *Put and Call Option*, called by the Americans the *Straddles*. There are options for the day, or for the account, or for the next account but one, and even for a longer time. Daily options expire at a quarter to three o'clock on the same day; other options at a quarter to three o'clock on the carrying over day of the account for which they are entered into.

The "*Call Option*" will be understood better by the novice if he consider it as a speculation in which he may gain indefinitely, and can only lose a fixed sum which he agrees to pay for the option or right of taking or not taking a certain quantity of stock at a certain price at a fixed future date.

In the following illustrations I have selected the stock that has been most dealt in by options, and have supposed the fluctuations to be moderate and probable.

The Working of a Call Option.—Suppose the speculator has given $\frac{1}{2}$ per cent., which would be a fair price for the call of 5000 Turkish 5 per cents. for the account at 23, he then stands to lose £25 if no rise occurs, and to win an indefinite sum from any rise that may occur, or from the way he works against his call option. I may just mention that most brokers only charge commission on the dealings, *i.e.*, if no chance of dealing has occurred all the time, they charge no commission. We have assumed that the speculator has given £25 for the call of 5000 Turks at 23. His object is now to profit by the rise. If after he has given the money the stock falls all the account and does not recover, he of course will lose his money. But had he given it just before the repudiation, when the stock was much higher, he would have lost no more than his £25. Suppose it rises from 23, the option price, to $23\frac{1}{2}$ buyers, the operator should sell 2000 of the 5000, because a relapse is likely, and the price already shows a profit of ½ per cent. If he sells 2000 he will have a profit on the account day of £10. Suppose the stock rises further to 23¾ buyers, he should sell 1000 more. This would show a profit against the call of £7 10s. If it rises to 24 buyers, he should sell another 1000, which would leave him still one thousand open and give another profit of £10. Now if I were the operator I should not close the last thousand unless it showed a rise of 2 per cent. or more, but the speculator must observe this. If, after his first sale, the stock dropped not less than ⅜ (it would hardly be worth his while to act if it did not), but as much more as might happen, he should disregard the call and treat his sale as an ordinary bear operation, closing at whatever profit the price would allow. Thus, instead of letting the sale of the first thousand at 23½ be reckoned as against the call price of 23, if it dropped after the sale to below 23, he should buy back, because he would gain more by so doing and still have the whole option open. Just so with the second, third, or fourth thousand sold. If it falls to near the option price or below it, he should treat the matter as a simple bear operation, closing at a profit and starting again with his option free to act against again. The operator must remember that he should enter into his option bargain as soon as the account begins, because he would have so much more time to act in, and not forget that $\frac{1}{8}$ commission per thousand stock is charged, and that he need not call the stock on the option day unless it shows a profit. As a general rule at least ⅔ should be sold on a fair rise, if the operator does not take the scale given above, and at

YE OUTSIDE FOOLS. 359

least one-fifth left open to catch a possible large fluctuation. The operator who simply does nothing while the market keeps moving up and down will never make options pay, and if he is so clear about the rise he had better be a bull of the stock and pay nothing but the commission.

The Working of a Put Option.—This will be better understood by the novice if looked upon as a speculation in which the loss is definite and the possible gain indefinite. The same amount is generally given not necessarily because the stock is so likely to rise as to fall, as because by a dealer in the House a *put* or *call* option can be made to act as a protection with equal ease.

We will suppose, then, that our operator has given ½ for the "put" of Turkish 5 per cents. at 23 believing that the stock will fall. If it rises all the account, he of course loses the money. But we will assume that after he has given for the *put* at 23 the stock falls ½ per cent. He might buy 2000, because he would make £10, reckoning against his *put*, less the commission of course of ⅛ per 1000. In all these examples the commission must be deducted. If after he has bought 2000 the market rallies to 22⅞, he would be wise to consider the previous operation as a bear sale closed at a profit of £7 10s., instead of reckoning 2000 of the put option as used, and a profit of £10 made. He would then have the put of 5000 to act against as before. Suppose the stock falls to 22⅜, he might buy 3000 this time, as he had already made £7 10s. of his £25. This, if reckoned against the put option, would give a profit of £18 15s. But if the market rallied after his purchase to 22⅞, he would do well to consider himself a protected bull of

3000 Turks at 22⅜, and to sell them at 22⅞, making a profit of £15, instead of £18 15s., if reckoned against 3000 of his option of 5000. He would have the whole 5000 to act against again, and on every moderate drop he should buy part of his 5000, and whenever it came near to the option price he should treat the operation as a simple bull, and sell to secure the profit and leave himself free to act. No amount of dealing and profit vitiates the option if each transaction be closed.

The Working of a Put and Call Option or Straddles.—The operator generally pays something less than twice the price of the single operation for this privilege. If the *Put or Call* of Turks were ½ per cent, as we assumed above, the put *and* call ought to be bought ⅞ for an account.

The novice will understand it better if he considers that he is both a protected bear and bull within certain limits, and that his object is to get his option money back, and a profit beside, by frequent dealings within the range of his option, or by the difference above or below the option price at a quarter to three on the first day of the account. His loss is definite. His gain depends upon the fluctuations in price and his skill in taking advantage of them.

We will suppose that a speculator has given ⅞ for the " put and call " of 5000 Turks for the account at 23. He can only lose £43 15s.

It does not matter to him whether the stock rise or fall, as long as it does one or the other.

Suppose, then, after he has given the money, that some one of the many causes at work knocks the price down from the option price of 23 to 22½. When I say 22½ I mean of course 22½ sellers. And *vice versâ* in the other reckonings. He should buy 2000, and reckoning it as against the put option at 23, there would be a profit of £10. So if the stock rose to $23\frac{1}{2}$, he should sell 2000, and reckoning that against the call option, there would be a profit of £10. But if in either case the price came within $\frac{1}{8}$ of the option price, viz., 23, it would be better to treat the first operation as a simple bull at $22\frac{1}{2}$, and to sell it at $22\frac{7}{8}$, or to treat the other operation as a simple bear operation at $23\frac{1}{2}$, and to buy at $23\frac{1}{8}$. He would in each case make $\frac{1}{8}$ per cent. less profit, but he would have the whole of his 5000 to operate against again, instead of only 3000, and would have still made $\frac{3}{8}$ per cent. profit.

In this way the operator should keep on taking advantage of the fluctuations, but not closing the whole 5000, except the profit be great enough to show a good profit after paying the option money. But all Stock Exchange speculation has so much to do with the unforeseen, that an operator should always have a small part open, unless provoked to close by a large fluctuation.

In theory it is a mistake to give for the *double option* in all cases where the stock is not very unsettled, and liable through special causes to violent fluctuations.

How to Turn a Single Option into a Double One. —Suppose the operator, as before, has given $\frac{1}{2}$ per cent. for the put *or* call of 5000 Turkish Fives at 23, and he feels uncertain about the probable fluctuations, and yet does not wish to incur the expense of the double option. To give himself the advantage of the " put *and* call option " (in a less degree, of course), he should act thus.

At the time when he gives for the *put* of 5000 at 23, he should buy 2000 at as near 23 as the jobbers' turn would permit; or, if he gave for the *call* of 5000 at 23, he should sell 2000 at the same time, and as near the price as the market would allow; the difference would only be $\frac{1}{16}$, or at most $\frac{1}{8}$. In the first case he would virtually be a protected *bear* of 3000, and a protected *bull* of 2000 Turks. In the other he would virtually be a protected *bull* of 3000, and a protected *bear* of 2000. If the stock rose above 23, he should sell slowly, not more than 1000 at a time, unless the rise was considerable, and take care, if a drop ensued to near the option price, to treat it as a simple bear transaction, while if the stock fell to below 23, he should buy still more slowly, as he has only 2000 to work with on this side, and remember, if the stock rallies to near the option price, he should treat it as a simple bull operation. He would then in both cases have his option of 3000 on the one side, and 2000 on the other, free to act against as before. The double option has this advantage, that there is no loss in the turn of the market, whereas in the single one there is.

The Working of Options in Practice.—Options are very interesting in theory, dear "Outside Fools," but they are not easy things to manage in practice, and I will tell you why.

In the first place, from our great experience we can estimate the value of them very much better than you can, and make the price accordingly.

Secondly, dealing by options is discouraged indirectly with "*outsiders*," and when an "outsider" does persist in trying to deal, he does so at great disadvantage in the price.

A jobber in options will make the price $\frac{1}{2}$-$\frac{3}{4}$, that is, he will take from the "outsider" $\frac{3}{4}$ per cent., or give him $\frac{1}{2}$. And observe, this is only in such a stock as Turkish 5 per cents., Peru, or Egypt; not now, mind, but when there was a comparatively steady market. In Spanish, the option can be had for about $\frac{3}{8}$, the double option for $\frac{5}{8}$ to $\frac{3}{4}$, as a rule.

But in any fluctuating stock, the jobber will most likely refuse to deal at all, or if he does offer to do so, he will make this sort of price 2–4. That is, he will take 4 per cent., or give 2 per cent.

In Consols the option varies from $\frac{1}{4}$ to $\frac{3}{8}$ per cent., and often the double option can be had for $\frac{1}{2}$ per cent. Take my advice, dear "Outside Fools," and keep clear of options, unless you have some good information about a movement likely to come off which others have not, and then you might as well act without the options.

Taking the Money in Options.—But if you must deal in "Options," whatever you do, don't take the money unless you have great confidence in the stock, and also possess the stock.

It is most dangerous. It can be done by "Insiders" because they can square their books as you cannot; but it is the worst operation possible to take the money.

We will suppose that a client has been rash enough to do so, and that he has taken 2 per cent. for the put of Egypt '73. The stock may drop 5 per cent. in a week with the greatest ease, and rise the same. Suppose you try to protect yourself by selling a bear of the same amount as you have taken money from the dealer for allowing him the right of *putting* the stock on you when the account day comes round. This is all very well; but suppose the stock never drops at all, but rises before option day 4 to 5 per cent. The dealer will not *put* the stock on you, of course, and you will be caught a bear, with a difference of 2 or 3 per cent. to pay after reckoning the 2 per cent. you receive from the jobber.

Suppose, on the other hand, that you have taken $1\frac{1}{4}$ per cent. for the call of Great Northern A, and have not the stock; you buy yourself a bull of the same amount to be ready for the dealer; but lo, the stock drops all the account instead of rising, and he never calls it of you, but leaves you a bull with a loss of 4 or 5, with only $1\frac{1}{4}$ to meet it.

If you hold a stock that fluctuates moderately, and you also believe in it, there is not much harm in taking for the put and call, if the dealers will give a fair price, which it is not often they will do. In this case, if the stock is called, you have it to deliver, and if it is put upon you, you have only got some more of what you believe in and a bonus for speculation in it.

Wide Price Options.—Some speculators prefer to give less money for the option and have it fixed at a more disadvantageous price to them.

Thus, suppose A gives $\frac{1}{4}$ for the *put* of 5000 Turks at 23 when the market is $23\frac{1}{2}$; he will only have to pay £12 10s. for his option; but the stock must fall more than $\frac{1}{2}$ per cent. before he can act at all. It looks cheap; but it does not often answer. So if he gave $\frac{1}{4}$ for the *call* at $23\frac{1}{2}$ when the market is 23, it must rise more than a half before he can deal.

Sometimes speculators will buy, say 1000 stock, and give $\frac{1}{4}$ per cent. for the *Call of more, i.e.,* the option of calling another thousand during the account.

Or they will give $\frac{1}{4}$ per cent. for the *Put of more* when they have sold 1000. If they can get a broker and a jobber to carry this out, it will sometimes answer; but in all cases where it would answer you will find both us and the jobbers fully alive to the fact, and we shall not let you have any great bargain, you may be sure.

Jobbers' Options.—As a rule most jobbers prefer to go home with their books even, and as they cannot always manage this, they will give or take from $\frac{1}{8}$ to $\frac{3}{8}$ for the *call* or *put* of the stocks they deal in, for the same day, or generally from the afternoon of one day till a quarter to three on the next. And the outsider who has a good nose for a market will, if his broker be smart and willing, find no trouble in getting options of this sort done, only he must remember that he will have to pay from $\frac{1}{16}$ to $\frac{1}{8}$ more than the jobber would, and when you consider that this is only for one day, even $\frac{1}{16}$ makes a good deal of difference.

From Saturday to Monday is a good time for these operations on the *Boulevards*, as it is sometimes called in Throgmorton Street, opposite MacLean's Exchange, a favorite *venue*.

CHAPTER LXXIX.

ENGLISH RAILWAY AS "MEDIA" FOR SPECULATION AND INVESTMENT.

But what are we to buy? say "Outside Fools."

Buy English Rails when they are not too high. They have been so, but they will soon be low enough. This season of the year is generally bad for bulls; but after March is past you may expect a bull to have his turn. Here are my reasons for advising you to buy the English Rails.

They are real property, and indestructible. They don't depend upon the name of some great magnate who at any moment may desert the ship and leave the passengers to drown, as is the case with Foreign loans.

The strife of politics, the panics of finance alike are powerless to damage them or permanently affect the price. There never will again be the same competition from the Foreign loans. That growing evil, over-population, does the railroads good. Extension manias are over now. There are no temporary loans to be renewed in panic times. They have been all converted into permanent Debenture Stock, which does not quite pay 4 per cent., so eagerly is it sought for. Even the Preferences cannot be bought to pay more than from $4\frac{1}{4}$ to $4\frac{1}{2}$ per cent., and where the full dividend is expected shortly to be made up, they cannot be bought to pay more than Consols.

Of course to a speculator a half per cent. more or less dividend is a matter of some consequence, but the investor may hold the best English Railways with the greatest confidence. All he has to do is to buy more when a heavy drop has occurred from temporary causes. A man does not give up the occupation of his farm because he has had one or two bad years, but waits for the average return. It should be so with Railway Stocks.

Only do, my dear "Outside Investing Fools" (for of all fools you mostly are the most ignorant, and often make the heaviest losses, because you hold till there is nothing left to hold), remember this. The time to buy is not when your *broker* is advising you to do so, when City editors are drawing attention to or when every one is talking loudly in praise of such and such a stock; but when there has been a fall, and when you feel inclined to think the soundest stocks are rotten at the core—that's the proper time to buy. Just now (I am speaking of January of the present year, 1876), all good securities have been forced up by the continued dulness of trade, the great scarcity of good investments, the general collapse in Foreign securities, and the ease of the money market. If you value your peace of mind, touch not a Foreign Bond, unless it be the few given in the list appended to this book. The great trunk lines of the country are the true investments for a man of sense who likes a sound and fluctuating security. Unless you believe that our country has passed the zenith of its prosperity, and that there is no revival of trade to come, or that the accounts have been so unfairly kept that a startling revelation of chicanery and fraud is in store for investors here, English Rails are the only true field for sensible operations, whether for speculation or investment. No doubt working expenses are now nearly at their lowest, but as soon as the coal and iron trades revive, so surely will the goods traffic largely increase, and whatever state trade may be in population will travel more and more each year that comes. More confidence is felt and more is known now about railroads than before.

The substitution of steel rails for iron will certainly tell very favorably in the cost of permanent way. They last from six to seven times as long. There is, too, a great saving in the substitution of iron for wood in the construction of bridges, stations, and other works. And whatever may be said of the block-system, and its defects, were it not for the indifference and carelessness of the company's servants themselves, who, like domestics, are getting too much the upper hand, there would be very much fewer accidents. No doubt in time machinery will free us still more from dependence on manual labor, where life is so concerned as it is here. Some of the larger companies have already supplemented the original double line with additional lines of rails, and are now in a position to deal properly with the large accession of business which the next revival of trade must bring; other large railway companies are paying heavy sums as interest on unproductive capital, all of which is borne by revenue, and as soon as that capital becomes productive the recovery in price will be great and permanent. Competitive schemes are neither fostered by the public nor by Parliament. See what the Brighton scheme has ended in, in spite of prophecies to the contrary. But a careful selection is necessary even in Rails.

The passenger lines have hitherto had it nearly all their own way, and we think that South-Western, Metropolitan District Preference, and Brighton will continue to improve. North British, at its present price of 103 *cum-div.*, is a good investment. Future prospects are often more important to look to than present dividends. Investors generally buy on the dividend declared, and by doing so they throw a great temptation in the way of directors to make things too pleasant. Great Eastern depends upon the development of the suburban traffic, Metropolitan may improve, Midland is a very improving property, and North-Western very safe; but the great trunk lines will not have their rise until trade revives, and then it will be considerable.

The reason why the passenger lines are the best speculative purchase now is because they are not committed to a heavy capital expenditure, as is the case with the goods lines, and are not so much affected by the bad trade of the country.

Investors and speculators should watch their opportunity here. The great men just now are unloading largely, but they will want their cargoes back again ere long.

CHAPTER LXXX.

WHY THE GREAT TRUNK LINES ARE PREFERABLE AS SPECULATIVE "MEDIA" TO THE SMALLER ONES.

IT is better for the sober speculator to buy the great trunk lines for these reasons. Directors and their friends cannot manipulate the stocks so easily. It is a very different thing to move a stock thirty millions in amount, which requires several hundred thousand pounds to pay one per cent. in dividend, and which is held more firmly by investors, than it is one to which £40,000 will give an extra two per cent. of dividend. A very different thing, dear "Outside Fools." Don't be a bear or bull of such small stocks, unless you can afford to lose considerably. One accident may sweep away the whole earnings of a year. In these close boroughs you are indeed on slippery ground.

Let me draw your attention to this fact. It is the direct interest of officials in high places to charge everything against revenue for as long a period as possible, and to pay small dividends or none at all while this is going on. And when this policy has brought the line into an efficient state of repair, and the working expenses up to a high rate, it is their interest to change the plan. Then they charge as much as can be charged to capital, and pay large dividends until they are compelled, for fear the ship should sink, to sail upon the other tack. An even uneventful prosperity, such as the South-Western enjoys, and an absence of serious market fluctuations, means a loss of several thousands a year to these officials, and, look here, you carping "Outside Fools," who call us Vampires, and other vulgar names, you all deserve as much abuse as we. There is a jobber in the House who could play hanky-panky tricks with this sound line, but never has. Why, he and his directors would soon kick riggers and their juggling tricks out of their offices.

As I have observed, the method of treating the accounts has much to do with the price of those railroads where a small sum influences dividend, and where the stock is small and easily handled by a syndicate. Now, if Erasmus Pinto had the management of one of these companies, his policy would be this. Suppose at the time of the inauguration of the Pinto rule the line was in a very bad condition, the first move would be this. To create a rise with the aid of the Pinto clique (directors' names need not appear on contracts), so as to give the "Outside Fools" the idea that the Pinto ability was great. To issue a large amount of stock to equip the line thoroughly, get the rolling stock in a fine condition, and prepare for the great rise to come. The next move would be to sell upon this rise and issue new stock, and even sell heavy bears besides. Then the

Pinto directorate would charge everything to revenue, discover flaws in the keeping of the accounts, lay in a wondrous stock of general stores, go in for steel rails, block-system, the newest sort of brake, and anything and everything that would give an excuse for paying no dividend and putting their own hands into the till. Every now and then, when the public had sold bears on the bad apparent prospects of the line, the clever magnates would buy back, and would be aided greatly by the fright of "Outside Fools." Then when the proper time arrived, the Pinto party would put all their rich friends into the stock, and have a comfortable long trot upwards varying from ten to fifty per cent., according to the flexibility of the raw material. The beauty of this *modus operandi* is its extreme simplicity, and the fact that there's no chance of being detected in the game. It is everyone's interest to keep the secret. As for you, dear "Ordinary Shareholding Outside Fools," you might as well attempt to fly up to the moon as to contend against such very clever specimens of that curious creature, man, as Pinto and his friends most surely are. We soon would show you what packed meetings, money's power, and proxies mean.

As soon as our stock had reached its first resting-place on its upward march, we should allow you, dear "Outside Shareholding Fools," to hear through touts and tips of the improved prospects of the line. The rise will have been put on so suddenly that you will not have had time, if you had had the idea, to buy before. You will then take our "tips," although of course you will not think you are taking them and buy when the stock is at its first resting-place. We shall sell to you, and after you have bought, most singular so say, the stock will drop. You, or most of you, will be frightened, and sell your bulls, and perhaps go in for a little bear as well. We, knowing beforehand what the future is to be, shall buy again and take the stock up to a second station, where it will stop and take refreshment as before. You will say, " What an ass I was to sell, there's something in the rise this time ; " and you will buy more eagerly than before. We then shall declare an unexpected dividend, and get out of our stock on that. These tactics will be repeated over and over again, and should you happen to be on the same side as Pinto and his party, you will find that out of a rise of 30 per cent. you will only have secured about 3 per cent. clear profit. We shall have puzzled you so much.

Now, my dear "Outside Fools," don't cry aloud, " Oh! how dishonorable! how shameful! What a cheat! Oh! what a rogue!" but give your EGOS a rap on the knuckles every time they make themselves such dolts and hypocrites in uttering such remarks. You nearly all would do the same, if but you had the chance. Just think to what temptations clever directors and railway magnates are exposed. Unless they be philosophers or very curious specimens, they must play their best cards until your knowledge makes the game more difficult. You have no other chance but that. The only difference between directors and shareholders is this—the former are far more exposed to temptation to abuse their trust, and have so many more facilities. Then wake, investors, ye that are the sleepy backbone of the wealthy speculator's tricks, awake, I say! make your directors aim at closing capital accounts, and cease to try to rival bigger companies. "Rest and be thankful" is the motto you should have. But hark ye, "Outside Fools." If this be your belief, that one man is an angel, and another a devil, that Mr. Plausible High-and-Mighty is many thousand times better and more honest than Mr. Bluntthief, you are the "Outside Fool" I want as a client. None will lose his money sooner than yourself. If you are impulsive, vain, or arrogant, make pets of stocks, hug your ideas, take tips and hate cold principles, try to pick others' brains, and deal in half a dozen things at once, and cannot bear that men should know how small a man you really are, advice is of no use to you, and though you be not ruined on 'Change, which certainly you will be if you do not keep away, still, like so many thousand other fools who do not speculate, but launch out in a thousand ways, and try to make the world believe how very big they are, you'll come to grief some other way. But if you take old Seesaw's *MIIΔEN AΓAN* as your guide, and act according to our rules, you will not lose, though you don't make, and you may be amused for years, and learn much wisdom from your close acquaintance with Satanic dragon sovereigns' ways.

The proper course for "outsiders" is this. To first study the stock they determine to operate in, or, better still, to study several stocks, and then to take the earliest eligible opportunity that offers of operating in any one of them. To buy, say from a fourth to a half of the amount of stock upon which they can afford to pay a difference of ten per cent., if necessary. If the stock rises after the first purchase, to sell half the amount bought, and hold the other until a further rise has taken place. If there should be a relapse instead of a rise, it would be wise to buy again.

But suppose after the first purchase there has been a fall instead of a rise, the speculator should then buy a second fourth of what he can afford to pay a ten per cent. difference upon, and sell that on a rally. But nothing is certain in finance. If, then, after he had purchased the second fourth, a fall should occur, he must then buy his third fourth, and sell that on a rally, and if the rally be strong enough to show a profit upon the second fourth also, he should sell that too. But we will put an extreme case, and suppose that, although he has bought three-fourths of what he can afford to pay his ten per cent. difference upon, the stock still falls through an extraordinary concatenation of unfavorable circumstances, or his having purchased on the top of a large and artificial rise, he must purchase his last fourth and wait for a rally. The three requisites to prevent loss, dear "Outside Fools," are judgment, nerve, and money. Now, in this case nerve is the one you want most, and money next. But your money has been fixed at ten per cent. of the nominal value of the stock purchased, therefore nerve is the thing most required. If I were in your case I should consider that I had certainly done my best, that circumstances had been peculiarly untoward, and that it was my duty to await the event with calmness. Do you not know that in all circumstances in life, not excluding speculation, if you have done your best according to your conscience, you are not morally expected to do any more? I am supposing that your conscience does not tell you to keep away, for if it do, and you still come, I consider you beyond the pale of salvation. A man who knows what's wrong and still does it, is clearly lost; but I don't believe most of us, dear "Outside Fools," act in this way. I have a better opinion of humanity. Well, let us hope, and I tell you honestly that if you had chosen such a stock as I will shortly point out to you, it would have been in the highest degree probable that before you purchased your second, or third, fourth there would have been a rally. Now mind, if you refuse in that event to take a profit, you alone are to blame. Never mind, if the stock rises afterwards—of course it may, but your plan must be right in the long run.

If you wish to gain confidence with regard to the probable fluctuations in Rails, just turn to the average rise and fall during each month for three years past. You will find that there is a strong tendency in all the best stocks to rally after a fall of two or three per cent., especially when there is a fair business doing in the stock-markets. Where the average fluctuation has been exceeded there has mostly been a considerable rise. But let me caution you to keep away altogether when there is stagnation, or, as perhaps such advice is not consistent with an accurate knowledge of human nature, to have so small an amount open that you practically do not care if a drop of ten or fifteen per cent. occurs. The powerful cliques who have forced up the price of some railway stocks beyond their intrinsic value, seeing that the investment demand has ceased, and that the event of the dividends has been, as we say on 'Change, fully *gone for*, are turning out their holdings in lumps, and that, coming upon a market bare of investors and full of weak bulls, has of course a very great effect. The money lost in foreign loans is actually gone, and there is so much less buying power left, for credit is buying power as well as cash.

General rules and theory are all very well, but more than that is required to be a successful speculator. Some men have the instinctive diagnostic faculty,—that is no doubt only the rapid summing up of the knowledge they possess, and then bringing it to bear at once; but few have this.

Every transaction requires special knowledge and special attention, and that is why outsiders who deal first in one thing and then another must be ruined, It is as though a man first opened a baker's shop. and then a butcher's, then a barber's, and then a tailor's. We don't do that inside. We have our market and keep to it, and as we know all about the stocks much better to begin with than you do, and get better information of what the cliques are about, why, it is a certainty that we shall beat you, who generally know next to nothing of the stock, take the tips of the cliques who want you to do the opposite, and have not, like us, the necessary capital to see it out or to look for the *mathematical expectation*, as the theorists would say. I had a High Wrangler on my books (he is dead now), who thought that with his knowledge of mathematices he must succeed. He was not a gambler, but an experimental philosopher. What he told me was this, and I tell you, dear " Outside Fools "—

." *Multiply each gain or loss by the probability on which it depends, compare the total results of gains and losses, and then you will have the required average, or, as it is termed, the mathematical expectation.*"

I professed to be greatly interested, and my interest continued until the Wrangler had lost six hundred pounds in experimental philosophy.

As he was tired, I explained to him the fallacy. His deductions were quite correct, but his premises were wrong. In fact, he started with a *petitio principii*. In other words, he assumed that he knew the probability on which the gain or loss depended, which was a totally unwarrantable assumption. In Stock Exchange speculation, and indeed, as I think, in all other things, it is impossible to gain such a complete knowledge of the "*sum of the conditions*" as to correctly predict the result of those conditions. The only people, my dear "Outside Fools," who have any approximate knowledge of this philosphical "*sum of the conditions*" are the powerful men who are behind the scenes, the directors, and wire-pullers, and financial magnates, who, possessing through their wealth enormous leverage on the markets, exercise it remorselessly; and I grant you this, that they, if any one, have this knowledge. And yet it would not be theoretically correct to say that they had this knowledge, for a war might suddenly break out, they might die, a money panic might suddenly occur, or a division in their own camp, to frustrate their plans. And if this way of making money be not more Satanic and dishonest than the gambling of "Outside Fools," and more pernicious in effect than the hocus-pocus of directors and jobbers, I know nothing of the principles of right and wrong. But as I am a broker myself, I suppose you will say that's likely enough.

Well, well, let that pass. I can't see what we have to do with weighing up one another's defects and excellences so nicely, when if the whole earth were swept clean away, split into fragments, and each fragment attracted into some other atmosphere, and all of us petty mannikins smothered with our fussy EGOS in the dust, it would make no more difference to the harmony of the universe than it does when a philosopher breaks wind. Away with you, joltheads, do your little duties and forget yourselves. But I have nothing to do with you; let me to my "Outside Fools" again.

As I said before, you must buy a small quantity of a sound stock, sell half of it if it rises, if it falls buy more, and so on till you have no more power to buy left, always selling as soon as your purchase shows a fair profit. Bless your worthy hearts, dear "Outside Fools," you have no idea of the means these official cliques have at their disposal to make a rise or fall, and drag you into it. Just call to mind how many of these movements you have witnessed, and how you were always just aware of the causes when the top was reached, or else had sold a bear just before the lowest point was touched. Does it not make your hair stand on end to find how numerous they are? Did not Erasmus Pinto recommend Great Westerns to you, when they were 120? Did he not show you how the weekly returns had four months' poor traffic to compare with, and how a bull must be safe—for had not the stock been 130? Well, if he did not, some other genius did! Did not Mac-Lean's, the Lombard, the Jerusalem, the Baltic, and all the other fashionable haunts of speculating fools buzz with the words? Buy Westerns, that's the tip. Was it not you, Mr. Verdant Green, who told me the other day that I must be an ass for saying that Midlands were cheaper than Caledonians? Did you not say to me Midlands are at 137, *cum-div.*, and only pay 6 per cent., and Caledonians paid 6¼ last summer, and are expected to pay 7½? Anyway, they are buying the dividend in the market at 7₁⁷₆ you said. Of course they never buy the dividend and sell the stock! Oh, no! I suppose it could not be made to pay. Oh, dear, what Verdant Greens you are, you "Outside Fools!" The jobbers in the House know you far better than you know yourselves. They know your tempers and pet weaknesses, your way of dealing and your means. Our intermediate agents never give us a hint or two! Oh, no, of course they don't!

And this is why we shake the tree so often just at the right time, because we know exactly how much fruit will fall, and how much will stay on the tree. Have you not frequently been sorely puzzled to observe those sudden falls or rises which occur inside the House in one whole group of stocks at once, and frequently without external cause? Of course you have. It means that we all see clearly from the state of the accounts ouside how to play our cards, and we then begin to play. We hold most trumps, and what is more, can mostly say what shall be trumps, and can look over our opponents' hand. The only time we can't is when a war breaks out or when a great revival from a period of long stagnation first sets in. The public at those times have a decided bent, and their investments or their sales continue in a current strong and well defined. Then bulls of Bashan, let your hearts be glad. Then, you may buy half what you can afford to pay a difference of 3 or 4 per cent. on if you will take profits like a bull of sense. Then any fool can make a little coin. Sometimes, if there is no market and we want to make an impression on the minds of "Outside Fools," the lively sinners like myself and poor old Seesaw, who is now at rest, would chalk dummy bargains on our books, send brokers out with quoted changes in the price, and even get them marked in the official list and brokers' printed evening touts. But hold, I've told you quite enough to frighten you. Why don't I tell you rather what to do to save yourself? There's sense in that, and I have orders not to stir your bile or to excite alarm too much.

But just one word. If an "Outside Investing Fool" cannot buy leasehold house property to bring in from 6 to 7 per cent. clear of all deductions, he is a dolt. And if he can, what on earth does he want to buy Russian, Brazil, and French, to pay 5 per cent.? Once let him see a general war, these 5 per cent. investments would look very queer, and, what is more, he then would sell, because he then would find for the first time that he knew nothing of the countries' state.

CHAPTER LXXXI.

CAUTIONS TO INTENDING SPECULATORS AND INVESTTORS IN RAILROADS.

Now, my dear "Foolish Outsiders," as the leading journal terms you, lest in our remarks on English Railways we should lead you to suppose that all you have to do is to buy for speculation or investment, and on a drop buy more, we address a few words of caution to you before we take our leave. We certainly do think that to the permanent holder there is no investment so good as English Railways; but although this be the case, it does not follow that now is the time to begin to buy. During the last two years there have been some very unusual circumstances to affect the price of Railroads. One of these circumstances has been the abnormal and continued ease in the money market. Another has been the universal distrust of all Foreign Bonds, aggravated by the partial repudiation of Turkey, and the collapse in the credit of the South American Republics. A third cause has been the great dulness of trade succeeding the prosperity of 1871, 1872, 1873, which made many of the large merchants decline unremunerative business, especially as the relations between labor and capital were so unpromising, and bring their money to the Stock Exchange. It may seem paradoxical to the tyro, but when trade is bad and money cheap, the prices of stocks are inflated, because there is no other outlet for capital. A fourth cause has been the reduction in the price of iron and coal; and a fifth, favorable traffic receipts on most of the lines, except those affected specially by the severity of the struggle between labor and capital. The passenger lines derived the greatest benefit from the increased traffic, because the increase was earned at less expense, less wear and tear to rolling stock and permanent way.

At the very time, then, that cautious speculators, whose blood was cool enough to see when a stock was too high, and to think of legitimate selling for a fall, which, as the City editor of the *Times* says, does good to the community, capital, as is often the case, became in direct antagonism to reason, and large purchases of Railway stock were made by wealthy speculators, who were of course soon followed by a host of minor speculators, with more or less means at command. Enormous quantities of stocks were bought and pawned at the various banks, which would never have made such fearful losses if they had only made advances on such solid property, with a respectable margin. Of course the principal operators, who went in at the commencement of the movement, have made very large profits, for they were enabled to effect partial realizations as the market rose, and then buy again on a temporary relapse. I can assure you, my dear "Outside Fools," that it took a very shrewd fellow to see that after 1875 came in, and when the rise in some stocks had been considerable, that still the tendency was upwards. Any "outsider" who was unfortunate enough to be caught a bear in the rise of Brighton, Dover A, Metropolitan, and others, will see clearly how useless proverbial wisdom is on 'Change. "Buy when they're low, and sell when they're high," is the old saw. Just so; be good enough to tell me when they're high, and when they're low. If any proof could be given of the folly of "outsiders" bearing without machinery to help them, for the good of the community forsooth, it certainly might have been derived from the sharp lesson of 1875. How many an honest speculator who listened to the broker's sage remark, "Rails are very high," and to the gabble of other speculators, or the statements of interested professionals, and the insidious suggestions thrown out from time to time in the newspapers, and always at the wrong time, have had great reason to rue the day when they tried to go against the grain, and sell a bear legitimately, for the good of themselves and the community. We can bear inside because we get our turns and a peep at the state of the account. You outside know nothing of the account, and get not much more than half as much as we do in contango, besides the danger of being frightened into closing just at the wrong time.

But to return. As soon as the wealthy speculators had bought, the accommodating Money Articles enunciated the theory that about four per cent. was sufficient return on all Railways that were improving, and that about ten per cent. might be safely added on to the price for the privilege of possessing, as the ordinary stocks do, the reversion of the whole earnings of the lines, after payment of the dividend to the Preferences. How much, dear " Outside Fools," do you think a City editor ought to have received who had the courage to speak thus to his readers, " *Although it is a fact that Railroad Stocks are high, it is also very probable that the rise will continue, because of the strength of the speculators and the dearth of other channels of investment and the plethora of money. Legitimate bears, be careful, or you will be pickled in a pungent and unreasonable brine !* "

Rogue as Erasmus Pinto is, he would have been proud to grasp the hand of a City editor whom his owners would have allowed to write such words as those. It is simply a question of strength on 'Change. Money will do anything for a time, and as we club together and are aided by the wealthy speculators, you have no chance unless you go with the stream. Has it never struck you how frequently a rise or fall occurs quite suddenly, inaugurated by us, and how the papers never say, "Such and such an event is likely to happen;" but always say "has happened;" and then use their knowledge of the combinations of words to give a plausible account of it. If ever they do prophesy, it is in the form of vague vaticination, which is always wrong. The ignorance or carelessness of City editors is wonderful.

Now, as a legitimate bear got a pretty pickling all last year, and is very likely to turn bull this, we lay before him and all whom it may concern the following considerations, and it is not our fault that the book was not before our readers at an earlier date. The difficulties a bull has to face are these:—

1. Traffics are diminishing.
2. Coal and iron are at their lowest.
3. Wages keep steadily increasing.
4. The public temper hostile and unjust to the Railways.
5. No immediate prospect of improvement in trade.
6. Further large amounts of capital required.
7. The fact that Government ministers have been asked by members to bring in a bill for shortening the hours of pointsmen, signal-men, and engine drivers, and to improve the service generally.

If only the jobbers parliamentary, directorial, and financial clubbed together and unfurled the banner, with "*compulsory doubling of the lines*" worked upon it, what would become of bulls who vainly tried to buy legitimately for the good of the community, and to oppose their puny common-sense against the powerful machinery of the protected bears? Ah! what indeed.

Although we have the greatest confidence in the indestructibility of Railway property, and although investors who do not mind a little temporary diminution of dividends will do well to stick to their holdings, and buy a little more when the storm looks very black, still we should fail in our duty if we did not warn you that an organized *Railway Scare* might easily be got up, in which case you would be sure to sell at somewhere near the lowest price. The man who holds English Railway stock will, in a few years' time, be richer than the holder of a similar amount of any other class of security. But it is quite possible that some very severe fluctuations may occur before that time. The bull's great opportunity will be on the eve and during the commencement of the next revival of trade. There is usually a strong rally in Rails about Easter or Whitsuntide; but it sometimes does not last, and this year, if it occur, it is very probable that it will not last.

The passenger lines must not be classed with the great trunk lines. As permanent investments we decidedly prefer the latter; as present speculations we should select some of the former. That ever-increasing item of wages falls more heavily on the great trunk lines; the expense, too, of the block-system and increased number of sidings to relieve the goods traffic falls heavier upon them. The passenger lines, on the other hand, are less affected by depression in the trade of the country, and can accommodate the increase of traffic derived from a growing population without incurring much extra expense. Of course any remission of passenger tax would benefit them much more; but we do not believe that any remission worth anything will be made, except it be in the case of what may be termed the Omnibus Lines, viz., the Metropolitan and the District. Their case is certainly very hard.

R

There is one point in which the great trunk lines have a most decided advantage over the passenger lines, and that is, that an accident, however bad, does not affect their dividends in the same ratio. A loss of twenty or thirty thousand pounds in this way is a very serious thing to a line that only requires about that sum to pay one per cent. of dividend for the half-year; but it makes little difference on lines that require from £130,000 to £310,000 to pay the same sum. Holders of Railway stock and speculators would do well to remember that, practically speaking, dividends are derived from maintenance charges —that is, the amount of dividend is increased or decreased according as the charges are low or high. Now when we see these charges very low, we do not, as you do, dear readers, feel bullish, and point with delight to that fact; but knowing that it will soon be time for the ship to be sailed on the opposite tack, to save her from sinking, we take our cut off the loaf thankfully, and, with our tongue tucked in our cheek, we pass it on to the public bull, or sometimes we even sell a legitimate bear for the good of the "end of all commerce and the community."

A speculator should remember this fact, that on 'Change, when the event "gone for" has actually come off, there is generally a movement in the opposite direction from bears closing or bulls realizing. Many a novice has lost his profit from being ignorant of this fact. With regard to the idea that seems to be gaining ground that directors are exposed to too severe temptations, as according to the City editor of the *Times* we brokers are, you must exercise your own judgment, my dear "outsiders." We explain, or try to explain, the system;

we do not attack men. We believe that one man is about as good as another in this respect all the world over.

CHAPTER LXXXII.

A BRIEF ACCOUNT OF A STOCK THAT HAS LATELY BEEN THE JOY AND GRIEF OF THE SPECULATOR BY MACHINERY AND THE RUIN OF THE SPECULATOR WITHOUT.

Egyptian 1873.

A STOCK *sui generis* is this, containing many hidden qualities and virtues. It should be the true gambler's delight, and has afforded even the *bonâ fide* investor the luxury of grief. A stock that must have sadly interfered with the doctor's melancholic patients; for has it not proved itself a narcotic, a tonic, a purgative, a diaphoretic, a stimulant, a noble searcher of the secretions, compared with which scammony and blue-pill are but as dirt, podophyllin and the world-famed Flatus-pills as dross ? Have we not seen red men turn pale and pale men turn red with the blush of excitement, through the magic influence of this glorious stock ? We have—yes, nearly every day. No " Inside Ass " this stock would dare to class. That's why we place it by itself. Its present and future value depends more upon parliamentary policy and the financiers' names that may endorse it than upon its intrinsic merits, which are as difficult to get at as a hedgehog is for a lady's poodle to unroll.

The present condition of Egyptian credit resembles that of a man who has gone down twice in deep water, and whom, just as he is sinking for the last time, a boat, arriving like a *Deus ex machina*, unexpectedly saves from a watery grave. Perfidious Albion was the boat; she rowed along the Suez Canal to save the drowning man. In such a hurry was perfidious Albion that, instead of rowing steadily in her true lifeboat, she must engage the services of Jewish boatmen at enormous cost to save the drowning man, although her coffers were all gorged with her perfidious sons' deposits, that could not have been employed more profitably.

How very odd it seems that the Bank of England could not have kept the secret as well as a financier, or as well as it was kept that afternoon until all had bought who ought to be allowed to buy. This surely proves that the bank's powers should be made a little flexible to suit the case.

Mr. Cave's report, we are told, implies that there is enough to pay seven per cent. on the Bonds, and that there is no necessity for the investors to lose anything. We are very glad to hear it. Of course Mr. Cave had access to all documents without reserve. He did not meet with any opposition in an attempt to probe the matter to the bottom. It was of course every one's interest to make things as smooth as possible for him. Well, it may be so, but it is very unlikely. The whole question, to our mind, with regard to Egypt lies in a nutshell. It is pleasant to hear that seven per cent. can now be paid on all Bonds; but more is required than that before investors are to be allowed to be again narcotized by the influence of a great financial name, which will undoubtedly be sought for soon to float another loan. It does not matter what the state of Egypt is; if once the name be got, the loan will be subscribed. What we think ought to be done is this. The entire floating debt funded and made known. There lies the element of danger, there is the usurer's delight, the Khedive's insecurity. What we want to know is, what chance has the Khedive of freeing himself from the army of usurious sharks who are daily entangling him more and more in the meshes of the Treasury Bills-Renewing Net? It is the direct interest of all concerned that he should not free himself. The French won't help him. The chances are that, wanting money for his personal expenditure and for his hobby-horse industrial enterprise, he will talk loudly of retrenchment, struggle nobly perhaps, as does a horse on asphalte pavement when he falls, to rise, and ultimately relapse into the usurer's bottomless morass. If he would do away with all drawings, and offer to pay 5 per cent. interest, and pay off the floating debt with the surplus, supposing he be able to pay 7 per cent., investors would be in a far safer position, and we on 'Change should recommend the stock with confidence. The four millions received for the Suez Canal shares will soon be spent if war with Abyssinia be not stopped. It is a pity, for the Khedive is, for an Oriental, an enlightened and liberal-minded man; but he is very human, and he cannot fight against the juggles of finance any better than investors can at home. But if the Khedive be wise, he will not quarrel with that very straightforward and energetic king, Johannes, and his tame lionesses. Money has not yet sapped the courage and strength of his people.

Let him wait until Abyssinia has had a Foreign loan floated here. Even the money to corrupt the frontier governors and the Remington Rifles were captured by this strong, determined king of Abyssinia in the Gundet narrows. A man who fasts and takes the Sacrament before he swoops upon his foes reminds one more of an old Jewish king, and surely is more than a match for soldiers who have seen so much of money's baneful influence. Besides, the Khedive certainly was in the wrong, and badly advised. He should give up his industrial enterprise for a time, and incur no fresh floating debt. Personally, the Khedive is quick-witted, and reminds one more of a French financier than an Oriental potentate. The dexterity with which he seized the idea of joining England as a friend of slaves and negroes, and posing before future possible investors in a fresh light, was amusing and instructive. No one will deny the great natural resources of the country; but, in the Khedive's own words, the people have been *exploités*, and are still exposed to *exploitation*. "Pressure," he goes on to say, "is always brought to bear upon me when I try to rescue my country from this embarrassment. The French usurers offered me money the other day at 22 per cent. Of course I refused. By consolidating all my state and floating debts at a reasonable percentage I could balance my income and expenditure without injuring any one, and should no longer need to borrow money upon extravagant and ruinous terms, which sooner or later must lead to national bankruptcy."

The above are not our words, dear readers, they are the Khedive's own, transmitted by a special correspondent to our agent's office, and to our mind they seem eminently true and sensible. In dealing in Egyptian stocks the great hidden force, or "unknown quantity," that speculators and investors have to contend against is the floating debt. It was just the same with the Turkish *mandats*. No one but the very biggest men who had just made an advance knew how much they came to, and so the calculators of the debt, although their inferences were right enough, had never any premises that could be safely trusted to. Mr. Cave's report will do no good at all unless our Government is prepared to go still further, and it already begins to see that it has gone quite far enough in stock-jobbing transactions, if it does not want to have the keen-sighted Liberal discover awkward flaws. The position of Egypt, speaking financially, will be just the same as it was before Mr. Cave's report. No doubt the Elliot project was defeated quite as much by French jealousy as by want of time to arrange with capitalists in England. We can well believe that Mr. Cave knows the financial condition of Egypt as well as the Khedive himself; but that some Egyptian officials and Levantine usurers do not know the condition better than both the Khedive and Mr. Cave, we do not believe. The Khedive has another great difficulty to face besides that with the usurers, viz., that he cannot control the collection and expenditure of his revenues properly, or retrench in the way that is absolutely necessary, without making concessions to constitutional principles of government. If as he ought to do, as far as the financial welfare of his country is concerned, he surrender the direction of his financial affairs to English or French officials, he must lose a portion of his personal and supreme authority. Humiliation, even when only apparent, is anything but pleasant to the Oriental mind. Indeed, it is scarcely politic to submit to it. Surrounded, as Ismail is, by insinuating flatterers, who ever tell him blandly that Egypt's wealth is inexhaustible, and knowing, as he does, that many an English investor believes the same; continually urged, as he is, by the seductive wiles of usury to issue loan after loan privately, and never mind the terms or interest, he would be more than human did he not succumb at last.

There is one point speculators will do well not to forget. The island of Candia is at the present moment ready for revolt. Its foreign instigators and protectors have but to give the word. At two or three days' notice its population would rise in arms. The Turkish Empire is the seat of future strife. The Sultan will more likely die fighting for his kingdom than submit to the tinkering of jealous foreign powers. These powers know that if the Turk but has his opium cut off for a short time he can fight with the best of them, for he is a fatalist. Your Christian gentleman don't make so good a soldier as a fatalist. He thinks too much of life. These Turks and Russians are automata, and now that "*villainous saltpetre hath been so long digged from the bowels of the harmless earth*"—there are more than you might suppose—who could declare with truth "*but for these vile guns, I had been myself a soldier.*"

The Khedive's birthday was on the 18th of last January, and at the theatre the Russian Envoy was engaged in close conversation with the Khedive in his box. He sympathizes more with France, and would be glad to see the British influence stop where it is.

The best thing under the circumstances would seem to be for the Khedive to hand over to an International Commission, after a National Bank has been established for the purpose of receiving and accounting for the funds, sufficient revenue to meet the interest agreed upon, and to leave the proceeds of the railways, which could be much increased if properly directed by Western agents, for the holders of the Bonds of 1873. The net revenue of the railways might be calculated at £750,000. The debt of the country is about £58,000,000, at the least. The floating debt we should guess to be nearly twenty millions, but it may be five millions out. It can but be a guess. What is wanted is to hoodwink the investor by one of the thousand tricks that *La Haute Finance* has at its command, so that these treasury bills may be duly met, and the same little game of usury played with the same success.

We are again pleased to notice, amid the venality and scurrility that has seized upon the financial columns of the press, that the *Economist* can still keep a clear head and proper notions of honesty. Thirteen years ago, Ismail Pacha succeeded his Uncle Said. The debt was then three millions. It is now nearly sixty millions. A good deal of the Khedive's money is locked up in unproductive works. The service of the debt is £7,500,000, and the revenue about £9,300,000. Capitalists, and schemers, whose only capital was their stock of impudence, flocked to Egypt after the arrival of Mr. Cave, and as all sorts of projects have flitted through the brains of these philanthropic gentlemen for the financial regeneration of the country, we will give them a valuable suggestion.

At present the Egyptians throw the Nile into the sea. Why is this? A grand industrial enterprise might surely be floated under the auspices of *La Haute Finance,* for the purpose of diverting the almost solid wealth of that wonderful river from its channel into dykes to intersect the country, and render it independent of the variable inundations. The fructifying deposit is wasted as it is. Any financier who is struck with the brilliant possibilities of this idea may communicate with Erasmus Pinto by advertisement in the Agony Column of the *Times,* on or after April 1st. Now, my dear " outsiders," do be sensible. Whatever Mr. Cave's mission may effect, Englishmen cannot restrain the personal expenditure of an Oriental despot. We cannot collect the taxes from the Fellahs. We cannot impose or remit the dues on Foreign goods. The purchase of the Suez Canal shares really means this, and nothing more—that England has purchased a virtual control over the short cut to India for the passage of her troops if necessary.

But a speculator must not forget that a country may compound with its Foreign creditors, and yet not be convulsed by political anarchy. And such a contingency is more to be regarded by our Government than the financial question, which, though it may bring profit to the magnates of finance, will never bring credit to our Parliament. At the very first attempt to move in the matter the country has had to pay £100,000 commission on a loan of four millions, and many reflecting men feel that we have been outwitted by French financiers' finesse, which only drew England on to get money to meet their bills then falling due. The purchase of the Canal shares is in itself an excellent thing, only the Government ought not to delay Mr. Cave's report, when the pith of it might have been made known long ago. Stock-jobbing should be discouraged not encouraged.

If any one had been at Cairo about January the 21st of this year, he might have seen some very lively sparring between the men of money and device. The representatives of the rival groups of financiers did not let the telegraph cables have much rest.

If Mr. Cave had not been there at all we believe that something further might have been done. Two things soon became quite clear to him. One was that the floating debt was much larger than any one had supposed, and that an immediate loan of from fifteen to twenty millions was necessary to grapple successfully with that. Of course he had no power to hold out hopes of England lending Egypt that sum on a mere promise to reform. Another point was equally clear to Mr. Cave, viz., that the country was substantially solvent. Just as young men are helped on to ruin by sharks who lend them money at 140 per cent., so is the Khedive being brought to bankruptcy, not by his country's insolvency or poverty, but by his inability to stay the ever-growing floating debt, the Eldorado of the usurers. If ever money can be justly called the "root of all evil," it can when it is in the hands of men who never do an honest day's work all through their lives, but trade on human weakness, misery, and necessity.

When, then, the solvency of the country was now

clear, the Alexandrine and Levantine army of philanthropists turned eager eyes again upon the Viceroy in need.

Sir George Elliot who is no financier, in a City sense, but an upright man, who really did in this case think there was another end to all commerce besides individual gain, is a man of large fortune. He has been connected with the docks at Alexandria and other public works for a long time. He believed he could command some of our great banking houses' influence. They thought that our Government meant more than it did. Each party overrated the other's influence. His plan was to raise a large loan in London for the purpose of converting the whole debt of the country into a uniform debt called Egyptian Consols. The bondholders were to be asked to accept a reduction of interest, and probably the suppression of drawings, to compensate for the increased security for the payment of the interest. For this purpose a commission was to have been appointed composed of nominees of England and Egypt, with the chief control vested in the hands of an English president. This was the right and only sensible plan; but if right could win its battles in this world so easily, the devil would soon have to migrate to another. The native financial agents raised the cry that "*annexation*" was our little game. They vowed that General Stanton and Mr. Cave were secretly abetting that idea. Of course neither of these gentlemen were doing anything of the kind. However it may be, the jealousy not only of the native officials but of the French was aroused by this cleverly-planned hue-and-cry. M. Outrey, who, although his manner is decidedly dictatorial, is a very able diplomatist, strenuously opposed the Elliot scheme. He "threatened" to propose an international commission and declare that the plan was tantamount to placing Egypt at the mercy of England. It frightened the Khedive. Then came the Franco-Levantine confederates' scheme, and as it was based upon a lower view of Egyptian and financiers' honesty, it was listened to with eagerness. Their plan is something like this. To establish a state Bank, with power of issue, to receive all income and pay all outgoings of the Government. To be allowed to charge ½ per cent. commission on all transactions. The Bank to be governed by a board elected by the shareholders. The President and two Vice-Presidents to be Frenchmen, Englishmen, or Italians. The Khedive to bind himself by special decree to issue no more Bonds. In return for this concession the Bank is to advance by degrees or at once about sixteen millions, to exchange the floating debt for Bonds, at a commission of 7 per cent. Ten per cent. of the projected loan is to be paid off yearly until it be completely discharged. The Khedive to be allowed a private account at the Bank, and to overdraw to the extent of two millions. The Bank to publish fortnightly statements of all receipts and payments.

Oh! how much more accurately the Franco-Levantine party understood the human weakness mixed up in the whole affair! How tenderly each big wig's EGO was dealt with.

But it was nervous work for the competitors to get this concession safely signed. Money down was wanted by the Khedive. Each party had to bid as low as possible and yet outbid the rival bid. Each party was obliged to throw a sprat to catch a herring, with a chance of losing sprat and getting nothing back.

Each bidder tried to get as good security for his advance as possible. I wish you could have seen the way the Khedive and his agents played off one against the other. You never would have wanted to go to a theatre for six months. It was the greatest comedy —a human comedy in real life. From day to day the astute Ismail played with his financing fish till Saturday, Feb. 12th., when the fish came to the scale. The Franco-Levantine fish weighed heavier through having coin to stick into the mouth of their fish at hand; while the English promises, though good, weighed lighter in the scale. So about five minutes to eleven the agreement was signed. It was pretty work, and very interesting to behold. Ismail Pacha is now 45 years old, and very stout, and generally dressed in plain unornamented black. He looks as like a Frenchman as an Egyptian.

What puzzled us the most was that *outré* policy of France. Why that high-handed dictatorial advice? It seemed so very like a mere caprice, or a desire of jealousy to administer a snub to British waxing influence. If so, it was a pity. Englishmen are friends of France, whatever injured *amour propre* may say of *perfide Albion*.

Now, my dear "outsiders," you see what sort of a stock you have to deal with, or if you don't I will just give you a brief recapitulation of the *pros* and *cons*.

Summary of the Commercial, Political, and Social Advantages possessed by Egypt.

1. A climate and soil of almost unrivalled excellence. The air would be perfect were it not that those who breathe it long find themselves possessed

with an automatic inclination for fiction, and a loathing of cold truth that cannot be described by those who have not resided at Cairo or Alexandria.

2. Egypt is not like Spain or Turkey. She is free from intestine trouble. There are no antagonistic religious creeds that know what *Odium Theologicum* means. Oh! happy country! Copt and Mahometan live there in harmony. Christians and Mussulmen hold office indiscriminately there. No powerful landowing interest opposes progress for its selfish sake. The only social classes are the Reigning Family and the Fellaheen. The fierce appeal of mad fanatics to unfurl the banners of Islam in a warlike sense would meet with slight response in Egypt now.

3. The political safety of Egypt is considerable. She is protected by the desert and the sea from troublesome neighbors. Her only danger is on the side of Turkey, or from Abyssinia. Mutual jealousy will keep foreigners from interfering without unusual cause. The Turkish rule is more likely to decline than increase. And this will allow the army to be still more reduced, and the soldiers to be employed on agricultural purposes.

4. The present dynasty is energetic and intelligent, whatever Oriental defects it may possess, and Prince Tewfik, the heir presumptive to the throne, is well educated, and considered to possess his father's abilities.

5. All traffic between Europe and India will now pass through Egypt. The Suez Canal has secured this advantage. The railway system of Middle and Lower Egypt is progressing fast. The value of the cotton exported last year was nine millions sterling.

The trade of Central Africa passes along the Nile in its passage to the outer world. A further development of trade with Syria and Arabia may be confidently looked for. Egypt may be considered a great commercial Exchange between the Eastern and the Western world, the emporium of Central Africa with Alexandria, a great trading harbor of the whole Levant and Cairo, an improving town, that will soon vie in luxury and outward civilization with many a Western city of much larger size.

6. Unskilled and agricultural labor can be performed as efficiently by the Fellahs as by English workmen.

Estimate of Revenue.

	£
Land Tax	5,800,000
Railways	1,000,000
Customs	600,000
Salt and Tobacco	560,000
Dates	180,000
Provincial Municipal Dues, Sheep Tax, Dues on Locks, Fish Sales, etc.	1,850,000
Licenses	400,000
	10,390,000

Disadvantages of Egypt.

1. The great amount of unproductive capital locked up in such works as the Great Water Canal in the Nile Valley, to irrigate portions of the country not periodically inundated by the river, the Suez Canal itself, the docks at Alexandria, the various railways, of which the Soudan is the most expensive.

2. The fact that an Oriental Court and expensive style of living are an absolute necessity, and that the harems continue to entail a great deal of unprofitable expense.

3. The likelihood of a disagreeable dispute arising between Egypt and Turkey about the tribute loans of 1854 and 1871.

4. The want of labor. Could not the "Heathen Chinee" be induced to become a commercial advantage to Egypt. A Chinaman works as hard and lives on as little as most other men. Both the mendacious atmosphere and the sort of living would just suit the "Heathen Chinee."

5. The great expanse of desert. This might be brought under cultivation with proper irrigation. Financiers, turn your inventive genius to that wasteful Nile.

6. The great scarcity of midwives and Infant Soothers. The Oriental babies die by thousands, like young turkeys not attended to at first. Now, Mrs. Crawshay, draw the Lady Helps' attention to this interesting fact. Under-population is the curse of Egypt, just as over-population is of England. Here you have a splendid field.

7. The fact that the Levantine usurers induce the Khedive to speculate upon the Stock Exchange, and that last year the English investing goose, that seemed an everlasting layer of golden eggs, is wearied out and nearly dead; and that when men who occupy a position where they can move the market, as the Khedive can, they seldom can resist the seductive interest of *Rigs and Wrecks*. I'll bet you a new hat, dear "Outside Fools," that the

Egyptian despot knows more than you do about Stock Exchange machinery.*

Estimate of the Annual Expenditure of Egypt.

	£
Kissing of Turkish Hands, etc., etc.	800,000
Civil List of Khedive and Family	400,000
Public Works	600,000
Army and Navy and Expeditions	1,000,000
Expense of Administration	1,160,000
Interest on Debt and Sinking Fund	6,400,000
	10,360,000

So that according to these figures the revenue is about equal to the present expenditure. But we probably do not know all the truth. If Parliament would take a humble broker's advice, it would resist the seductive hopes of safe speculation held out by the appointment of an English director to the National Bank that is projected, and would take up an honest and dignified position by holding entirely aloof from this fresh raid upon investors' pockets.

By so doing they would also return the snub given by French financiers to British influence.

---

* If the new system be not carried out, which, in the above estimate of disadvantages, we assume will be, there must be added this worst of all disadvantages, viz., that at present it requires nearly one million and a half every month to keep the financial sharks from attacking a vital part. A mass of bills are ever falling due, which must be met, and wonderful will be the system which can cope successfully with Oriental love of fiction and of usury. We shall soon see; but be careful of the few poor eggs you still may lay, poor weak, exhausted goose. They're going to try and make you lay once more.

Such a course would undoubtedly conduce to commercial morality. Unless the English Government be identified in some way or other with the business, investors will not be caught. The astute Parisians are already beginning to see that. Let them fail to float their loan, and then come to England for advice and assistance. (If perfidious, stupid England's money-bags do not entitle her to that deference from Franco-Levantine usurers, she must indeed be besotted to let herself be plundered first and then called "stupid fool.") In that event, let our Government stipulate for effective guarantees, a reduction of the interest to 6 per cent. at least, and the total suppression of the drawings. The *bonâ fide* investor would never miss a drawing from which it is so very unlikely that he will derive any profit. Poor ill-used soul, he would be very pleased if he could think his 6 per cent. was nearly safe. The Khedive is indeed a clever man. Just have a talk with him, and you will find that you never know whether his language be the language of diplomacy, or whether it be that of one who shows you his real heart. He has learnt something at that desk at which he spends so large a portion of his time. But our Government should clearly know what is proposed to them. In plain English it is this. To indirectly help the financiers and bankers of Egypt and the Levant to get their advances repaid out of fresh money drawn from the investor, and called, if you like, a funded loan. It matters not what the term may be. That is what is meant, and we think it augurs rather ill for foreigners' estimate of England's honesty of Government, to say nothing of commercial morality, for no doubt, as the City editor of the *Times* has clearly and coldly stated, "*The end of all commerce is individual gain.*" But surely the Government of the country is not going to join the universal gamble and stock-jobbing that is all the fashion now. The Conservatives should know that *money is the root of all evil*, and if they be not careful that evil will take a tangible form which will cost them their seats. They are on very slippery ground just now, and have already tripped too much. It is surely unwise to allow bits of Mr. Cave's report to keep oozing out from day to day, and to be made a handle for the wealthy gamblers in Egyptian stocks, when long ago the pith of the report might have completely stayed such questionable games. And surely when it is shown how the country is solvent in itself, a caution from those in power will be given to the plundered Englishman, that if he lends his money, the old plan of short-dated bills and secret floating debt may soon be started by the usurers again.

The Khedive is indeed a clever man. Although he has accepted the French offer, he well knows that England's influence is wanted much to float the loan. In France there are few clergymen and few professional men who have not studied money far too well to be caught in anything so dangerous as Foreign loans. They buy their own.

Now, for fear you should in these remarks, dear readers, think you see an undertone that plainly leans one way, we will speak plainer still. Do nothing till you see if Paris can unaided float the loan. You may buy yourselves a trifle if it can. But you would not take our advice if you did anything just now. No doubt the chances are they will make some slight rise to dazzle the investing mind.

YE OUTSIDE FOOLS. 405

I wish, if any of you should be lucky enough to meet with a young jobber or broker who is anxious to take 2 per cent. for the *put* and *call* of Egyptian '73 for a month on, from the date when you find him, you would kindly communicate with Erasmus Pinto, through the Agony Column, not of the *Misleading Age*, but of the *Times*, the leading journal of the age. Erasmus Pinto will give you a trifle if you find him a safe man to take the coin, and sign a contract according to our rules.

Now if your speculative itching will not let you wait, and there are many cases where it won't, just buy a very little stock, watch it, nurse it, play with it as dogs play with a bone. And if it drop, say two or three per cent., repeat the dose. But for goodness' sake divide the contents of your medicine bottle into at least eight or ten doses, or the medicine may kill you instead of curing the itch.

In conclusion, don't forget one fact, which is just now of more importance than any other financial fact. More than one hundred millions of money has been lost by investors in Foreign loans, which has not gone into the pockets of other investors or speculators, but has simply vanished. There is, therefore, all that buying power less, and as the speculators have been busily turning out the stocks pawned with the banks, all things, both good and bad, are coming down with a run. We brokers are finding out the ugly fact that the goose is laying nothing now. And so it must be *dog eat dog*, until at least the puppies are all eaten up. By that time I feel sure that business will have quite revived.

Till then, ye speculative roach, try not the early worm. What a nice gay month was January last for all those speculators in Egyptian Bonds whom the previous twenty per cent. bear panic left with a skin still on. Well-conducted journals were in splendid form. Exciting telegrams were plenty at the news rooms and exchanges where the "Outside Fools" do congregate, which telegrams were promply contradicted when they had worked out their end.

"*The Austrian troops are mobilized.*" These words scared out unnumbered bulls and 'ticed in many bears. "*It is a lie.*" These words next day made bears close and bulls buy again.

"*Nubar Pasha has resigned. Oh, dread calamity!*" These words made men sell Egypts by fifty thousand at a time, and by twenty thousand in the streets.

"*Terrible discovery of over issue of Treasury Bonds.*" This rumor drove the bulls insane, and almost strangled some large bears with laughing at their luck.

"*Quarrel between the Right Honorable Stephen Cave and the Khedive of Egypt.*" This statement brought in still more bears who had a pickling the next day, when out came, "*'Tis a lie.*"

Ursa Major, who had been a bull just for a little space in the best of company, was *Ursa Major* once again, and made the spirits of the bulls most fearfully depressed.

The house put up the stock to spite and try to pickle *Ursa Major*, but in vain. Still some bulls bellowed with delight.

The mention of the Elliot Loan and National bank made bears' heads very sore, Ursa Major still held on.

A little less excitement after this. I do assure you, my dear "Outside Fools," both bulls and bears had one of the prettiest speculative jaunts in January that any mind that craved for mystery or excitement could wish to have. The highest price touched was 70¼, on Jan. 3rd, and the lowest price 61, on the 11th.

But surely the Conservatives will look upon that Burials Bill with careful eyes. A poor majority of thirty-one, when whip and spur had been so freely used, and pressing circulars sent out, and when the House was full, is very, very like defeat. Once let the Liberals get hold of a financial muddle, which Egyptian usurers seem anxious to supply, and the odd trick is theirs. Look here, dear readers. There is voting by machinery and speculating by machinery (is it not, odd?), and it looks almost as if burying would have to be done by machinery. If a dead man could but come to life and see how important he is, would he not be surprised. And should not we, too, be surprised if we but knew how many voted against the bill from party-feeling, not from consciousness of being in the right?

Yes, man is a fighting animal and nowhere more than when in Parliament.

OUTSIDE CRITICISM.

"The *end of all commerce is individual gain.*" So says the present City editor of the *Times* in his work on "Speculation," which many of us brokers and jobbers have read with attention, especially the chapter on "*The Selfishness and Hard-heartedness of the Professional Speculator,*" although that chapter does not give you much comfort, dear "Outside Fools." But how is it that, although this gentleman is eloquent enough about the danger of listening to advice from brokers, and taking "tips" qualified or unqualified, and although there are signs in the 136 pages of his work of a decidedly pessimistic view of human nature, and although there is a whole chapter devoted to the *Pitfalls* and *Hidden Forces opposed to the Speculator,* nothing is said about the greatest of all dangers, viz., interested advice given through the medium of the *Money Articles* and in other ways? Does not the City editor of the *Times* know that this is *the one Hidden Force* of all others of which the least hard-hearted and selfish, the best educated and the most gentlemanly speculators and investors have absolutely no idea. Plenty of us brokers could tell the City editor of the *Times* of hundreds of clergymen and professional men, some speculators and others investors, who lost nearly all they had through the implicit reliance they placed upon their paper and its financial advice. Oh well he says, "*The end of all commerce is individual gain. People engaged in commerce in all its multifarious ramifications care only for themselves and for no other single soul.*" Were this not so terribly true, those commercial speculations, in the truest and fullest sense of the words, the Money Columns and financial articles in the newspapers would not only be wise after the event, but would say to the "*foolish outsider,*" for which term I am indebted to the City editor of the *Times,* " Beware, there are sharks about. You will tumble headlong down a precipice there, not through your own folly, but through your ignorance and the idea that we should tell you if anything were very wrong."

Were it not so fatally true that unless one be a

"*foolish outsider*" one must not take financial advice either in a newspaper or out of it, there would not have been that cynical indifference manifested by City editors at the mysterious jugglery of *La Haute Finance*, through which so many millions of "*foolish outsiders*" have been made poorer, if not wiser, by the gigantic issues of foreign I O U's.

The capitalists' great names which floated these Foreign loans, these devouring abysses of a nation of "foolish outsiders'" saving, have worked far more mischief than the advice of brokers, against which the City editor of the *Times* cautions the "*foolish outsider.*"

Yes, we confess that we are disappointed not to have met with a chapter on "*The Tender-heartedness of the Professional City Editor,*" and a refutation or corroboration of the assertion made by another author of a work on "Speculation," who, not being a tender-hearted City editor, thus speaks of the *Hidden Dangers of the Money Articles.* He says,—

"*Many place the most implicit reliance on their statements. Few, however, are acquainted with the fact that there are those intimately connected with the Press who are great speculators in railway shares, etc. The 'leading' articles are couched in language intended only to mislead, and that which appears to convey 'bonâ fide' information is only meant to serve the purpose of some interested parties. They venture on prophetic rumors of peace or war. And the power of the Press in this respect is enormous,*" etc.

Now it is obvious that either the author of the work we quote from, who professes to have had large experience, must be quite in error, or else that the City editor of the *Times*, who says in the opening
s

lines of his book on "Speculation," "*Our object is to show people how improbable it is that they will be able to speculate successfully,*" and who has a chapter on *Pitfalls*, has certainly made a most grave omission in not drawing his readers' attention to this deepest and most treacherous of all speculators' and investors' pitfalls.

The daily telegrams published by "well-conducted papers"—term, alas, too vague and general—the "growling despatches" of foreign potentates' understrappers, dear foolish "outsiders," are only part of the machinery of powerful continental speculators often working in league with home operators, through whose ominous vaticinations you lose your money, and we undeservedly get the blame.

Are the Money Columns of the well-conducted papers to be looked upon as threepenny or penny diurnal trustworthy advisers, or are they not? Hear what the same gentleman says of *Successful Diplomatists*, who of course have no telegrams or growling despatches to insert in the well-conducted journals.

He says:—

"*Successful Diplomatists in all times, with few exceptions, have been men who have never scrupled to resort to finessing, chicanery, and the 'ruse de guerre' in every form, under cover of a saintly innocence that would shame the devil.*"

Oh, Hard-hearted and Selfish Diplomatists! Oh! noble-hearted and disinterested City editors, to resist the temptations of that saintly innocence that shames the devil!

Again he remarks with regard to Erasmus Pinto and his brothers that,—

"*It is idle to put any other construction upon a broker's*

advice than that it is to serve directly or indirectly the purpose of him who recommends."

Then what about the "*foolish outsiders*" estimate of the City editor's advice? For the sake of charity let its value be clearly understood. This gentleman is so interested in us that he says, "*Brokers should not be exposed to such temptation.*"

We retort that, except in the case of the City editor of the *Times*, whose greatest pleasure is no doubt to resist temptation, neither should City editors be so exposed.

Did not the strong man fail to resist the charms of that siren Money? Yes, and there are many no better than he.

Well, as we have said, we have read the City editor of the *Times*' book, addressed to the "foolish outsider," and as he seems to dislike "*Outside Criticism,*" we offer him a few "*Inside*" and impartial critical remarks. The book on "Speculation" is evidently written by a cool-headed shrewd person, who thoroughly understands the value of "*keeping his own counsel,*" the "*folly of foolish outsiders,*" and the *true character of Brokers and Jobbers*, who has a considerable respect for aggregated capital, and whose speculative proclivities, if he had any, would be decidedly "bearish."

But we do not think that the gentleman should have been hard-hearted to us brokers, and so soft-hearted to the great ones of finance, and so afraid of including in his chapter on Pitfalls that *barathrum* which so few "foolish outsiders" fathom till they have lost their all.

Even though he can so clearly perceive that "*the number of really sound Brokers who have a steady legiti-*

mate business, upon which pure speculation is an excrescence not particularly encouraged or liked, is small compared with the entire body, and that by far the greater number depend very much for their means of support upon purely speculative time-bargains," he need not have indirectly told the "foolish outsiders" that they are much less likely to lose by "bearing" than by "bulling." It is one thing to bear when you know much more than the ordinary speculator about what the great men are about, and another when you are a "foolish outsider." All bears that Erasmus Pinto has known to have made money have been persons whose position gave them superior information. Otherwise their bear speculations would have ended as foolishly as those of the "foolish outsider."

We cannot conclude without quoting a paragraph that occurs in some extraneous matter appended to the 136 pages which constitute the work on "Speculation,"—

"Could there be anything more highly eloquent of the sound management of the banks in the City, of the prudent caution shown by the large lending establishments, of the unruffled attitude of the A 1 mercantile houses, to whom 10 per cent. for a month is occasionally more a subject for rejoicing than anything else, as it clips the wings of reckless traders, than the fact that such 'agony and disaster' left the City still in the most flourishing possible condition, where, very shortly after, some large Foreign loans were covered immediately several times over?"

You have been well vindicated, Mr. Bonamy Price, since that was penned.

The prudent caution of the A 1 banks has been indeed commendable, when the loss from such caution on the part of one banking institution alone was not far short of a million sterling, for the half year. Of course the person, not the system, is to blame. That's how the progress of education is checked. We are horrified when a Collie oversteps the line, and pretend that we had no idea such persons could be found. What snug hypocrisy, and miserable cant. There are hundreds of Collies walking about daily undiscovered.

But to return. No doubt a ten per cent. rate is not much to those who aid materially, by their manipulation of " Other Securities" and " Other Deposits," the high rate requisite to enable them to buy good things cheap or close their bears of stocks that won't go down by ordinary means, and not until the *reckless traders* have been all cleared out. If the City is to be thought prosperous, " where, shortly after, some large Foreign loans were covered immediately several times over," how about the unhappy country-flies' prosperity that the City-spiders induced to rush into their treacherous webs, those Foreign loans? How diametrically opposed the prosperity of the City seems to be to that of the country! Well, well, I was born to be a poor devil of a broker, whose advice must not be taken. Would to heaven I had been lucky enough to have been a City editor! Would I not have shown the "foolish outsiders" a thing or two in hard-hearted and selfish " bearing ? " Ay, indeed, I would!

But we have advertised the gentleman's book on " Speculation " more than enough, and as " *the end of all commercial transactions is individual gain,*" and of course, according to a pessimist, a writer of a book has no other motive but his own gain, Erasmus Pinto is empowered by the *Very Highest Authority* to inform the City editor of the *Times* that if he thinks this advertisement worth a cheque, he has only to send one under cover to the chairman of our Committee, and the brokers and jobbers of the Stock Exchange pledge their honor as gentlemen that such cheque shall not be photographed, but shall be the first donation towards a fund for the establishment of a Reformatory for hard-hearted and selfish *wealthy* Speculators.

Now, dear "Outside Fools," just hear what advice Sir George Campbell has just had given him by the *Daily Telegraph* of Feb. 28th.

"We," says the writer, "will tell Sir George Campbell what to do, if he desires to win for himself lasting renown, and draw down upon his head showers of blessings from every English investor. Let him get a Select Committee to take evidence on what in the jargon of the Stock Exchange are known as bear sales, or speculative operations for the fall in particular stocks. This is the kind of '*wrecking*' which causes so much loss to persons who are neither brokers nor dealers, well able to take care of themselves, and who have, moreover, no protection from the law or from Stock Exchange regulations. The practice of selling what one has not got for the express purpose of depreciating prices, and thus frightening holders into sacrificing stock for the sole profit of the conspirators who seek to compass their ruin, has now developed into a fine art, and people talk openly of the next assault which is to be made on a particular security, and of the exact procedure by sap and mining that is to precede the grand attack. Inasmuch as 'bear operations' are held by their supporters" (our friend, the City editor of the *Times*, I suppose, is meant by the writer) "to exert a highly moral influence and to exercise a mysteriously purifying effect on the market, let evidence be taken beforehand on the matter."

We sincerely trust and believe that Sir George Campbell's good sense will not be blinded by the words of this fond enthusiast, who in imagination appears to see some hostile editorial EGO tumbled from his "bearing pedestal," while Sir George Campbell is winning lasting renown from British investors, who vie with one another in showering down blessings on his head.

Now we are not like certain spiteful reviewers, who, having drawn attention to the defects of a work, and meeting with a passage that is certainly apposite and likely to do good, say nothing about it, although these critics, dear readers of books, look upon you pretty much as the *Times* does upon the "foolish outsider," as good easy folk, not overmuch blessed with sense or judgment, who can be led by the nose as critics, publishers, and tradesmen will. Why don't you wake up and show these "inside" fussy, cynical, critical, and editorial bodies that you are no more "foolish outsiders" than they, but for their position, and learn so fast that their cynicism shall be changed to fear, if not to admiration and esteem.

No, we are not like spiteful reviewers, who bring out the bad and suppress the good; and we thank the City editor of the *Times* for having the courage to say that "selling for the fall," or "bearing," is legitimate; but we do not agree with him that the small bear is the man who does the harm, or is, so to speak, the illegitimate bear. Our experience tells us that this is anything but the case. He harms himself, not the community. Every man of common sense who knows anything of the subject will admit that the speculator who sells for immediate or future delivery a commodity or stock that is *too high* does good to the community. So does every man who buys a stock or commodity that is *too low*, whether he pay for it then or at a future date.

But before we go any further we must just premise that there is no such thing as a bullion basis in the business of the world, and that what are called *Time-bargains* on 'Change enter into every form of business in the world, in one form or other. If people only recognized this fact, what seems so hard to understand would be as clear as the day. There never will be such a thing as a bullion basis. The whole world over-trades, and if the books of three fourths of the members of any trading community were strictly scrutinized, they would show a very different state of things from what is mostly supposed by those who know nothing about it. It is just the same with the house-holder. It is quite the exception for men to live within their means.

Most over-trade, and want to be thought bigger than they are. There is a delightful narcotism, an exciting mystery, in this over trading on the part of the whole world that entirely eludes these radical reformers who want to alter human nature as a cook would mould a piece of paste. It never will be done. Anyone who will honestly forget his EGO, and, seeing the flaws in a system, will point them out and use his influence to get them removed, does a public good.

Noisy declaimers and assertive assailants of a

system about which they probably know nothing, except that they have lost money in trying to work it without study and self-restraint, do a great deal of harm.

"*Dum vitant stulti vitia in contraria currunt,*" says the satirist. "*Ne quid nimis,*" says the philosopher.

If fussy enthusiasts would have the moral courage to refuse the enticing narcotism that would make their judgment drunk with the vain idea that they are going to save their fellow-creatures by thousands at a time, and would give their assertive EGOS a good box on the ears every time they feel inclined to forget the meaning of these words of the satirist and philosopher, education would be much less hampered than it is.

The enthusiast of the *Telegraph* says nothing about *Riggers*.

His brother of the *Times* says nothing about *Wreckers*, who work by machinery, but lays the blame on little bears, who have scarcely more than they stand up in.

As it seems so difficult to arrive at the truth, we will tell you our experience.

"Bearing," when attempted by a little man, almost always ends in his losing his money, whether he bears a good or a bad stock.

It is only the wealthy speculator, such as a large financier, or those who possess superior information who can bear to make a profit. Why? Because as soon as there are sufficient little bears in a stock, that, on its merits, is too high, it becomes worth the while of capital to fight against reason and make the bears close by its power. Unless it happens that capital is on the bears' side, the theoretical bear, who would do the community good by his sales, has less chance than the bull. Any broker of experience will tell you this.

Why? Because aggregated capital is not content with legitimate 'bearing," but prefers to get Reason to sell, say a limited stock that is too high, and then to corner the bears, who would otherwise do good by their sales, and to force up the price until they must close for want of further means. If this were not so, I can assure you that whatever Mr. Crump may say about "bearing going against the grain," there are plenty of "foolish outsiders" who would sell "legitimate bears," and would even make money. But the public must not be allowed to make money, even if they free themselves from their own ignorance and greed, except such portion of them as are friends of directors, secretaries, accountants, and large financiers. The men who do harm by "bearing" are the large capitalists, who combine to force down the good, in order to buy when they find the public has bought, and who combine to force up the bad when the public has sold. Here you have the whole mischief, and the cause is, aggregated capital in the hands of financiers. Why should we suppose one man to be so much more able to withstand the temptations of money than another.

Is not this what is meant by the phrase, "How hardly shall a rich man enter into the kingdom of heaven."

If legislation can reduce the power of money when aggregated in large sums in financiers' hands, it will do something worth talking about; but I believe no legislation will ever do anything of the kind. But if you learn the tricks and dishonesty of such men, and the machinery of their system, dear "foolish outsiders," and rely more on yourselves, and less on interested advisers, you may do something. But if you can get the better of money, why, you are a match for the devil.

I was asked by an "Outside Fool" the other day why the City editor of the *Times* last year calculated the price of Railway stocks on a five per cent. basis, and implied that they were too dear.

I could not tell him. He said Midlands were put down at 120, and yet they afterwards went to 149, and paid a $\frac{1}{2}$ per cent. more dividend.

They were 145 some two months ago, and nearly all Railway stocks were on the eve of a great fall. But no calculations on a five per cent. basis appeared then, although this was the time to have said, "The bear may now do good to the community." This should have been done, or the other left undone.

Theoretical Bears of Brighton, North British, Dover A, Metropolitan, District, Caledonian, Chatham Preference would have made a nice thing of it the last two years if they had gone against the grain, and tried honestly to do a little good to the community, disregarding what capital might do with them.

I fear the chance there was, dear "foolish outsiders," for you to bear some Rails and do good to the community will be over before you read this book. If not, it will be a northern line that is left. And mind you don't pick the wrong one.

And hark ye. I am instructed to tell you nothing but blunt truth and shame the devil. Don't listen to the advice of City editors. They are clever fellows, and if you go to dine with them they will treat you well and give you a very fair glass of wine; but the "end of all commerce is individual gain." They can't afford any more than a broker or a jobber can to give you the straight tip, especially when our commission is from $\frac{1}{16}$ to $\frac{1}{2}$ per cent., and the charge for their advice from sixpence to a penny per week or day.

Our advice to you, Sir George Campbell, is this. When you are on the subject of the *Wreckers*, don't forget the *Riggers*. A *Rigger* to-day is often a *Wrecker* to-morrow. And, most of all, remember that if you do not inquire into the doings of the most wealthy magnates of finance you will never put the saddle on the right horse.

Why, Sir George Campbell and Sir Henry James, your philanthropic hair would stand on end and positively bristle with indignant horror if you knew the class of men who directly and indirectly solicit us brokers and jobbers to aid in Working *Rigs* or *Wrecks*, as the case may be. The men who work these interesting *ups* and *downs* do anything but good to the community. And yet they are not the "*reckless speculators with little more than they stand up in, who impose upon the weak and credulous.*" Bless your innocent hearts, my good reformers, we very soon settle the hash of these little speculative "bearikins." But I can tell you that we are often terribly afraid of the highly respectable, wealthy, and powerful *Riggers* and *Wreckers*, with ample machinery at their command, and not unfrequently a column or two of press leverage to help the wheels round faster. We have to mind lest we, too, be not caught by the silent wheels and *Hidden Forces* of this machinery that has cost the nation so very, very dear, and will do still till money in the hands of very few financial hands is better understood.

How often does this money in the hands of few financial hands say to us brokers, "Come and help to shake the tree or raise the kite." And we admit that often we do help. We must co-operate or lose our living; for if we refused, the money would soon find some others ready for its dirty work.

If Sir George Campbell, or any other worthy member of Parliament, tries to suppress "bearing" altogether, he will only act like poor deluded "Mother Stewart" and the Whisky Warriors, or like those fond reformers who suppose that our salvation depends upon the closing of Cremorne, the Alhambra, and the theatres where any girl who has a decent leg to show, believing that "*the end of all commerce is individual gain,*" shows all the leg she dare, because she knows so many like to see it, if it be a well-shaped leg, although they afterwards cry shame. Poor girl, is she to blame more than these Moneymongers and Financial Acrobats? At all events, she is more honest than they are.

Repressive measures that would close one vent for human nature's weakness without opening another are the worst of all the measures of conceited, egotistic, and insane reform.

And with regard to "*the drawing down of showers of blessings upon Sir George's head from investors,*" let us give a word of warning to Sir George and Parliament, for fear such waggish scribes should turn some honest head with hope of winning an undying fame —a nation's gratitude. The suppression of "*legitimate bearing*" would certainly enable the financial acrobat to keep his foreign rubbish up at a most dangerous price for a short time, and probably to blind once more those most foolish and ignorant people, the investing class. It might enable them to bolster Egypt up, and vow that its securities were cheap at par. I do not say they're not; but all I say is that it makes just all the difference whose name is at the back of these fine foreign promises to pay, so seldom kept. Just make it worth some good firm's while to take up Spanish, you would soon have articles to show that Spain was rich in mines and only wanted peace, and soon have fools to buy at 25. Then down would come the rubbish to its former price, in spite of peace and mines. Good names are never wanted when the game is worth the candle. But suppose that the investor has been lulled again into a false security, and that he has again dreamt golden dreams in his fool's paradise, that clergymen once more can help to spoil (as they, poor souls, so vainly thought) these Moslem countries by lending at high interest, will these deluded creatures, when they wake, as wake they surely must ere long, when the astute loan-monger found the orange losing nearly all its juice, and felt inclined to throw it by, would these investors, whose experience had been so roughly bought, draw blessings down upon reformers' heads, who took away by suppressing "honest and professional inside bearing" the only check there was to these financial acrobats? Why, they would execrate, not bless.

Investors, take a practical man's advice! If "bearing" is to be suppressed, sell what you hold at once. You'll get it back much cheaper, mark my words. Don't mind the price at what you sell. Why, but for bears such as the jobbers of the House are, the very soundest of all stocks would rule from ten to twenty per cent. lower in their price. Just controvert that fact, ye waggish scribes. It's true enough, ye members of our Parliament, and many of you know it is. But even in your august body there are gambling, jobbing, vain, conceited animals, just as in any other class of men. Deal gently with us brokers, I implore you, my good sirs. The devil is not much blacker in our House than in your own. The most pernicious sort of " bearing " is that conducted by men who occupy high places of trust both on the continent and at home, and who use their superior knowledge of the future course of politics, and the secret plans of finance to make a raid on investors' pockets so as to aggrandize themselves, who, as the City editor's own happy phrase has it, *" care for no other single soul."* These men send round false tips by bribed touts and runners, for well they know the weakness of human nature to follow a bigger man in all matters connected with finance. The bigger man repays their flattery by luring them to ruin, seeing that *" he cares for no other single soul, and that the end of all commerce is individual gain."* Look here, joltheads, and jobbernols, it is not this fact that does the mischief, but it is the *wide-spread* ignorance of this fact. Get ye, then, as fast as brain can learn, the wisdom of the serpent, and still retain your dove-like innocence, if but ye can, ye " Outside Fools." The cure rests with you more than with Parliament.

One more word. In Foreign stocks you have all the continent to fight against, as well as selfish and hard-hearted speculators here. In Rails you have only directors and a few organized cliques who now and again like to get hold of a good thing cheap. Stick fast to what you've bought, and buy a little more, and then you'll come out right enough, if you buy good stocks. Directors and officials, who have superior knowledge of the dividends they mean to pay, the prospects of their stocks, the hidden causes quite beyond the traffic returns that can make a half or one per cent. difference in the dividend, of course sell for a fall at the right time. You see I do not call it "bearing," though the effect is quite as startling. They hold the stock, dear "Outside Fools," and their name is not seen on contract notes. There's no necessity. A friend will do the job. Money will do almost anything. They don't deliver, but take back the stock when all the bulls who thought the price was low have been obliged to sell. If old Nathaniel Seesaw had not quarrelled with his cook, and died so suddenly through her device, he could have told you some rare tales about directors' tricks. Mind, dead directors; not you, dear sir, alive and hearty, who seem so fain to put the cap upon your head. This is the safe and the patrician way to bear a stock, enthusiasts.

But hold; I feel that I must not say more about directors, and be careful how I dare to breathe the august name of City editors. Our age is fearfully sensitive. The EGO now seems more important than it used to be. If, then, any tender-hearted City editor or director thinks that we refer to him, he is mistaken. It is the system, not the men, that we have to do with. And we ask our critics to remember this in their estimate of us brokers and jobbers. We may be the vampires and villains some have called us, but we must in common justice call attention to the fact that we, like the Admiralty's scape-goat the other day, have to bear all the blame, while there are men whose money and position and nothing else make them thought better than ourselves.

And as for bears, you need not be afraid, investors, of the "foolish outsider," who bears in his small way, or of the legitimate bear, which I consider to be a jobber who stands in the market to be shot at, and exercises his judgment as to whether a stock is too high or too low. He is undoubtedly a legitimate jobber. If you can do anything by legislation, prevent his being "got at," as the saying is, by wealthy speculators, who know so well that the end of all commerce is individual gain, and who, to use the words of the gentleman referred to before, cuts his way to his profit regardless of obstacles, just as the surgeon's knife is plunged into the flesh, severing arteries, muscles, and sinews that surround the bone he wants to reach and saw.

If Parliament be really in earnest, the best thing it could do would be this. To insist on all the newspapers containing in the money articles some such sentences as the following:—

1. The end of all commerce is individual gain.

2. Brokers, jobbers, and City editors ought not to be so exposed to temptation.

3. "Foolish outsiders" ought to know more of the the stocks in which they invest their money.

4. To further this end, that a sum be granted by Parliament for the establishment of professorial chairs at the Universities to explain the Hidden Forces arrayed against investors, and the peculiar power of

capital aggregated in the hands of great financiers, and the, so to speak, Satanic personality of a dragon sovereign.

5. That rectors, vicars, and all the clergymen be requested by their bishops to enlighten their congregations more upon a subject that seems so interesting to themselves.

6. That every investor, or "foolish outsider," who can be proved to have taken a "tip" from a chairman, director, broker or jobber, be put in the stocks publicly to be gazed upon, or have his head shaved by his family, and kept in close confinement.

7. That all shareholders be advised that it is their real interest to combine together, and insist upon their directors giving up extension-schemes, and pitting their EGOS one against the other so, and that the best way to effect this is for the large shareholders not to side with the speculative element on the Board, but with the ordinary shareholders.

8. That Speculation and Investment Bees be established in all the towns of any consequence.

9. That the owners of newspapers be implored by a deputation from an impoverished and dispirited nation of investors and "foolish outsiders" to allow their City editors, without fear of consequences, to explain honestly and graphically to their readers the working of rigs, wrecks, cliques, rings, pools, corners, bangs, pocket orders, and all the *jargon* of the Exchange, as the writer in the *Daily Telegraph* calls it, and that they discourse now and again upon the temptations to which directors are exposed, and show how triumphantly they resist such temptations, and scorn the idea that their commercial end is individual gain.

YE OUTSIDE FOOLS. 427

10. Let every "Outside Fool" say to himself, or aloud to his family, if he have one, "*Ignorance, greed of gain, and desire for mysterious excitement are my foes, but the greatest of these three is ignorance.*"

CHAPTER LXXXIII.

THE SCALE OF COMMISSION.

THE proper place, my dear "outsiders," to arrange this interesting little matter is the broker's sanctum. Much depends upon the amount and character of the business done, the means and stability of the client, whether he attend personally or reside at a distance, so as to be conveniently shot at by wire. I love the country client myself. As a rule he is safer, greener, gives less trouble, and pays much more commission. Some idiots who attend every day worry one to death with ridiculous questions, are continually asking prices without doing business, and making themselves generally nuisances and asses. Never mind. Erasmus Pinto is even with these boobies before he has done with them.

Be straight with your brokers, and give as little trouble as possible, dear "outsiders," and remember that the commission, after all, is only a secondary affair. If a man tries to screw his broker down, he will more than take it out in the price, or if he do not, it is time the Lunacy Commissioners looked into his case.

I will give you my scale, although, mind, I do this entirely on my own responsibility. If the client be an investor, the price will be double or more, according to his means and knowledge of the world:—

A sixteenth per cent. on Consols and Foreign bonds.

An eighth per cent. on English Rails.

Sixpence per share of £1 in value or under.

A shilling per share of £5 in value or under.

One and sixpence per share of £10 in value or under.

Two and sixpence per share of £20 in value or under.

Five shillings per share of £50 in value or under.

Ten shillings per share for all shares above £50 in value.

CHAPTER LXXXIV.

QUERIES.

Can any learned "Outside Fool" or sapient "Inside Ass" answer the following questions for Erasmus Pinto? They quite gravel him, they do:—

1. Why do the South-Eastern directors charge £90 per mile, the Brighton directors £102, the South-Western £120, and the Chatham £156 for the maintenance of permanent way? Oh, those able, clever men!

2. What is the precise psychological effect of a fee of £8,000 on the EGO of a professional Railway Doctor?

3. Why has a Railway, which, according to its chairman, is better managed than those extremely well-managed concerns, the North-Western and the Lancashire and Yorkshire, dropped from 90 to 71¾

after declaring a dividend of one per cent. more than that for the corresponding period last year?

4. Wanted to find the exact amount of Egotism in a very clever savior of derelict Railway-ships, and a mean plutocrat, whatever that may mean. Also a dinner with a real aristocrat who keeps good wine.

5. Wanted to know the number of investing fools who are comparing the price of North-Western, which pays about $4\frac{3}{4}$ per cent. on the money, with that of Caledonian, which pays about $5\frac{5}{8}$.

What is the canny Scot about? For 1874 Caledonians paid 2 and $5\frac{1}{2}$ per cent. in dividend. For 1875 they paid $6\frac{1}{4}$ and $7\frac{1}{4}$. In the summer of 1874 the price was $90\frac{1}{4}$. In the summer of 1875 it was 130. After declaring $1\frac{3}{4}$ more dividend it has fallen from $137\frac{1}{2}$ to 125. What are the Scotch investors about? Oh! I have it. The ship is only tacking. They are going to work it in a fairly liberal way. Well, it is time. Erasmus Pinto recommends this remarkable stock to the notice of investors and speculators who require an elegant diuretic, a nice diaphoretic, a brisk purgative, or a powerful stimulant. Three months' experience will be full of lively incident.

6. Wanted to know the exact number of men who sold the North British dividend at more than $5\frac{1}{2}$ per cent., and also the exact number of those who bought the dividend at about $5\frac{1}{4}$ to $5\frac{3}{4}$, and sold bears of the stock. The hand is not yet played out. If you would learn how small a man you are, dear "outsider," measure your speculative address against North British wit.

7. Wanted to know why the shareholders in English Railways do not hold a monster meeting to

discuss these important questions: The alarming growth of new capital, the extraórdinary effect of projectors' pestering efforts to promote competitive schemes that only suck the blood from the parent line, the overweening influence of directors in Parliament as elsewhere, and the increasing contempt in which the ordinary shareholder is held by Directorial EGO, which is becoming too clever by half, and has already learnt by heart this fearful, terrible truth, that "THE END OF ALL COMMERCE IS INDIVIDUAL GAIN." As this is the case, dear "Outside Fools," never be tempted to deal in dividends. In other kinds of speculation you probably will lose, but in this you must.

Let investors give up their insane habits of playing into the hands of Directors, who, as a large shareholder aptly remarked, are more injurious to the large interests committed to their trust than Parliament, the public, or even the press. The half-year's dividend is often a very unsafe guide. Dividends before now have come out of worn-out sleepers, corroding boilers, and carriages fast falling to decay. A close examination of the accounts is necessary to see how the dividend has been earned.

THE AUTHOR'S FAREWELL TO THE READER.

SHOULD any "Outside Fool" or "Inside Ass,"
Dreaming he sees himself, and not his class,
Depicted in these pages, say, "*I swear
'Tis mine own face I see*," why, let him wear
The Fool's cap, if it prove so true a fit.
Blame not the unoffending author's wit.
Let Malice censure Truth, and not the pen,
If what men do should seem so like the men.
How strange when KNOW THYSELF is call'd the end
Of human knowledge, it should so offend
The EGO to be shown itself,—that self
Which more than all it loves, ay, more than pelf!
How strange that Ignorance is sore afraid
Lest Truth should clip the profits of its trade.
All ignorance is vice : the rogue's the fool
Of fools in true philosophy's great school.
His realms of plunder are his curse and bane,
His selfish roguery brings loss, not gain.
Dear reader, if you're curious to see
The truth of this, just come and deal with me.
Erasmus Pinto has but lash'd himself,—
The rogue reform'd loves knowledge more than pelf.
Reader, good-bye, though cheating's now in vogue,
I love your "Outside Fool" more than your rogue.
Good-bye Grammaticus, my prince of snobs,
The venal critic's worse than one who jobs.
I'd rather, as a broker, win my bread,
Than drug with clever lies blind fools who read.
Good-bye, dear brothers of our Inside Hall,
Your humble spokesman, Pinto, thanks you all.

www.ingramcontent.com/pod-product-compliance
Lightning Source LLC
Chambersburg PA
CBHW051740300426
44115CB00007B/634